Masculinity and Sexuality in Modern Mexico

SERIES ADVISORY EDITOR:
Lyman L. Johnson,
University of North Carolina at Charlotte

Masculinity and Sexuality in Modern Mexico

Edited by

Víctor M. Macías-González and Anne Rubenstein

University of New Mexico Press ✣ Albuquerque

Printed in the United States of America
17 16 15 14 13 12 1 2 3 4 5 6

LIBRARY OF CONGRESS CATALOGING-IN-PUBLICATION DATA

Masculinity and sexuality in modern Mexico / edited by Víctor M. Macías-González and Anne Rubenstein.
p. cm. — (Diálogos series)
Includes bibliographical references and index.
ISBN 978-0-8263-2905-9 (pbk. : alk. paper) — ISBN 978-0-8263-2906-6 (electronic)
1. Masculinity—Mexico—History. 2. Men—Mexico—Identity.
3. Machismo—Mexico. 4. Sex—Mexico—History. 5. Sex role—Mexico—History.
6. Men—Mexico—Social life and customs. 7. Mexico—Civilization.
I. Macías-González, Víctor M., 1970– II. Rubenstein, Anne.
HQ1090.7.M6M37 2012
155.3'320972—dc23

2012013072

BOOK DESIGN
Composed in 10.25/13.5 Minion Pro Regular
Display type is Minion Pro

To the men in our lives,

Scott Sweeden and Patrick McGraw

Contents

Illustrations

Acknowledgments

AS IS TRADITIONAL, THE EDITORS OF THIS BOOK ACCEPT ALL RESPONsibility for errors of fact and interpretation herein. Having said that, we want to name and thank some of the many people who helped make the book what it is.

This book exists because Lyman Johnson and David Holtby talked us into doing it over the course of a coffee break at the 2001 meeting of the Rocky Mountain Council of Latin American Studies. We thank them for the coffee and for so much more: excellent advice, rigorous editing, support, and patience. Clark Whitehorn, who has not had such a long history with this project, has nonetheless been invaluable to it, and we thank him as well.

We thank the friends, students, teachers, and colleagues who have helped shape our thinking about gender history. For Anne, that includes especially her colleagues and students in York University's graduate history program, particularly those involved with the reading group in Gender and Women's History, everyone involved with the Toronto Area Latin American Research Group, and all the Latin Americanist students she has had the good fortune to work with, especially Melanie Huska, Dilaila Longo, Sophia Koutsoyannis, Pamela Fuentes, Frank Peddie, Brigitte Khadija Cairus, José Tufy Cairus, Brad Skopyk, Mary-Lee Mullholland, Liz Polak, Maurice Demers, and James Cullingham. Víctor thanks the University of Minnesota's Comparative Women's History Workshop and the UW-La Crosse History Writers' Group, especially Jodi Vandenberg-Daves and Marti Lybeck.

We have been in dialogue with the authors in this book for some years now, and we thank them for their patience and even more for how their ideas have challenged and changed our own. Other scholars outside our own institutions also have pushed us to think more clearly about these murky topics, and we are especially grateful to Glenn Avent, Bill Beezley, Gabriela Cano, Eileen Ford, Asunción Lavrin, María Teresa Fernández Aceves, Bill French,

Ramón A. Gutiérrez, Matthew Gutmann, Donna Guy, Rodrigo Laguarda, Robert McKee-Irwin, Pablo Piccato, Carmen Ramos, Sonya Lipsett Rivera, Susie Porter, Ageeth Sluis, Camilla Townsend, Mary-Kay Vaughan, and Pamela Voekel for timely interventions and helpful disagreements. Much of this collective thinking has happened in the context of the Coloquio Internacional de Estudios de la Mujer y Género en México (Red MuGen), and like everyone who thinks about gender in Mexico, we owe all the scholars connected to that organization an enormous debt.

Víctor M. Macías-González thanks the International Development Fund and the College of Liberal Studies of the University of Wisconsin–La Crosse (UW-L) for the research and travel funds that made this book possible. Larry Sleznikow of the UW-L Office of Academic Technology Services lent his technical expertise to assist with the formatting of illustrations.

Robert Buffington thanks Valerie Bhat for her assistance editing and formatting the images in his chapter.

Finally, we thank our extended families, who made gender interesting to us in the first place and who continue to keep it that way.

Introduction

Masculinity and History in Modern Mexico

VÍCTOR M. MACÍAS-GONZÁLEZ
AND ANNE RUBENSTEIN

FOR CATALINA DE ERAUSO, MEXICO WAS THE PROMISED LAND OF masculinity. The novice nun ran away from her Basque convent to live for several years as a cross-dressed conquistador in Peru, until she was caught in 1619. She was sent to Spain for trial, not for the murders of several men (to which she cheerfully confessed), but because she was suspected of having broken her vows as a nun. Having proved both that she never had taken her final oaths—or perhaps at this point in her story one should say *he*—and that he remained virginal, he was freed and allowed to travel to Rome, where he explained himself to Pope Urban VIII in 1626. In his written testimony, and probably in his confession too, de Erauso pointed to his manly behavior in the Andes, where he had seduced women and murdered men who questioned his masculine honor, as evidence that he truly was male and thus should not be returned forcibly to the convent. In the end, the Pope granted him permission to live as a man for the rest of his life. He then chose not to return to Peru but to try out life in the Valley of Mexico. In 1630, he started anew as the proprietor of a medium-sized ranch in New Spain. There he vanished from the historical record for the most part, although he entered Mexican folklore as *la monja alférez* ("second lieutenant nun"). Historians assume that he lived the rest of his long life in peace among people who, it seems, did not trouble themselves overmuch about disjunctions between biological sex and social gender, but did strongly privilege masculinity over femininity.[1]

Historians and anthropologists, unlike la monja alférez, do care deeply about the difference between biological sex and social gender. From our point of view, sex is the small set of physical traits, mostly related to reproduction, that make up the spectrum that has "male" at one end and "female" at the other. Biological sex—the actual makeup of human bodies—is hard to think about historically because it has not changed much in thousands of years. But what people *mean* when they say "I am a woman" or "I am a man," and also how important and how unchanging they believe that statement to be, does vary radically from place to place and time to time: that is what historians mean by gender. People build gender identities collectively from codes of behavior, attitudes, memories, stories, and emotions. Individuals learn to express their genders though interactions with other people, social institutions, and physical spaces. As societies and landscapes change over time, so do the constraints and parameters of gender. Gender is in constant flux, never static, always unstable. Individuals like Catalina de Erauso can challenge their society's gender ideology by resisting the constraints it places on their lives. But more often, it is groups of people who transform the terms by which their society understands and enforces gender norms, whether through deliberate political action or through incremental change in the patterns of everyday life.

In the present day, almost five centuries after Catalina de Erauso moved to Mexico, the Mexican word *macho* has entered the global lexicon. From Beijing to Brussels, the word connotes men who expect the superior place in a vigorously defended gender hierarchy and the societies informed by such a hierarchy.[2] It is easy to assume that, as the word is Mexican, *macho* described (and still describes) Mexicans and Mexico. If Mexico were such a timeless world of male power—still the world where Catalina de Erauso hoped to live as a man—this book would have no point. But the scholars whose work is included here, though we may disagree on some points, all believe that both men and masculinity (which are not the same thing) have been part of Mexico's historical transformations; countless political, social, economic, and cultural events shaped the meaning of *masculine*, while arguments over gender, in turn, helped shape Mexican history. Thus, *macho* may be a useful category for understanding some kinds of gendered identities and interactions, but it is far from being the only useful category. What this book is about, then, is how the relationship between biological sex and social gender (which anthropologists call a sex-gender system) has changed over time, and how changes in Mexico's sex-gender system both created and reflected other kinds of political, social, cultural, and spatial transformations.

Scholars who study many places and times agree that gender helps make history. Nearly two decades ago, feminist historian Joan Wallach Scott argued for the importance of gender as a category of historical analysis. Scott defined gender as a "constitutive element of social relationships based on perceived differences between the sexes [that] . . . is a primary way of signifying relationships of power."[3] Gender serves to structure and give meaning to social groups, particularly when those groups interact with each other. It creates relations of power—domination and subordination—that change over time. Various social actors transform and deploy these relationships to create order in society; societies invoke gender to imbue practices, policies, institutions, and people with meaning.

Masculinity in Mexican History: Some Case Studies

The articles in this book cover a geographical range from Texas to Oaxaca, a chronological range from the early days of the Porfirio Díaz dictatorship through the present, and a very wide range of social actors. These essays tell stories of file clerks and movie stars, wealthy world travelers, and ordinary people who seldom ventured farther than a bar in the middle of town. Many of the essays discuss men who thought of themselves as men and ordinarily had sex with women. But two take up cases of women whose sexual aggression suggests that they acted, and perhaps identified themselves, as men. Six other chapters describe men who had sex with other men (at least some of the time) and perhaps identified themselves as gay, as well as men who dressed like women and perhaps identified as women too. This should remind us that—like Catalina de Erauso's neighbors—we should avoid confusing sex with gender. Even more, it should make us recognize the diversity of political, economic, social, and cultural circumstances—and spaces—that have shaped Mexicans' experiences of and ideas about masculinity.

The first part of the book offers five case studies of how some Mexicans in different places and times enacted masculine identities. In the first, "The Bathhouse and Male Homosexuality in Porfirian Mexico," Víctor M. Macías-González describes how the Mexican government, hoping to create economic and cultural modernity by encouraging cleanliness, supported the construction of public bathhouses, which Mexican men instead used as sites for erotic encounters with each other. The second, Kathryn A. Sloan's "Runaway Daughters: Women's Masculine Roles in Elopement Cases in Nineteenth-Century Mexico," deals with *rapto*, a type of crime that covered a spectrum of illicit contact between men and women from elopement to rape. Committing this crime was a way for young Oaxacan men to show their neighbors how manly they could be. In some cases of rapto—those more closely resembling elopement—women's participation in arranging abductions suggests that women, too, sometimes took on public male roles. In the third article, "Dominance and Submission in Don Porfirio's Belle Époque: The Case of Luis and Piedad," James A. Garza analyzes a love triangle that led to a murder. The particulars of this case reveal unease and confusion about morality and masculine honor in turn-of-the-century Mexico City. Next, Eric Schantz's article, "Meretricious Mexicali: Exalted Masculinities and the Crafting of Male Desire in a Border Red-Light District, 1908–1925," investigates how female prostitutes and their male clients moved across borders—both the physical lines between nations and the symbolic ones between racial, gender, and moral categories—while conducting their business in a post-Revolutionary northern boomtown. The last article in this section, "Theaters of Masculinity: Moviegoing and Male Roles in Mexico Before 1960" by Anne Rubenstein, discusses how Mexican men going to the movies used movie theaters as stages for a range of roles from dependable provider to wild juvenile delinquent: masculinity was not a single thing, but could take many forms in urban, twentieth-century Mexico.

The second part of this book concerns the way that mass-media depictions of Mexican masculinity changed across space and over time. Robert Buffington's "Toward a Modern Sacrificial Economy: Violence Against Women and Male Subjectivity in Turn-of-the-Century Mexico City" examines how working-class men constructed their subjectivity using representations of women in the penny press. "Nationalizing the Bohemian: The Mythogenesis of Agustín Lara," by Andrew G. Wood, examines the fictions that the great songwriter and star crafted about his own origins, having to do with his birthplace, his early career, and the origins of his famous facial scar. Wood concludes that Lara's fame owed much to his clever recasting of his own life into a more romantic (and less socially acceptable) mold. Jeffrey M. Pilcher's article "The Gay Caballero: Machismo, Homosexuality, and the Nation in Golden Age Film" analyzes an incident of labor conflict in which movie stars Mario Moreno (Cantinflas) and Jorge Negrete tried to prevent a Spanish folkloric dancer, Miguel de Molina, from performing in Mexico City. Pilcher views the rhetoric around this event as revealing the discursive limits of acceptable masculinity in midcentury Mexico. Finally, Mary-Lee Mulholland studies contemporary performances by Guadalajara mariachi musicians in her article "Mariachis Machos and Charros Gays: Masculinities in Guadalajara." She suggests that the city has two landscapes in which male sexuality can be performed—one is the territory of the cowboy singers, who are supposed to be profoundly and authentically masculine, and the other is Guadalajara's famous gay scene, its *ambiente*—and that mariachi performance, though it takes place in the first of these territories, is infused with new meaning by its proximity to the second.

The new scholarship on masculinity in Mexico represented in this book obviously concerns itself with questions of male sexual behavior and sexual identity. But we have also identified three other threads that link many new studies of masculinities in modern Mexico.

The first thread linking these articles has to do with performance and mass media: historians and others looking at cinema, television, comic books, pop music, dance, vaudeville theater, sports, and the tabloid press, among other genres, have begun to see how gender controversies have shaped—and been shaped by—popular culture.[4] Judith Butler has described gender as resulting from "performances that congeal over time to produce appearance of substance, of a natural sort of being."[5] In Butler's view, performances of gender, especially when popular culture makes them visible, can be analyzed to reveal how seemingly natural and unchangeable facts of life are really part of a socially constructed heterosexual matrix. Mass media is one of the key locations for this matrix, a cultural framework through which communities "make sense of the ways that our bodies, genders, and desires seem to naturally appear heterosexual."[6] As they analyze key forms of media from different points in Mexico's past, the essays of Buffington, Mulholland, Pilcher, Rubenstein, and Wood describe how popular culture encodes gender identity and how people sometimes use popular culture to challenge or uphold local gender ideologies.

Another thread joins articles on the relations between individuals and powerful institutions. In studying this complicated set of relationships, scholars are following the lead of French philosopher Michel Foucault. Many historians of gender have agreed with Foucault that people sometimes make claims based on gender status to get what they need from political, cultural, or religious institutions. That is, they deploy the set of words, images, stories, and ideas about gender that are already available to them to form their arguments. (Foucault called this set, in its totality, a discourse.) The success or failure of such claims then acts to undermine or reinforce the existing gender discourse; but every time a relatively powerless person resorts to using that discourse, Foucault would claim, he or she also reinforces existing hierarchies—helping the powerful to remain powerful.[7] Essays in this volume that explore how this process worked in Mexico include those by Buffington, Garza, Macías-González, Schantz, and Sloan.

The last thread connecting recent studies of Mexican masculinities takes spatial mobility as a marker, or cause, of modernity—that ambiguous and highly gendered condition. Historians of gender have begun to focus on the role of social spaces in shaping identities.[8] Contributors to this volume have gone further than that by interesting themselves in much more than static geographic locations; they also examine the ideologies that restrict and inhibit dynamic movement within and across spaces. In this book, such movements through space occur around and across Mexico's northern border, as in Schantz's article; between Europe and Mexico, as in the chapter by Macías-González; between an imagined rural Bajío and urban reality, as in Mulholland and Pilcher's contributions, or an equally imaginary small-town Veracruz and the movie version of Mexico City, as in Wood's essay; and simply in and around Mexico City, as Garza's article suggests.

The "separate spheres" model—which argues that the advent of industrial modernity divided the male world of street, workplace, and political participation from the female domain of the home, religion, and the emotions—implies that the history of Mexican masculinities could best be studied through analyzing what men did at work.[9] But the model has come in for a great deal of criticism: historians have complained that it confuses cultural ideals with social realities and does not account for the ways in which race and class hierarchies existed alongside (and intersected with) gender hierarchy.[10] Historians of Mexico seem to have taken these critiques to heart; very few scholars of masculinity have taken up the topic of work and the workplace.[11] Certainly the essays here rest on the assumption that masculinities exist only in relation to femininities; to other hierarchies of race, ethnicity, and class; and in movement from place to place. They also distinguish carefully between a culture's idealized depictions of family and gender and a society's everyday, material realities of life inside and outside the home. For the scholars who have contributed to this book, workplaces, especially single-sex workplaces, would not be the most useful sites to consider issues of gender formation and transformation.

Yet social spaces that exclude women entirely or that are primarily intended for male use have great historical importance. Physical spaces, like social structures, can shape specific ways of being masculine and understanding masculinity. So the contributors to this volume are asking this: Did the "modern" spaces that were being created by economic and cultural change throughout this period have an impact on masculine identities? If so, how did that process work? In particular, public and private spaces intended exclusively or primarily for male use—bathhouses, cantinas, cafés, schools, clubhouses, barracks, factories, sports arenas, courtrooms, movie theater balconies, and many more—intrigue historians. Places like these facilitated the formation of male social networks and masculine identities; by studying them we hope to understand how the evolving relationship between gender ideologies and cultural understandings of physical space helped cause political transformations from the triumph of nineteenth-century Liberalism through the fall of the Partido Revolucionario Institucional (PRI).

"Even the Virgin Could Have Something of the Masculine": Politicians, Artists, and Scholars Debate Mexican Masculinity, 1820–1911

Masculinity and male sexuality in Mexico (and in Mexican communities in the United States) have been topics of literary and social-scientific discussion for at least a century and a half but have not until recently drawn the attention of historians.[12] Scholars of colonial Latin America, however, have made questions of gender central to their field.[13] They suggest that the struggle for male honor and familial respectability motivated Spaniards in the Americas to behave in otherwise inexplicable ways, as with the horsemen crossing the Andes who, according to Catalina de Erauso, preferred the risk of starvation to the certain blot on their honor that would have resulted from being seen planting potatoes.[14] More importantly, the shared obsession with family honor that spread in the late colonial era from elite conquistadores to enslaved Africans and impoverished native people gave cultural unity (and therefore political strength) to an otherwise tottering empire. Historians concur that the honor/shame complex was an ideology, not a reality; many forms of seemingly unacceptable behavior—out-of-wedlock births, for instance—could be made licit after the fact as long as everyone within the community could plausibly pretend ignorance, through such face-saving devices as the "private pregnancies" described by historian Ann Twinam.[15] As several essays in this book suggest, the ideology of honor—though it changed over time—continued to shape male experience and thought well past 1821, when Mexico gained its political independence from Spain.

The challenges to state formation and economic development that marked the 1810–1870 period problematized masculinity in a new way. The former "New Spain" had little binding it together beyond the name *Mexico*. And most nineteenth-century Mexicans used that name to refer, not to their *patria*, but to Mexico City (as has remained true in parts of the state of Yucatán, for example, into the present day). Political and military leaders like Antonio López de Santa Anna, trying to hold the new nation together, deployed or created religious and political mythologies that they hoped all their countrymen would share. They used highly gendered images, especially that of the Virgin of Guadalupe and of the political leader as "the man on horseback," or *caudillo*, who had defeated the less manly Spaniards. Gradually *Mexico* took on a masculine persona connected to older ideas about honor and respect.[16] So, for instance, the Liberal writers of the Constitution of 1857 conceptualized proper citizenship using a gendered and class-specific language, referring to "persons of honesty, of legality, and [of] use to the Republic."[17]

This *honesty* referred to the composure, demeanor, and self-possession of ideal male citizens. This ideal Mexican who represented the nation (and was represented by it as well) had to partake of masculine honor and respectability. But, in the minds of Mexican elites, race was equally important in defining the ideal citizen: he had to be white. In one comic but telling 1853 incident, President López de Santa Anna attempted to create an elite guard corps in imitation of those that protected European monarchs. Unfortunately for him, he could not hire enough guards of a convincingly European appearance—meaning not only pale-skinned, but hairy as well. López de Santa Anna had to order blond wigs, beards, and cosmetics from abroad to change the appearance of the beardless, dark-skinned, Indian and mestizo men who applied to serve as his guard.[18]

The nineteenth-century caudillos and statesmen who struggled against each other (and against the Church) in the battlefields, the congress chambers, and the newspapers to define the country's political agenda did so in homosocial spaces. Raised and educated in the company of other males—whether in colleges, professional schools, or seminaries—they frequently did not marry until later in life. Instead they turned to friendship and practiced forms of fictive kinship among their peers to satisfy their desire for companionship and emotional intimacy. Senior military officers related to their aides-de-camp in a paternal fashion, mentoring the young men in their service and establishing close emotional bonds with them. For instance, Guillermo Prieto, while serving President Anastasio Bustamante from 1840 to 1841, slept in the presidential bedchamber, referring to the room in his memoirs as *nuestra habitación*—"our room."[19] Bustamante, in turn, had modeled his relationship with Prieto after one he had enjoyed with Emperor Agustín I, whom he so loved and admired that he left instructions in his will for his heart to be extracted and placed amidst the emperor's remains in the Metropolitan Cathedral.[20] Intergenerational connections like these provided participants with valuable social capital; they helped men enter a political, military, cultural, and economic elite. Such friendships—encoded in a language of fraternity, filial piety, and emotion—created a new masculine sensibility.[21] At a time of frequent political turmoil and military conflict, these brotherhoods provided a degree of stability and continuity among Mexican elites.

Mexicans interpreted the painful loss of half the nation's territory to the United States at midcentury, followed by the humbling experience of French occupation (1862–1867), as crushing blows to the national brotherhood's honor as a (symbolic) white man. So, when Porfirio Díaz took power in 1877, the new regime inherited this gendered political culture and a national sense (at least among elites) that Mexico faced a gender crisis at the same time that it had to face its overwhelming problems of underdevelopment and instability. Díaz and his advisors, *los científicos*, envisioned a future in which male citizens of Mexico would resemble what they believed Frenchmen to be: hardworking, "modern," and white. Meanwhile, the Mexican state faced the problem of shifting the blame for the recent disasters. The hypermasculinized political culture of the day, along with new French ideas about science, modernity, and the body, led Mexico's ruling elite to believe that the nation's troubles had been caused by insufficient manliness. They pointed to the newly invented figure of the homosexual man as a central political problem.[22]

Thus at the beginning of the time period under consideration in this book, we can see a marked rise in elite Mexican debate about masculinity. Were Mexicans manly enough? Could effeminate men be identified and cast out of the body politic? During the Porfiriato, elites marginalized people whose behavior and appearance mixed aspects of both genders. Liberal literary critic and statesman Ignacio Manuel Altamirano, for example, criticized painters who in their works depicted individuals of ambiguous gender. In his notes on an exhibition he visited in 1879, Altamirano indicated his disapproval of a biblical scene where the Virgin Mary's femininity was lacking and "[had] something of the masculine."[23] Such comments were not simply expressions of disagreements over esthetic issues; they also communicated the ideological content of images—particularly historical and allegorical paintings. So visual art, aided by critics, served as a mechanism of ideological persuasion that could "create reality . . . to legitimate their present."[24]

By 1900 narratives about and images of sexually deviant men seemed to be everywhere. Social scientists like Carlos Roumagnac, Andrés Molina Enríquez, and Julio Guerrero had begun to write on homosexuality, describing, classifying, and stigmatizing it in clinical terms.[25] At the same time folk artists and penny press journalists like José Guadalupe Posada titillated their lower-middle-class and proletarian readers with scandalous tales of male sexual deviance. And naturalist novelists like Eduardo A. Castrejón, in his 1906 *Los 41: Novela crítica-social*, described homosexuality as a "social ill" that threatened polite society. Castrejón's novel portrayed a real-life scandal. In November 1901, a late-night police raid on a house party in a central Mexico City residential district netted forty-one of the city's most prominent young men, half of them dressed as women. Gossips whispered that don Ignacio de la Torre y Mier, Porfirio Díaz's son-in-law, had also been present but had escaped. The ensuing scandal made the number *forty-one* a dirty joke among Mexicans, but more importantly, it brought the figure of the homosexual further into public view and gave ordinary Mexicans proof of their rulers' decadence. During the regime's last years, journalists and scandalmongers increasingly accused the country's upper classes of effeminacy and homosexuality—including accusations against Porfirio Díaz himself.[26] This kind of gossip reflected public acceptance of the elite discourse on the political value of masculinity; at the same time, it shows the Mexican public adapting elite gender ideology to its own political purposes.

Cantinflas as Revolutionary Role Model: Politicians, Artists, and Scholars Debate Mexican Masculinity, 1911–1970

The Revolution that brought the Porfiriato to an end—as with the other total wars of the twentieth century throughout the world—brought with it a relaxation of social and moral strictures. Historians have noted how some women seized the chance to experiment with new forms of dress, comportment, behavior, and thought (though most simply scrambled to survive times of violence, dearth, and chaos).[27] Male leaders of various revolutionary factions, however—especially those like Emiliano Zapata and Pancho Villa followed by armies of peasants and indigenous people—tacitly accepted the Porfirian conflation of nation, state, family honor, and male power.[28] Indeed, by arranging to be photographed, filmed, and gossiped about in poses of exaggerated masculinity—wearing big hats, sporting large guns, and in Villa's case surrounded by his many wives and even more children—these revolutionary heroes manipulated this masculinist ideology. They seemed to be saying that their exaggerated manliness made up for their lesser class and ethnic status, marking them as true citizens of the nation they were hoping to remake.

Even a woman who rose to command a troop in Zapata's army ended up maintaining her position (and, eventually, her pension) by proving herself as a man who could ride and shoot better than anyone who followed her. She then decided to lead the rest of her life as a man, known to all as el coronel Amelio Robles. Her story demonstrates the unusual opportunities the Revolution offered some women to claim better positions in the hierarchy of gender privilege. But it also indicates how these individuals' skills, resourcefulness, and luck reinforced the existing sex-gender system too: for instance, the unusual case of *la coronela*'s pension helped justify the more general refusal of pensions to women veterans.[29]

This masculinist national ideology evolved to fit new political, cultural, and economic circumstances in the post-Revolutionary period. In the 1920s and 1930s, some artists and intellectuals aligned themselves with the Revolutionary state through their attacks on other avant-garde literary and artistic figures (like those who wrote in the periodical *Los Contemporáneos* or worked for the Teatro Ulíses) as antinational, decadent, and effete. Poet and playwright Salvador Novo was almost unique in his positive writings about homosexuality, scandalously questioning the hypermasculinity that *Estridentista* writers like Manuel Maples Arce and Germán List Arzubide championed as the Revolutionary model.[30] The youthful Novo bravely prowled Mexico City's main streets while in makeup, with plucked eyebrows and effete mannerisms. But by 1940 such actions had discredited him as a critic of heteronormative masculinity; he spent the rest of his long career in literature, theater, film, advertising, and journalism acting as a mouthpiece and prop for the increasingly ossified post-Revolutionary state.[31]

Novo aside, in the post-Revolutionary era the identification of heterosexual masculinity with political authority and national identity was so powerful that even some young, Revolution-minded women began wearing their hair cut short and playing sports formerly reserved for men. This may have started out as elite women's gesture of affiliation with the international New Women (who were also called *flappers* in the United States), but by the middle of the 1920s the middle- and working-class young women who adopted the style were making a claim on the national government as a new kind of masculine national subject. Thus in the summer of 1924, a Mexico City newspaper estimated that at one of the biggest new public high schools for women in Mexico, almost all the young women—including the principal—sported the new short haircuts; it was no coincidence that in the same summer, male students from Mexico City's upper-class medical school and Preparatoria Nacional started physically attacking such short-haired young women who wandered too near to these bastions of traditional male privilege.[32]

Revolutionary rhetoric enabled women like *las pelonas* to lay claim to the category of "masculine." At the same time, by emphasizing the masculinity of mestizo and indigenous Mexicans, it changed the relationship between ideologies of gender and race in Mexico. The country's Creole and Europhile mestizo elites had long identified whiteness with masculinity (and vice versa), but the culture of the Revolutionary era depicted the ideal Mexican man as darker skinned.[33] Artists initiated this process even before the Revolution began, as in Saturnino Herrán's 1910 allegorical paintings *De la construcción* and *Del trabajo*, which presented dark-skinned, muscular men as Westernized, thrifty, and hardworking citizens.[34] But this esthetic shift became state policy in the early 1920s, when José Vasconcelos launched a cultural revolution that aimed to forge a cross-class national union through education of the poor and acculturation of the indigenous population.[35] Accordingly, teachers carried out literacy campaigns, provided life-skill training, reevaluated folk traditions as an authentic component of the national culture, and instituted physical education and precision drills in the name of national integration, social improvement, and modernization. Through exercise and an "improved" diet that replaced indigenous corn with European wheat, the Revolutionary state hoped to transform the bodies of the lower orders to better resemble those of modern Europeans.[36] Visual artists joined in this radical reinterpretation of the bodies of Indians and poor people; they began to include indigenous people, women, and the poor in their iconography and narrative of the nation. And some of the muralists—notably Diego Rivera, on the walls of the National Palace—portrayed Indian men in pre-Cortesian Mexico (and afterward) as powerful, cultured, and beautiful, a view that was further legitimated in the research of anthropologists like Manuel Gamio.

Social commentators and literary critics like Samuel Ramos, Antonio Caso, and Octavio Paz recodified Mexico's masculinity and sexuality in the mid-twentieth century in response to changing social and economic conditions. Between 1940 and 1960 Mexico transformed itself from a predominantly rural nation to an overwhelmingly urban one. The stunningly rapid urbanization that marked the 1940s and 1950s brought social problems in its wake: uneven economic development and inadequate urban infrastructure, as well as an increasingly corrupt, powerful, and unresponsive central government, made Mexican cities violent, uncomfortable, and unhealthy places to live. As in the past, Mexican intellectuals (and observers from outside Mexico too) blamed these national problems on a particular group of Mexican men: in this case, blame fell on working-class urban men, often referred to as *pelados* or—when they were migrants to or from the United States—*pachucos*. These imaginary male figures (like their equally imaginary female counterpart, the overly religious, fearful, conservative, family-obsessed "traditional Mexican woman") supposedly blocked progress and development in Mexico because they were violent, touchy, suspicious, womanizing loners who would not commit themselves to a marriage or a job. Writings about the failings of the Mexican national character—above all, Paz's essay "Los hijos de la Malinche"—became the cognitive filters through which Mexicans and others, beginning with anthropologist Oscar Lewis, approached gender: they equated masculinity with *machismo*, and assumed that all Mexican men were (or wanted to be) violence-prone, overly emotional, fatalistic *machos*.[37] Intellectuals blamed Mexico's social and economic ills on the figure of the urban working-class macho, much like contemporaneous social critics in the United States and England blamed many social problems on the figure of the juvenile delinquent.

The 1940s and 1950s were also the Golden Age of the Mexican film industry, and some of the most popular comedies and melodramas of the era reflected intellectuals' ideas about working-class masculinity. But where Octavio Paz and Oscar Lewis linked Mexican manhood to Mexico's troubles, the movies celebrated the same stereotypical vision of masculinity. Stars like Jorge Negrete, Pedro Infante, Luis Aguilar, Tin-Tan, and Cantinflas, among others, played roles ranging from singing cowboys to singing cops and singing automobile mechanics, and they always showed these men as heroic. Even when they were comic figures, these stars played characters who were bold, tough, competent, loyal, loving, and resourceful. The movies transformed the stereotype of the Mexican macho from a national menace to a source of national pride.

The model of Mexican masculinity proposed by Paz and popularized in Golden Age cinema served important political functions. The leaders of the 1968 student movement, which ended in the disaster at Tlatelolco when the government opened fire on a massive gathering of peaceful demonstrators, were relatively privileged young men; they deployed the signs and behaviors they believed to be typical of working-class machismo, as Paz had described it and the movies had portrayed it, as a way to find common ground with other Mexicans.[38] The male leaders of the Chicano movement in the United States similarly made claims to political power and a Mexican identity through exaggerated displays of Pedro Infante–like machismo.[39] Even Che Guevara was reported to have modeled his public behavior on the famous Mexican film comedian Cantinflas.[40]

So the Revolutionary-era debates over masculinity, femininity, and citizenship appeared to have been decided as the 1970s began. Mexicans appeared to agree on what typical male behavior was and seemed to know, too, what constituted exemplary male character. A broad political consensus seemed to have been reached about how the Mexican state should relate to both. Yet gender did not cease to be the object of intense intellectual debate in Mexico, nor did masculinity cease to have powerful, conflicting political uses.

Conclusion: Masculinity and Political Change

The view of Mexican masculinity and national character proposed by Octavio Paz first began to be challenged at precisely the moment when it seemed most widely accepted, both by intellectuals and as popularized in mass media. From the perspectives of feminist, gay and lesbian, and postcolonialist studies, three basic critiques emerged.[41] First, critics observed that the image of the Mexican macho was just that—an image. It did not reflect most people's daily lives, or their self-perceptions. Second, they pointed out that collapsing the categories of *Mexican* and *male* disenfranchised women. Third, they noted that this model assumed that the macho always behaved heterosexually, but the increasing visibility of urban gay communities (especially in Guadalajara and Mexico City) and the rise of a gay liberation movement made it clear that while the *ideal* of Mexican masculinity proposed by Paz might be straight, many Mexican men were not.

So, by the end of the 1970s, gender studies—and especially the study of masculinity—had taken on a new urgency in Mexico. Some of the most interesting responses to this intellectual challenge came from anthropologists. They turned away from abstract considerations of the national character as a whole (as in Octavio Paz's essays) and Freudian efforts to decode the Mexican family romance (as in Oscar Lewis's ethnographies). Instead, this new generation of writers attempted to describe clearly how gender identities and gender relations played themselves out in the everyday lives of ordinary Mexicans. Although they have disagreed sharply on many questions, most anthropologists writing about Mexican men, masculinity, and sexuality have come to understand gender in Mexico as performative—a deliberate series of theatrical acts intended for an audience—rather than seeing it as a reflection of national character or family history. Much ethnographic attention, therefore, has been paid to the lives of those who perform their gender in the most public, theatrical ways: drag queens and male sex workers.[42] Even those anthropologists who have looked at the lives of more ordinary Mexican men, however, have seen masculinity as more than a single thing; in their ethnographic accounts, masculinity encompasses a wide range of behaviors and understandings, all more or less socially comprehensible (if not always perfectly acceptable).[43] Furthermore, these anthropologists see gendered behavior as contingent: men can pick and choose among this wide set of possible actions, habits, and ideas according to their circumstances. What counts as masculine depends on where a person is, what he or she is doing, and who might see the person doing it.

These new anthropological accounts of masculinity as plural and performative have been echoed in the work of other Mexican writers: critics and journalists like Carlos Monsiváis, Elena Poniatowska, and Alma Guillermoprieto; novelists like José Emilio Pacheco and Luis Zapata; and performance artists and filmmakers like Astrid Hadad, Jaime Humberto Hermosillo, and Jesusa Rodríguez. Observing and reworking narratives they have found everywhere from elementary school textbooks to professional wrestling, they have analyzed the shared mythology of twentieth-century Mexico. Their writings have moved in two directions. First, they have described and critiqued the gendering of daily life, carefully separating gender mythologies (especially the stereotypes of the self-abnegating woman and the violently macho man) from lived experiences of femininity and masculinity, while examining how the national mythos shapes gendered behavior. Second, they have described and critiqued the ways that the national mythology—not just the pantheon of military heroes, but also stock comic characters like the pachuco and the naive Indian servant girl—has served the needs of the most powerful people in Mexico, maintaining hierarchies of power along lines of race and class, as well as gender.[44] By insisting on writing about the national mythology *as mythology*, these writers strengthened social movements—notably, feminist and gay liberationist movements—that started from a critique of Mexican gender ideology.

The period after the deadly 1985 Mexico City earthquake saw the rise of new social movements in response to the perceived immobility and corruption of the government, which had been led by the same political party since 1922. Not all such movements were directly concerned with gender politics, but even those that seemed most remote from these issues, like the Zapatistas in Chiapas, also made a point of their feminist politics and made gleeful sport of the mythology of machismo. Yet when the Partido Revolucionario Institucional finally lost power in the year 2000, Mexican voters picked a new president, Vicente Fox, who seemed more stereotypically macho than any Mexican leader of the past fifty years. Fox seemed to embody the *charro*, the cowboy who had been the protagonist of so many Golden Age movies and mariachi tunes. This irony underlines the continuing importance of masculinity as a category of analysis in the study of Mexican politics and Mexican history, as well as the need for further analysis and critique of the ideology, discourse, and reality of masculinity in Mexico.

NOTES

1. Catalina de Erauso's testimony was published, in translation, as *The Lieutenant Nun: Memoir of a Basque Transvestite in the New World*, trans. Michele Stepto and Gabriel Stepto (Boston: Beacon Press, 1996).
2. Just as an example, we have heard the word used in conversation over the last few years to describe Argentines, Chinese, Germans, Russians, and—yes—even Mexicans.
3. Joan Wallach Scott, "Gender, A Useful Category of Historical Analysis," in *Gender and the Politics of History* (New York: Columbia University Press, 1988), 28–50. Scott's ideas were first formulated in 1985 and subsequently appeared in the *American Historical Review* 91, no. 5 (December 1986). Scott revisits her distinction between biological sex and social gender in her book *The Fantasy of Feminist History* (Durham, NC: Duke University Press, 2011) to warn us against oversimplification of this formulation, reminding us that experiences of the biological are also historically contingent. See especially pp. 7–11.
4. Most of the work so far that connects gender history to mass-media history in Mexico has concerned women rather than men. See, for example, Anne Rubenstein, *Bad Language, Naked Ladies, and Other Threats to the Nation: A Political History of Comic Books in Mexico* (Durham, NC: Duke University Press, 1998); Patience Schell, *Church and State Education in Revolutionary Mexico City* (Tucson: University of Arizona Press, 2003); and Julia Tuñón, *Mujeres de luz y sombra en el cine mexicano: La construcción de una imagen, 1939–1952* (Mexico City: Colegio de México/INCIME, 1998). But see also Eric Zolov, *Refried Elvis: The Rise of the Mexican Counterculture* (Berkeley: University of California, 1999).
5. Judith Butler, *Gender Trouble: Feminism and the Subversion of Identity* (New York: Routledge, 1990), 190, cited in Anny Cranny-Francis, Wendy Waring, Pam Stavropoulos, and Joan Kirby, *Gender Studies, Terms and Debates* (New York: Palgrave-Macmillan, 2003), 168–69.
6. Butler, *Gender Trouble*, 151, cited in Cranny-Francis et al., *Gender Studies*, 20.
7. Luther H. H. Martin and Patrick H. Hutton, eds., *Technologies of the Self: A Seminar with Michel Foucault* (London: Tavistock, 1988), 17–49.
8. Stephen M. Whitehead, *Men and Masculinities* (Cambridge, UK: Polity Press, 2002), 138–40; Michel Foucault, "Space, Knowledge and Power," interview by Paul Rabinow, in *Skyline: The Architecture and Design Review*, March 5, 1982: 16–20.
9. The notion of separate spheres (a male public sphere and a female private sphere) was initially developed in the seminal article of Barbara Welter, "The Cult of True Womanhood: 1820–1860," *American Historical Quarterly* 18 (1966): 151–74.
10. This view has since been challenged by a number of its early adherents; see Linda K. Kerber et al., "Beyond Roles, Beyond Spheres: Thinking About Gender in the Early Republic," *The William and Mary Quarterly*, 3rd Ser., 46, no. 3 (July 1989): 565–85.
11. An important exception to this rule: Steven Bachelor, "Toiling for the 'New Invaders': Autoworkers, Transnational Corporations, and Working-Class Culture

in Mexico City, 1955–1968," in *Fragments of a Golden Age*, ed. Gil Joseph, Anne Rubenstein, and Eric Zolov (Durham, NC: Duke University Press, 2000).

12. Sueann Caulfield wrote that "gender analysis has not been as central a concern" to Latin American historians who work at Latin American universities as it has been to historians of Latin America working in the United States and Canada, which has limited the amount of historical research published on Mexican masculinities. Sueann Caulfield, "The History of Gender in the Historiography of Latin America," *Hispanic American Historical Review* 81, no. 3–4 (August–November 2001): 450. However, several more recently published books have established masculinity as a key topic among historians of Latin America and especially modern Mexico: see Robert McKee Irwin, *Mexican Masculinities* (Minneapolis: University of Minnesota Press, 2003); Sergio de la Mora, *Cinemachismo: Masculinities and Sexuality in Mexican Film* (Austin: University of Texas Press, 2006); and Katherine Bliss and William French, eds., *Gender, Sexuality, and Power in Latin America Since Independence* (Boston: Rowman and Littlefield, 2006).
13. See, for example, these edited collections: Asunción Lavrin, *Sexuality and Marriage in Colonial Latin America* (Lincoln: University of Nebraska Press, 1989); and Lyman L. Johnson and Sonya Lipsett-Rivera, eds., *The Faces of Honor: Sex, Shame, and Violence in Colonial Latin America* (Albuquerque: University of New Mexico Press, 1998). Important early work on the gender history of colonial New Spain includes Patricia Seed, *To Love, Honor, and Obey in Colonial Mexico: Conflicts over Marriage Choice, 1574–1821* (Stanford, CA: Stanford University Press, 1988); and Ramón A. Gutiérrez, *When Jesus Came, the Corn Mothers Went Away: Marriage, Sexuality, and Power in New Mexico, 1500–1846* (Stanford, CA: Stanford University Press, 1991).
14. De Erauso, *Lieutenant Nun*, 87.
15. Anne Twinam, *Public Lives, Private Secrets: Gender, Honor, Sexuality, and Illegitimacy in Colonial Spanish America* (Stanford, CA: Stanford University Press, 1999).
16. For the visual aspects of this myth making, see Stacie G. Widdifield, *The Embodiment of the National in Late Nineteenth-Century Mexican Painting* (Tucson: University of Arizona Press, 1996).
17. Mexico, Laws, Statutes, "Constitución Federal de los Estados Unidos Mexicanos, sancionada y jurada por el Congreso General constituyente el día cinco de febrero de 1857," in *Derechos del Pueblo Mexicano: México a través de sus constituciones. Historia constitucional, 1847–1917* (Mexico City: XLVI Legislatura de la Cámara de Diputados, 1967), 2:406–40.
18. Victoriano Salado Álvarez, *De Santa Anna a la Reforma. Memorias de un veterano. Relato anecdótico de nuestras luchas y de la vida nacional desde 1851 a 1861*, 2 vols. (Mexico City: J. Ballescá y Cía., 1902), 1:234–35 and 275.
19. Guillermo Prieto, *Memorias de mis tiempos* (Mexico City: Consejo Nacional para la Cultura y las Artes, 1992), 288.

20. Víctor M. Macías-González, "*El hermano de amor que tu mismo elegiste:* Masculine Friendships in Nineteenth-Century Mexico." Paper presented on April 16, 2004, at the Colloquium on Race, Class, and Gender in Latin American Civil Society of the Center for Latin American Studies of the Ohio State University.
21. The literature on masculine friendship and intimacy draws on the oft-anthologized seminal essay of Carroll Smith-Rosenberg, "The Female World of Love and Ritual: Relations Between Women in Nineteenth-Century America," *Signs* 1 (1975): 1–29. For a recent application of Smith-Rosenberg to Latin American male friendships, see Andrew J. Kerkendall, *Class Mates: Male Student Culture and the Making of a Political Class in Nineteenth-Century Brazil* (Lincoln: University of Nebraska Press, 2002).
22. Men had sex with other men in Mexico before 1870, of course; people recognized the existence of male effeminacy as well. A few texts mentioned homosexual preferences or behaviors, if only to ridicule them, as occurred in a one-act operetta that Melchor Ocampo wrote in 1840 that featured an effeminate man—don Primoroso—who "preferred to lay with men." (Melchor Ocampo, "Don Primoroso. Sainete," *Obras Completas de Melchor Ocampo*, 3 vols., ed. Ángel Polá and Aurelio J. Venegas [México: F. Vázquez, 1900], 3:253). But the *category* (or identity) of "the homosexual man"—as opposed to a set of behaviors—had only just entered public discourse in the Americas at this time.
23. Ignacio Manuel Altamirano, *Obras completas, vol. XX: Diarios* (Mexico City: Consejo Nacional para la Cultura y las Artes, 1992), 182.
24. Tomás Pérez Vejo, "Pintura de historia e imaginario nacional: el pasado en imágenes," *Historia y Grafía* 16 (2001): 73.
25. Pablo Piccato, *City of Suspects: Crime in Mexico City, 1900–1931* (Durham, NC: Duke University Press, 2001), 50–72.
26. Victoriano Salado Álvarez, *Memorias. Tiempo viejo* (Mexico City: Ediapsa Editores, 1946), 245.
27. Carlos Monsiváis, "Los que tenemos unas manos que no nos pertenecen," *Debate Feminista* 8, no. 16 (October 1997): 15.
28. On hypermasculinity of Zapata and Villa, see Samuel Brunk, *Emiliano Zapata: Revolution and Betrayal in Mexico* (Albuquerque: University of New Mexico Press, 1995); and Friedrich Katz, *The Life and Times of Pancho Villa* (Stanford, CA: Stanford University Press, 1998), respectively. On public image of Villa, see Margarita de Orellana, *La mirada circular. El cine norteamericano de la Revolución Mexicana, 1911–1917* (Mexico City: Joaquín Mortiz, 1991); and Mark Cronlund Anderson, *Pancho Villa's Revolution by Headlines* (Norman: University of Oklahoma Press, 2001).
29. Gabriela Cano, "*Soldaderas* and *coronelas*," in *Encyclopedia of Mexico: History, Society, and Culture*, ed. Michael S. Werner (Chicago: Fitzroy Dearborn, 1997), 2:1357–60; and Gabriela Cano, "Unconcealable Realities of Desire: Amelio Robles's (Transgender) Masculinity in the Mexican Revolution," in *Sex in Revolution:*

Gender, Politics, and Power in Modern Mexico, ed. Gabriela Cano, Jocelyn Olcott, and Mary Kay Vaughan (Durham, NC: Duke University Press, 2008), 25–56.

30. On the *Contemporáneos* and *Estridentistas*, consult Guillermo Sheridan, *Los Contemporáneos ayer* (Mexico City: Fondo de Cultura Económica, 1993); and Luis Mario Schneider, *El estridentismo o una literatura de la estrategia* (Mexico City: INBA, 1968), respectively.
31. Carlos Monsiváis, *Salvador Novo: Lo marginal en el centro* (Mexico City: Era, 2000).
32. Anne Rubenstein, "The War on *las pelonas*: Modern Women and Their Enemies, Mexico City, 1924," in *Sex in Revolution: Gender, Politics, and Power in Modern Mexico*, ed. Gabriela Cano, Jocelyn Olcott, and Mary Kay Vaughan (Durham, NC: Duke University Press, 2008), 57–80.
33. Liberal literary and artistic figures had already begun to transform the image of the ideal man in the nineteenth century, making soldiers and workers emblematic of valor, patriotism, moral strength, hard work, and honor. Ignacio M. Altamirano, *El zarco*, 20th ed. (Mexico City: Editorial Porrúa, 1995), xxi–xxii, 49, and 52.
34. Víctor M. Macías-González, "Apuntes sobre la construcción de la masculinidad en México a través del arte decimonónico," in *Hacia una nueva historia del arte mexicano, Vol. II*, ed. Stacie Widdifield and Esther Acevedo (Mexico City: Consejo Nacional para la Cultura y las Artes, 2004), 329–50.
35. Alexander S. Dawson, "From Models for the Nation to Model Citizens: *Indigenismo* and the 'Revindication' of the Mexican Indian, 1920–1940," *Journal of Latin American Studies* 30, no. 2 (1998): 279–308.
36. David E. Lorey, "Postrevolutionary Contexts for Independence Day: The 'Problem' of Order and the Invention of Revolution Day, 1920s–1940s," in *Viva Mexico! Viva la Independencia! Celebrations of September 16*, ed. William H. Beezley and David E. Lorey (Wilmington, DE: Scholarly Resources Books, 2001), 233–48.
37. Octavio Paz, *The Labyrinth of Solitude*, trans. Lysander Kemp (New York: Grove Press, 1962); Oscar Lewis, *Children of Sanchez* (New York: Random House, 1961).
38. For masculinity and youth culture of the 1960s, see Eric Zolov, *Refried Elvis*.
39. Ilan Stavans, *Bandido: Oscar "Zeta" Acosta and the Chicano Experience* (New York: Perseus Book Group, 1995).
40. Paco Ignacio Taíbo II, *Ernesto Guevara, también conocido como el Che* (Mexico: Editorial Planeta, 1996), 105–6.
41. An early and important feminist analysis of the Paz and Lewis writings on masculinity can be found in Jean Franco, *Plotting Women: Gender and Representation in Mexico* (New York: Columbia University Press, 1989).
42. Joseph Carrier, *De los otros: Intimacy and Homosexuality among Mexican Men* (New York: Columbia University Press, 1995); G. Núñez Noriega, *Sexo entre varones. Poder y resistencia en el campo sexual*, 2nd ed. (Mexico City: Programa universitario para estudios de género/UNAM, 2000); Annick Prieur, *Mema's House, Mexico City: On Transvestites, Queens, and Machos* (Chicago: University of Chicago Press, 1998).

43. Matthew C. Gutmann, *The Meanings of Macho: Being a Man in Mexico City* (Berkeley: University of California Press, 1996); Roger Magazine, "Both Husbands and *Banda* (Gang) Members: Conceptualizing Marital Conflict and Instability Among Young Rural Migrants in Mexico City," *Men and Masculinities* 7, no. 2 (October 2004): 144–56.
44. See, for example, Alma Guillermoprieto, "Mexico City, 1992," in *The Heart That Bleeds* (New York: Vintage Books, 1995), 47–67; Carlos Monsiváis, *Entrada libre. Crónicas de la sociedad que se organiza* (Mexico City: Ediciones Era, 1987) and *Los rituales del caos* (Mexico City: Ediciones Era, 1995); and Elena Poniatowska, *La noche de Tlatelolco* (Mexico City: Ediciones Era, 1968) and *Nada, nadie. Voces de temblor* (Mexico City: Ediciones Era, 1988).

PART 1

EXPERIENCES

CHAPTER 1

The Bathhouse and Male Homosexuality in Porfirian Mexico

VÍCTOR M. MACÍAS-GONZÁLEZ

ON A WARM JUNE AFTERNOON IN 1908, A GROUP OF TEENAGERS congregated after school on a dusty town plaza in Jalisco, waiting for the five o'clock prayers.[1] As the youngest of the boys—Elías Nandino, age eight—contemplated buying five cents' worth of flower-scented water to sprinkle in front of the Sacred Heart, his friend Lencho showed up—a brawny, tall, hairy older boy with an outgoing personality, charming smile, and great singing voice. Instead of going to church, Lencho suggested that the boys go for a bath. The heat must have been overwhelming, because they immediately forgot God and rushed down to the river. On its banks, they stripped, and using handfuls of the grasses that grew there, scrubbed and lathered. As the bathers frolicked in the water, Lencho, "who had a really big body and used both hands to cover his privates," would, when swimming past Nandino, pinch his thighs:

> I liked it, and with each lap, he would pinch higher and higher, until he caressed my peepee. He did this—I do not know how many times—until my peepee got hard and then, intentionally, stroked it with his big hand.[2]

Over the next three or four years Nandino continued to bathe with his classmates, either at the river or in the large pool of a bathhouse next to the town's electrical plant. While he relished these occasions—he wrote about "the beauty of their bodies"—he also felt awkward, not knowing what to make of emotions he felt for his chums, hesitating about "what I so much wanted to tell them."[3]

Not until 1914 would Nandino, now a young man of fourteen, finally grasp the meaning of the sensations he felt. That year, he had two sexual encounters with different men at bathhouses in Cocula, Jalisco. The first encounter—with a handsome, timid young man who was on his way to the United States seeking refuge from the Revolution—culminated in a brief romance that Nandino later described as "beautiful days of sincere love . . . I do not remember who started it, but it began with a hungry kiss . . . it was the first time I kissed a man."[4] The second incident occurred at "Los Baños del Pensil." Instead of bathing in the open with others, Nandino opted for a private tub—and into it he invited another young man, whom he had long admired from afar. With him, Nandino would develop his first relationship:

> I invited him and he accepted. We undressed, I saw his body and he saw mine. We were like rifles . . . We got into the water. We played and without meaning to, our bodies touched. I already knew how to kiss. I knew its impact, its meaning. We shared one. We got out of the tub, and in that place where we were supposed to scrub and cleanse ourselves, we pleasured each other . . . Thereafter, each week, he came looking for me . . . to bathe.[5]

Some seventy years after these incidents, in the 1980s, as Nandino drafted his memoirs reflecting on his life as a prominent physician, bureaucrat, poet—and homosexual—his memories of bathing helped Nandino to frame or conceptualize same-sex love between men. Bathhouses and similar aquatic recreation spaces helped individuals to imagine themselves as belonging to a distinct community of same-sex attracted men. These bathing spaces allowed the crystallization of abstract identities, becoming "showcases" that made possible and tangible desires and identities that until then had not been as easily manifested.[6] As such a "showcase," the bathhouse transformed same-sex desire from a behavior into an objective identity. Although the evidence is not conclusive, it appears that a few men did define themselves that way and that they did so exactly at the point in Mexican history when public discourse around homosexual acts peaked: 1901, the year of the "41" scandal.

Late in the evening of Saturday, November 16, 1901, from his post at the street corner, the neighborhood watchman observed an unusual degree of traffic at the entrance to No. 4, La Paz Street; many elegant people were alighting from carriages, dressed as for a ball. He did not recall anyone filing a permit for a dance at his precinct, so he moved closer to investigate . . . and to his disbelief, he saw that the persons whom he had taken for women were actually men wearing heavy makeup and wigs! He alerted his superiors, and within minutes, undercover police had the place surrounded. In the ensuing raid, forty-one men were arrested—nineteen dressed as women—and over the next week, the lurid details seeped to the public.[7] Authorities moved quickly to punish the arrested men, publicly humiliating them before exiling them to the Yucatán, where they served as conscripts. Newspapers and handbills informed the public of the crime, condemning the forty-one's subversion of society's gender order. The scandal—at a time when the world's attention was on Mexico City owing to its hosting of the Second Pan American Conference—even gave rise to corridos and a novel, transforming "41" into the euphemism for homosexuality that it remains to this day. Many people feared that the scandal threatened a gender disruption that might undermine the regime through its implication of elite effeminacy. Politicians, intellectuals, social critics, businessmen, clergy, and others responded, increasing their surveillance of public spaces where they suspected homosexual acts occurred—including bathhouses.

Bathing, Class, Gender, and the Nation

When Porfirian educators, social reformers, politicians, and entrepreneurs discussed bathing practices and spaces, they did so in relationship to the regime's goal of transforming Mexico into a modern society. Bathrooms, washhouses, and public baths became crucial sites of encounter between individuals of humble social origins and their social superiors. There, it was hoped, the poor would acquire not only the elite's superior sanitary practices, but also their notions about how bathing could potentially be an object of national pride.[8] Elites may have also hoped that in adopting the daily bath or shower, the lower orders would accelerate their "Westernization" (and this would be measured by the degree that their appearance and dress conformed to the styles in Europe and the United States and other visible markers of difference) that foreigners found lacking. This introduced a racial dimension to bathing. For the white (and whitish) members of the *gente decente*, this may have implied that the symbolic superiority connoted through bathing—a practice that economics restricted to the middle and upper classes—also defined the mestizo underclass as dirty. Ironically, Mexicans also made proud, boastful nationalistic observations about the bathing habits of the predominantly Indian peasantry. Porfirian efforts to disseminate statistical reports of water consumption and bathhouse modernization abroad, together with the travel accounts of middle- and upper-class Mexicans disdainful of foreign hygiene practices, suggest that Mexicans may have regarded their modern baths as superior to those of a dirty Europe.[9]

The Porfirian elite understood bathing as a gendered activity. The sumptuous settings of the bathhouse somehow transgressed the gender order and consequently feminized the males that spent too much time there. This, clearly, contradicted elite expectations that the bathing experience would teach the lower orders the gente decente's superior values of cleanliness and morality.[10]

Social classes in Mexico perceived the morality of bathing and bathhouses differently. While the socially redeeming value that the upper classes saw in the daily bath echoed Enlightenment-era notions of ablutions as therapeutic, the lower orders espoused medieval superstitions associating immorality, disrepute, and ill health with full-body immersions.[11] Bathing—because it required the human body to be unclothed—has historically been regarded as an ambivalent, dangerous, morally threatening activity. During the Reconquista, one of the first things that kings did upon taking possession of a newly liberated Moorish town was to close the bathhouses, because in the dark shadows of the steam rooms, the Devil could easily lure the Christians to commit nefarious acts.[12] Early modern Spanish *dichos* (folk wisdom) are perhaps the best measure of the traditional Hispanic mentality toward bathing: "De los baños, menos provechos que daños" ("You have more to fear than gain from bathing"), "La corteza guarda el palo" ("Bark protects the stick"—*bark* as in encrusted grime), "Más vale tierra en cuerpo que cuerpo en tierra" ("It is better to have dirt on your body than for your body to be six feet under"), and "Más vale oler a puerco que a muerto" ("It is better to stink like a pig than like a corpse").[13] Thus, even when authorities or philanthropists funded free public baths, the poor shied away. When authorities decreed in 1901 that all guests of the public shelters should wash themselves in order to secure a bed, over half of the people vacated the premises. By 1905, the municipal government of Mexico City closed its free public bathhouse in La Lagunilla for lack of use.[14]

Porfirian Mexico's bathhouses thus tended to attract men of the middle and upper classes—a small but demanding clientele. These urbane, well-heeled males converged at bathhouses for reasons beside hygiene. They primarily used balneal establishments as a space where they could socialize with friends and pamper themselves with steam baths, treat themselves to a massage, and get a haircut while having a drink, gossiping, and closing business and political deals. According to numerous testimonials, the baths were a popular meeting place that drew men from intellectual, professional, business, political, military, and artistic circles. José Juan Tablada related in his memoirs—in rhymed verses, no less!—the good times he spent in the company of bohemians like Julio Ruelas and Bernardo Couto y Castillo swimming in the pools of the Military College at Chapultepec or washing himself in the showers at the Club Ugartechea, one of the first public gyms in Mexico City.[15] Tablada also commented amply on the bathing routines of his contemporaries, like the millionaire don Sebastián Camacho, who took cold morning baths in order to prevent pneumonia.[16] Jesús E. Valenzuela, primary financial backer of the literary journal *Revista Moderna*, described in his memoirs the dinners and musical soirées that frequently followed his baths at the Alberca Pane, where he assiduously swam in the company of General Carlos Pacheco, Secretary of War and Development. Of Pacheco, Valenzuela said, "He [was] a man that liked pleasure . . . one day I went to bathe with him, because he had a bathroom in his home, but we also bathed together frequently at the Alberca Pane Baths, from where we usually went to eat menudo."[17]

Porfirian Mexico's contemporary European societies understood balneal practices and spaces within the context of a complex interplay of social, economic, political, and cultural phenomena. As the leisurely and hygienic bathing practices of western European elites spread to the rest of society, the middle and working classes reinterpreted the meaning and practice of bathing.[18] Originally regarded as dangerous, barbaric, or immoral, by 1750 river or sea bathing became more acceptable and was increasingly practiced with therapeutic aims.[19] Maladies as varied as venereal disease, cardiovascular afflictions, or dyspepsia were treated through medically supervised bathing regimens and the ingestion of mineral waters, leading to the development of spas and similar health resorts throughout Europe and the Americas.[20] By the *fin de siècle*, the French middle classes increasingly rationalized "therapeutic vacations as a sensible, even productive way of spending time."[21]

Bathing practices and spaces formed individual identities in Mexico as in Europe. A person's ablutions provide us with an opportunity to dissect her or his ideas (and those of his or her society) about class, gender, nationality, and consumption.[22] Taking "the cure" at a genteel spa—European resorts like Karlsbad or Évian were ideal, but those that developed in Tehuacán, Puebla, were just as exclusive, if more accessible—allowed the upwardly mobile individual to define his or her sense of self-worth as a member of a neat, tidy, and washed proper society.[23] Personal cleanliness—and acquisition of the cultivated aquatic leisure—distinguished the rising middling sorts from unclean masses widely regarded as the culprits for the precarious state of public health. Philanthropists in Liverpool and London, for example, funded the first public baths and washhouses between 1850 and 1890 to curb disease in working-class districts adjacent to middle-class neighborhoods.[24] Building on the efforts of the British reformers, the bourgeoisie of France and Germany targeted their laboring classes for a much-needed soak and wash, hoping to thus combat disease in crowded tenements—and to consequently diminish any threat by the unwashed poor to the middle classes. These imposing public baths, through their grand scale and luxurious appointments, also prompted a feeling of civic pride among their patrons.[25]

As sites of consumption, leisure, sociability, civic pride, and identity formation, the numerous bathhouses, clubs, and gyms that Mexican entrepreneurs developed for the expanding numbers of affluent, otiose, sophisticated male consumers in search of modern, chic locales also served to affirm middle- and upper-class manhood.[26] These new bathing and leisure spaces answered the need for sites where new models of masculinity emerging in response to economic, social, and cultural changes could be performed. Elite migration to urban areas during the Porfiriato, coupled with a growing distaste for blood sports and the adoption of novel forms of athletic leisure, made the traditional physically exerting activities of cattle roping and branding, horse breaking, and feats of equestrian skill, alongside cockfighting and bullfighting, obsolete as articulators of elite masculinity.[27] Whereas the upper class had been renowned for their equestrian skills in the 1830s and 1840s—Guillermo Prieto described a youthful Manuel Payno as "a good rider"—by the 1880s pampered young men began to develop sumptuous, decadent interests, like amassing vast collections of art, shopping, drugs, and travel.[28] Telesforo García, writing to Emilio Castelar in 1897, complained of his son's lack of energy and direction, underlining, instead, his skill and interest in mysticism and painting.[29] Like urban male professionals, technicians, shopkeepers, and clerks, the newly "citified" *hacendados* now turned to "the strenuous life"—which Gail Bederman refers to the performance of hard physical movements, primarily through sports and body building—to prop up a sagging sense of self resulting from their abandonment of exhausting physical agrarian feats and growing reliance on exertionless mental tasks.[30] Since urban males of the middle and upper classes could not affirm their masculinity either through physical exertion at work or at leisure, they instead turned to body building, exercise, and competitive sports.[31] Entrepreneurs developed athletic clubs, gymnasiums, and bathhouses to turn a profit from the same masculine affliction that prompted the state and a number of social groups to incorporate more physical education into the educational curriculum, as well as to sponsor groups like the YMCA.[32]

However, neither entrepreneurs, nor policymakers, nor philanthropists, nor any other advocate of the strenuous life foresaw that the geography and practices of these sites of masculine affirmation would present the ideal situation for the emergence of a hedonist subculture that could potentially backfire on their intent to establish these places as bastions of modern Porfirian manhood. While these spaces sported some of the latest and fanciest exercise and weight training equipment, they were also spaces of great sumptuousness and extreme indulgence where men soaked, scrubbed, steamed, sweated, and swam before having a massage, manicure, or pedicure. Here they also coifed their hair or had their moustaches trimmed and waxed. The entire ritual of primping and preening before going out on the town took as long as three or four hours amid a comfort that evoked a sultan's harem. Advertisements touted "modern comfort and Oriental luxury with fluffy pillows, divans, magazines, newspapers, books, and a well-stocked buffet table."[33]

But while some regarded the dandified middle- and upper-class male bather's indulgence as evidence of Mexico's economic, social, and industrial progress, others saw in it a sinister feminization of the elite. Public opinion scorned the luxurious lifestyle of *lagartijos* (fops) because they blurred traditional gender boundaries and represented a sterile or unproductive—and thus unmasculine—use of capital that violated the values of frugality, modesty, decorum, and capital accumulation that the regime advocated.[34] This effete material decadence of the bathhouse, combined with its homosocial dynamic, ultimately queered the very space that society had hoped would serve to overcome men's anxieties toward modernization. Male nudity abounded in the dressing rooms, showers, steam rooms, pools, and exercise rooms of bathhouses, gymnasiums, and athletic clubs. Male nakedness may ultimately have become, alongside bathers' hedonistic material excesses, the Achilles heel of masculine affirmation. Male nudity destroyed any performance of whiteness that mestizos contrived through costly European-style clothes, scents, and cosmetics, making evident how the mixed-race individuals were darker and less hirsute than whites (on average), thus destroying the power that clothing and grooming normally created. Moreover, complete male exposure also freed the body of its usual "bearers of prestige"—wealth, status, and class—making the bathing experience a somewhat democratizing experience.[35] So the nudity Porfirians witnessed while bathing and exercising was probably the source of some anxiety linked to race, class, and ethnicity. But the presence of so many naked male bodies in dressing rooms, massage parlors, pools, showers, and other such spaces transformed these sites into places where, potentially, men who were sexually attracted to other men could easily meet. What chill the Porfirian establishment must have felt when Mexico City's luxurious bathhouses (and other aquatic recreational facilities), instead of showcasing the regime's advances, became known as spaces of same-sex desire.

Porfirian medical and social discourses, if not political practices, established a clear correlation between a person's cleanliness and his or her moral character, class, race, and gender. Julio Guerrero's sociological treatise *La génesis del crímen en México* (1901) noted how the dirtiest classes were the poor, who could not afford "to even buy soap with which to wash, as it would consume 25% of their income."[36] The Mexican pariahs—*léperos, soldaderas*, beggars, and the like—were not only immoral, promiscuous, thieving, miserable drunks, but according to Guerrero, had such a disregard for hygiene that their dirt-colored, sore-covered bodies gave off a most fetid stench since the city's barefoot downtrodden bathed "only when it rains."[37] Guerrero's claims that the unclean were also morally depraved were echoed by his contemporary, criminologist Carlos Roumagnac.[38]

In contradistinction, the moral elements of society consisted of the washed. The socially precarious middling sorts—artisans, shopkeepers, army officers, and other *gente menuda*—while promiscuous, prone to infidelity, and barely cultured, were admirable because they lived in the neat and tidy central districts of Mexico City.[39] Cleanliness being next to godliness was clearly a motto that Porfirians understood. Being well-scrubbed and squeaky-clean earned one social acceptance. Having a *buena presentación* would open up doors; individuals applying for work as palace guards, for example, were required to have a pleasant appearance.[40] Etiquette books reminded readers that they could never spend enough time grooming themselves; time invested tidying up was time well spent, because it contributed to improving one's public persona or reputation.[41] Young boys were urged to make cleanliness their sole adornment and that through it, they would obtain virtue and health.[42] Nineteenth-century Mexicans thus privileged cleanliness alongside moral, honor, class, racial, and gender lines. To be manly was to be clean—but the high costs related with the cleanliness practiced in Mexico City's bathhouses restricted this masculinity to a small number of privileged men.

However, just as individuals in the eighteenth century had found ways to transgress race and honor as markers of status through wealth and notoriety, Porfirians also found ways to contravene the new masculine hierarchy that bathing seemed to be instilling. Cleanliness could allow members of the underclass to transcend certain racial, class, and cultural biases that would normally have predisposed middle- and upper-class families against them. While the gente decente may have read dirty, working-class people as immoral, criminally suspect individuals, they may have been willing to disregard the ethnic or class origins of a person if he or she appeared clean. Guerrero, for example, described Indians not only as healthy, robust, honest, faithful, and moral, but also as "hard-working lovers of cleanliness."[43] The country's *criollo* elite were paragons of moral and hygienic cleanliness, according to Guerrero, as evidenced by their predilection for protecting their bodies from contact with filth through their use of gloves, perfumes, and fastidious changing of undergarments. The women of this class, he hinted, were immaculate, noting that they followed "all of the prescriptions of hygiene" and that they even kept abreast of the latest scientific sanitary developments by reading newspaper and journal articles analyzing housekeeping methods.[44] But what about the men? Guerrero said relatively little about the bathing practices of upper-class males beyond implying that they were talented, tidy, and fastidious individuals who ordered everyone in their households to "hygienically observe cleanliness."[45]

The prescriptive literature that these middle- and upper-class men would have purportedly used to guide themselves and other members of their households on cleanliness gave little information on the type of conduct that one was to observe while bathing at a public establishment, or how one was to behave when nude. While Spanish books of etiquette advised readers to wash their faces and hands but little else, Mexican and other Latin American *manuales de urbanidad* urged readers to bathe daily—or at least, weekly—given the tropical conditions of the New World.[46] With the exception of specialized guidebooks for thermal stations or bathhouses, the prescriptive literature remained silent on the matter of male nudity in public bathhouses, although the state of undress was generally frowned upon. It was not unusual for some to bathe dressed lest they transgress modesty, particularly if they did so in the company of others, as one would do in a school dormitory or a bathhouse.[47]

Whether they gave much thought to their state of undress or not, Porfirian males measured, quantified, and scrutinized their cleanliness. Perhaps because they believed there existed a high correlation between cleanliness and modernity, the Porfirian "Wizards of Progress" incorporated references to sanitary conditions to the displays and propagandistic literature exhibited in Mexican pavilions at world fairs.[48] The Superior Sanitation Council, a federal entity entrusted with health policy, proved particularly zealous in disseminating evidence of hygienic advances in the country. Its studies, guides, and codes were widely distributed. Models of waterworks, bathing facilities, and restrooms built in various public edifices were proudly put on display.[49] Organizers proudly pointed out that the hydrotherapy department in Mexico City's General Hospital was based on the specifications the French government had designated for similar establishments in its army hospitals.[50]

The cleanliness of the middle and upper urban classes, and of rural folk in general, was a matter of national pride. Mexico could very well be backward or even inferior, the gente decente might acknowledge, but at least it was a clean country. As early as 1885, government reports proudly noted how per capita consumption of water in Mexico City and Puebla (at eighty and seventy liters, respectively, per person daily) was comparable with Berlin, Brussels, or Vienna. By 1904, new pumping stations and an expanded sewer system allowed those living in Mexico City an average per capita use of 244 liters, a figure nearly thrice that of Berlin, twice that of Brussels or Vienna, and a full seventy liters ahead of the average Londoner. By 1909, with the completion of a new aqueduct from Xochimilco, the populace of Mexico City increased its water use to 400 liters, levels comparable with Rome, Chicago, or New York.[51] All of this evidence clearly illustrates that Mexicans were consuming larger amounts of water than ever before, but just how much of this was devoted to bathing? Undoubtedly, industry—such as the paper mill in San Ángel—probably used a substantial amount of this additional water, as did probably the growing number of fountains and artificial lakes in the city's parks and the rapidly expanding grounds of Chapultepec forest. Surely, as Guerrero suggests, the masses remained unclean during this time, much as they remained elsewhere. In Europe, Mexican travelers were shocked to learn that the laboring masses were equally unclean as those of their homeland, a fact made evident in studies outlining the many subterfuges to which German and French civic leaders recurred to lure workers into the public baths built for their use.[52]

Middle- and upper-class Mexicans returning from prolonged stays abroad proudly noted their hygienic superiority to Europeans. Manuel F. Madrazo, nephew of Toribio Esquivel Obregón, noted in his correspondence the lack of "basic comforts in Europe" and greatly celebrated that while in Belgium, he was able to obtain "what passes for luxury accommodations here, since my room has a bathroom, an extraordinary thing here, since people do not bathe with the frequency that we do at home."[53] While travelers recorded their shock at Europeans' infrequent bathing, they were especially stunned to discover that Spaniards were filthy.[54] Mexicans' bathing culture was inherited from their indigenous forefathers, not from the conquistadores.[55] Gachupines, if they bathed at all, did so only in the summer and at that, fully clothed and in rivers, streams, or lakes—never at home, least of all in a bathtub. In the 1870s, doña Isabel Pesado y de la Llave, duquesa de Mier, was scandalized to discover that not even in the best hotels of Spain could she secure a wash basin.[56] Similarly, the aristocratic don Juan Sánchez-Navarro y Peón, consummate financial assessor to Mexican presidents, smugly noted in his memoirs how Madrid innkeepers, during the 1930s, refused to provide him with the daily hot-water bath without which his daily morning routine was incomplete.[57]

Bathing Spaces

Porfirian bathing establishments thus constituted important cultural sites. They allowed for the propagation of new cultural and consumption patterns that helped the middle and upper classes to express and participate in nationalist comparisons of the bathing culture of a clean Mexico vis-à-vis a dirty western Europe. But bathing also helped the Porfirian elite to articulate their sense of self in terms of race, class, and ethnicity and, most significantly (as argued in the second part of this chapter), helped them to negotiate new ideas about masculine propriety. Bathhouses were not only places of modernity, chauvinism, hygiene, and leisure; they were also spaces of homosociability. And while these were locales where people of the same gender socialized—frequently while disrobed—they also allowed middle- and upper-class men to experiment with novel forms of masculinity. How did gender and space function in the bathhouse?

While government statistics proclaimed the superiority of Mexican bathing practices vis-à-vis western Europe, analysis of balneal literature from 1880 to 1890 reveals a certain anxiety at the state of bathhouses in major urban areas. A guidebook that Romualdo de Zamora y Duque, Mexico City's bathhouse tycoon, commissioned in the late 1880s is particularly telling. De Zamora y Duque's hired pen, *ingeniero* Alberto Malo, was under instructions to "diligently" study bathing establishments in the United States and Europe in order to assess the quality of bathhouses in Mexico City. After much consideration, Malo concluded that the capital's bathhouses were inferior—and frankly, decrepit. With most establishments installed in buildings dating from the eighteenth century, few offered comfort. They consisted of a reception area, a dressing room, and a long, cold, dark gallery where a shivering clientele took its ablutions in hand-filled talavera-tiled tubs with little or no privacy. Modesty was lacking, as the employees who delivered the barely heated water to customers were often men who ogled female bathers.[58] Few had showers or steam rooms and, for the most part, they reflected bathing technology from the beginning of the nineteenth century.

Manuel Olaguíbel, the general manager of the Alberca Pane—the flagship establishment of de Zamora y Duque's balneal emporium—subsequently attempted to remedy the conditions that Malo had observed. When it finally opened in 1895 after years of remodeling, the pompously named Baños turco-romanos de la Gran Alberca Pane became the most modern and luxurious bathhouse of Mexico City. No expenses were spared. Located on the city's most elegant avenue, the Paseo de la Reforma, in front of the monument to Christopher Columbus, the Alberca Pane featured the latest hydrotherapeutic gadgets, steam baths, and saunas on facilities that also housed a massage parlor, barber shop, bar, reading lounges, and refreshingly cold spring-fed pools. Local and imported marbles, fine furnishings, and exotic paintings glamorized the establishment.[59] In the formal gardens, a small orchestra—directed by one of Mexico's leading composers, Juventino Rosas—delighted customers with waltzes, schottisches, and other tunes.

Other bathing entrepreneurs soon followed suit. Eduardo Dublán, owner of the Factor Baths, located in front of the Mexican Congress, had the courtyard gardens of his establishment replanted with flowering bushes and hired a string ensemble to "harmonize" the conversations of its all-male Sunday clientele. To the sides of the elegantly statued, classically ornamented indoor pool—where Mexican congressmen could imagine themselves to be Roman senators—led off a series of mazelike hallways with private bathing alcoves. The innovative private tubs, which had helped to establish the Alberca Pane as the premier bathing establishment in the city, were touted most boastfully by Dublán: "We guarantee the privacy of our clients." The Hidalgo Baths, owned by Salvador Miranda, advertised the elegance of its installations, stressed the beauty of its gardens, and called attention to the great beauty of its oriental pool.[60]

The sumptuous redecoration, redistribution, and redesign of bathhouse spaces in the 1890s attracted the attention of authorities to spaces that they had long since neglected. This had not always been the case. During the colonial era, authorities had closely monitored balneal establishments and had gone to great extents to discourage same-gender desire and practices in spaces of aquatic entertainment. Fearful that such occurrences of the "nefarious sin" (*pecado nefando*) would offend God and bring divine wrath upon the realm, as stated in a royal order dating from 1624, the Church and the Crown placed under pronounced and secret surveillance the turbid waters and dark corners of convent baths, college pools, steam rooms (*temascales*), and suburban watering holes where bathers threw themselves into lust and concupiscence. Until a series of high-profile bathhouse raids in the mid-seventeenth century exposed the relative ease with which individuals engaged in homosexual acts in bathhouses, these spaces facilitated the development of same-sex-attracted male social networks and affective ties.[61] But perhaps because many of the arrested turned out to be students and clerics, the Inquisition dropped the subject and, subsequently, policed what we would call heterosexual bathers, discouraging mixed-gender bathing through the establishment of men-only and women-only baths—and ignored same-sex attracted bathhouse patrons altogether, perhaps hoping that by not drawing attention to the phenomenon, it would go away.[62]

From independence in 1821 until the 1870s, the perpetual penury and weakness of the state diminished authorities' surveillance of bathing establishments altogether. Only gradually did the Porfirian state begin to pay attention to balneal spaces as sites of sanitary concern and corporal scrutiny. Since public hygienists thought that inadequately maintained bathhouses could pose a public health threat—epidemics of cholera and typhus were frequent prior to the multimillion-dollar overhaul of public utilities in

Mexico City and other urban areas—they asked bathers, bathhouse attendants, and managers to report any people whose bodies exhibited the telltale signs of contagious diseases. By the 1890s, new sanitary codes ordered bathhouse owners and managers to immediately report the names of clients whose bodies showed signs of cholera, bubonic plague, yellow fever, typhus, smallpox, scarlet fever, and diphtheria.[63] But no mention was made of homosexuality; it had not been pathologized—yet. It had not occurred to anyone that the new, modern, luxurious bathhouses provided a place where scantily clad same-sex-attracted men could congregate and, through careful observation, lingering looks, furtive glances, and guarded comments, contact others who shared their same-sex attraction. What passed unperceived to attendants turned into a mating ritual for those "in the know." The bathhouse had been queered.

The geography of the bathhouse greatly facilitated this "cruising" through its new layout. Gone were the dark, small, noisy galleries full of shivering bathers. In their place, there emerged palatial compounds comprised of a series of well-lit, highly compartmentalized, quite large rooms from which radiated a series of dark hallways and private bathing booths with locking doors. A soft gurgling sound from the large volumes of water that flowed and splashed throughout the establishment, together with the plush carpeting, the profusion of indoor plants, and the noises that the exercise machinery emitted, probably muffled any noises that the walls of compartments failed to contain. At the heart of the baths, there was a large central pool where dozens, if not hundreds, of men swam or floated. Unbeknownst to its designers, same-sex-attracted bathers used the layout to their advantage, looking around until a handsome man held their gaze; the hunted became the hunter. Once mutual interest was established, the couple could safely, discretely, and separately leave the pool and rendezvous in private bathing cabinets. Once behind closed doors, and perhaps in collusion with a well-bribed bath attendant, they could safely carry on.

Contacts could also be made in the exercise rooms, where conversation about weightlifting techniques or carefully phrased compliments about someone's musculature could safely evolve into a pick-up line. After all, research suggests that late-nineteenth-century males had not yet internalized homophobic impulses that would discourage them from public demonstrations of affection.[64] Mexican men in this period seemed to have few inhibitions about touching each other in public. Jesús A. Valenzuela relates the affections he and others of his contemporaries received from

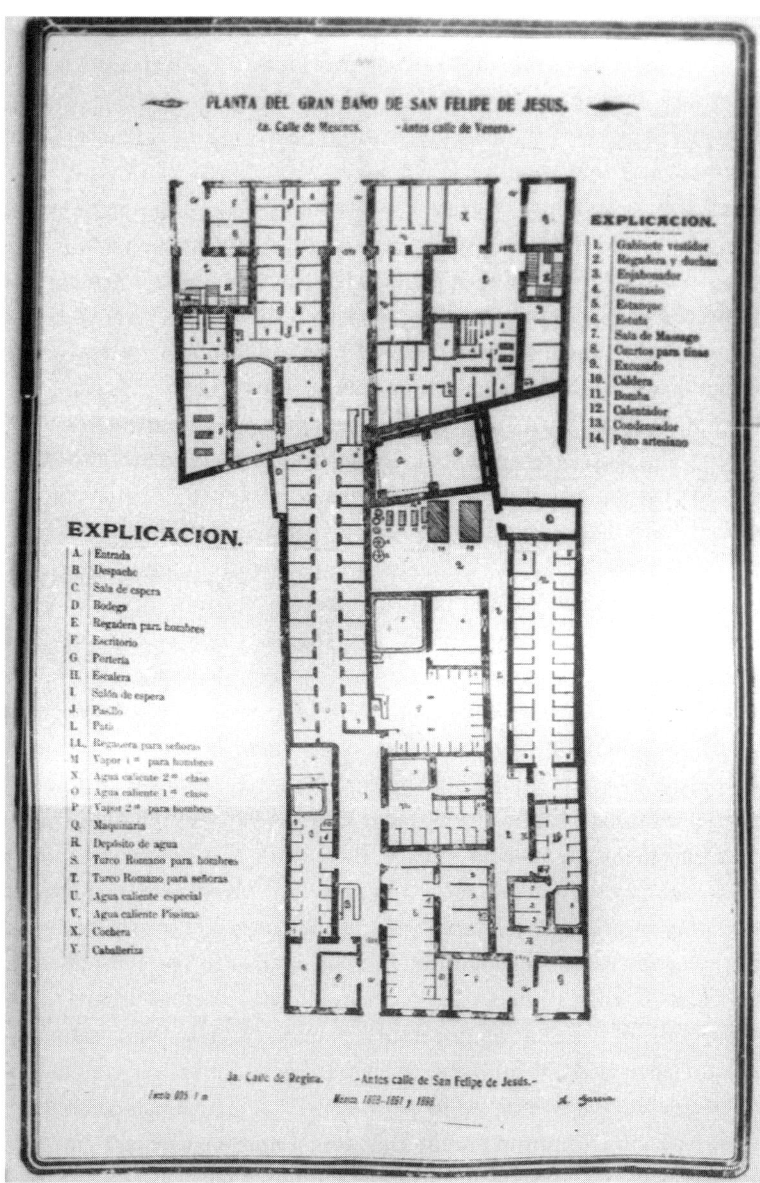

Figure 1.1. Bathhouses featured large public areas for cruising and small cubicles that could be used for trysts. Notice the multiple entrances. Map, "El gran baño de San Felipe de Jesús," from anonymous, *Ligeros apuntes históricos sobre el baño en México y datos históricos y estadísticos del gran baño de san Felipe de Jesús en la capital de la República* (Mexico City: Tipografía Vázquez e hijos, 1911), unpaginated.

other men. Manuel Gutiérrez Nájera once gave Valenzuela "loud smacking kisses" on his hands while on a railway car; Manuel González Jr. kissed the painter Julio Ruelas on the forehead.[65] Such instances of public tactile intimacy—particularly if they occurred while men were nude and in a bathhouse—suggest that should individuals be so inclined, the frequency and acceptability with which Porfirian society regarded public, same-sex displays of affection made it possible for some to express their fondness for another man. If the intended object of desire did not object and allowed the other to continue touching him—or even reciprocated and or increased the intimacy of the touching—a man could very well erotically caress another man publicly while bathing or working out. A slap on the back, a careless slip of the palm while measuring a muscle, could become a tender caress.

For those who were not as daring as the Lencho that the youthful Elías Nandino encountered in this chapter's opening vignette, the layout of the bathhouse afforded other methods, such as lying about the reading room and noticing what books and magazines bathers read while lounging about. From this, an educated guess could be made about a person's interests. Was he reading a homoerotic foreign journal, like *Physical Culture Magazine*?[66] Was he engrossed reading a newspaper account of the homosexual scandals that were rocking the German Empire, or was he following the Oscar Wilde trial?

The geography of the bathhouse allowed homosexual men to find others like themselves; its sumptuous space and leisurely practices facilitated the formation of same-sex affective ties and sense of self. Commonly used pejoratives for effeminate men in nineteenth-century Mexico—*perfumado* (the well-scented or perfumed one) or *polveado* (powdered)—suggest that contemporaries thought gay men spent too much time grooming themselves and hence frequented first-class bathing establishments. In the collective mind, being clean, finicky, and an avid bather made one queer. Melchor Ocampo, in the middle of the nineteenth century, penned a one-act play featuring an *adamado* (effeminate) youth who, when faced with the task of confronting a band of thieves that was trying to break into his home, panicked because he did not have time to primp and preen.[67] José Tomás de Cuéllar's *Historia de Chucho el Ninfo* (1871) similarly portrays—although Cuéllar never comes out and says so—an effeminate, seemingly gay man (a queen) who is consumed with his appearance. He uses makeup, curls his hair, uses cold cream, and drives his valet crazy with the fastidiousness of his costume and cleanliness.[68] A book of advice for young boys summarizes this argument quite clearly:

Pero no por el temor
De parecer incivil,
El afeite femenil
Uses á mas y mejor;
Que el hombre que fátuo y nécio
Como mujer se engalana
Y en perfumarse se afana,
Solo merece desprecio.

(Do not for the fear of
Appearing uncivil
Abuse the cosmetics of women
Because the man
Who stubbornly and vainly
Adorns himself as a woman
And likes to scent himself
Deserves only scorn.)[69]

A guidebook dating from the 1890s, suggests—in luxuriant detail—the homoerotically charged environment of bathhouses. In a brief testimonial, a visitor to the Gran Alberca Pane described his experiences there in a most sensual manner. "I disencumbered myself of my clothing," he begins his tale, insinuating the undesirability of clothing and the naturality of nudity. Upon entering the first of the tri-chambered Turkish bath (tepidarium, caldarium, and laconicum), "I felt the warm air caressing, overpowering me." The air is pleasurable and puts him in a mood whereby he can offer himself to something that is more powerful than he. As his eyes adjust to the dim light, he notices the play of colored lights. "These," he wrote, "idealize the spectacle of other bathers, who seemed to dance and turn nude all about me. I lay down on a divan and entered a most pleasant somnolence free of all physical or moral restraint. My thoughts began to wander."[70] And that was only the beginning. His sensual experience was heightened in the massage room, where a member of the "pleasant, smiling, refined, and exquisitely gallant" staff scrubbed and gave him such a good kneading that "I began to fall under a spell." With the masseur's hands running all over his body, he noticed the dim lights changing color:

> beginning a rhythmic dance evocative of the arabesque designs on the walls, giving a rainbow hue to the drops of water dripping from the faucets [as fast] as the [beating] of the wings of a hummingbird . . . [the hands] of the most able and pleasant masseur, washes and lathers all of your body, and I know not where he is more tenderly gentle, if at the top, middle, or bottom.[71]

One cannot but wonder whether the language here used is a veiled reference by the delirious bather to being tactilely stimulated by the bath boy, particularly given the pulsating phallic imagery (the hummingbird beating his wings and the faucet dripping). Lest one make such a conjecture, the narrator of the testimonial assures the reader that the stimulation the young man is making of his body is guided by "all the movements that science dictates." Once he is thus reinvigorated, most fittingly, the much-aroused bather takes a cold water plunge and upon emerging from the pool, another young man envelops his naked body in a white towel.[72]

Washing the Queer Away

It did not take long for authorities to catch on to the "dirty dealings" at the bathhouses. The behavior, practices, and sumptuous trappings of the same-sex-attracted male bathing culture of the 1890s became unacceptable by 1905 owing to increased elite anxiety stemming from widespread claims that upper-class males were becoming too soft, self-serving, and hedonist to be entrusted with the country.[73] The Porfirian bonanza had corrupted the morality and the spirit of enterprise of the golden youth, who had instead taken up drugs, alcohol, sex, materialism, and a life of sinful pleasures.[74] This had turned them into weak, immoral, decadent, frivolous, effeminate men. During a heated discussion with Rubén M. Campos at the famed bar "Wondracek," Alberto Leduc questioned the masculinity of Mexico City literary circles, claiming that the country could do without poofs: "We need men, not effeminate poets like Walt Whitman."[75] Moreover, a series of homosexual scandals at the turn of the century implicating members of the country's highest social, industrial, military, and political circles forced health authorities, journalists, bathhouse entrepreneurs, and others to more closely scrutinize steam rooms, gymnasiums, swimming pools, and showers as sites that endangered public health and morality.[76] It was not a phenomenon that was exclusive to Mexico City; the authors of the 1905 Chihuahua civil code not only criminalized same-sex rape and persecuted all forms of *contra-natura* intercourse with stiff fines and penalties, but also sought to provide protection, both to men and to women, from any unsolicited sexual innuendos or advances in public spaces. Article 769, which sanctioned individuals who engaged in public behavior "contrary to decency" with fines of up to five hundred pesos, criminalized homosexuality. Article 771, which guaranteed freedom from any unwanted sexual advances from individuals of the opposite or same sex, also penalized homosexuality.[77] Authorities and business owners consequently elaborated regulations outlining what was considered proper and improper public behavior.

So by the beginning of the twentieth century Mexican bathhouses—much like gay baths in the United States in the late 1970s and during the 1980s—symbolized sexual license, irresponsibility, degeneracy, and scandal.[78] Authors of bathing advertisements and guidebooks reassured the public of the safety and morality of first-class balneary establishments. In his prologue to the guide to the Gran Baño de San Felipe de Jesús, literary figure Luis G. Urbina stressed that unlike its competitors, this establishment was characterized by cleanliness, order, and propriety. Special attention was drawn to the employees' honorable behavior, as well as their attention to detail and constant vigilance against physical and moral dangers. Facilities were well-lit, privacy was guaranteed, and most interestingly, noted the amplitude of all departments. At the San Felipe de Jesús Baths, its propaganda proclaimed, bathers were not so crowded that they would unnecessarily and uncomfortably rub up against each other. Rather, they could circulate freely and not be in close proximity to strangers, as was the case in "dubious" establishments. A set of rules was strictly enforced to guarantee safety, hygiene, and a "moral environment" to clients. This included a prohibition against the mixing of genders, precluded the presence of prostitutes, and strictly banned the sharing of tubs or the scrubbing or handling of other bathers in any way.[79]

Moreover, loiterers were warned against dawdling about; they were to rapidly proceed about their business and vacate the premises within forty-five minutes of entering. Anyone who took too long in the baths was fined; patrons were asked to not congregate in the gymnasium and to only use the equipment for fifteen minutes. The harshness of these policies, the guidebook noted, was to curb the occurrence of improper behavior that apparently discombobulated polite society: "These procedures are meant to preserve order and morality in this establishment, in order to avoid any dangers or inconveniences to the customers."[80]

Given the great symbolic value of bathhouses to Porfirian elites, measures had to be taken to contain the grave danger that homosexual cruising posed for an unsuspecting population. The regulations and language employed suggests that baths without adequate means to guarantee privacy, inappropriate or insufficient lighting or surveillance, and with crowded conditions, could lend themselves to bathers cruising the baths, inappropriately touching themselves or each other. Policymakers perhaps hoped that individuals would cease to cruise each other out of fear that society was now on the lookout for their transgressions.

Conclusion

Through analysis of the geography of leisure and hygiene, we can interrogate quotidian practices that allow us to understand how societies set the standards through which individuals measure their self-worth. The balneal practices of Porfirian Mexico offer insight into the much-examined discourses of hygiene, morality, leisure, and class, but they also increase our understanding of how Díaz's regime transformed Mexican society—whether through increased contact with the outside world or through the expansion of traditional definitions and manifestations of gender. The bathing culture of the gente decente not only allowed them to define and articulate the boundaries of polite society, but it also provided them with a way of expressing, through a banal quotidian practice, a sense of national pride. From depths of their soapy bathtubs and dark steam baths, the middle classes could carry out their civic duty and personally contribute to the regime's modernizing goals. A daily bath regimen not only gave them health and membership in the country's moral majority, but it also allowed them to perform Mexico's balneal superiority vis-à-vis an unwashed Europe.

But in the site that proclaimed the country's civilization also lurked the sinister specter of moral danger. Bathhouses were instrumental in making public, visible, or evident the artificiality of heterosexual masculinity. In the steamy darkness of the balneal establishment, as the many regulations and prohibitions reviewed here suggest, Porfirian males could sexually satisfy themselves with other men. These regulations, clearly aimed at suppressing opportunities for same-gender sensuality, reveal a much more widespread practice of homosexuality than historians have seen previously. Whether or not the men who sought out the affection of other men thought of themselves as members of a separate subculture is irrelevant to this point; we can leave the genealogy of a gay identity for another time. What is evident is that bathhouse regulations sought to discourage or hide the public display or flaunting of non-reproductive, non-heterosexual sensuality. Rather, the enactment of these policies made evident that societal unease about the revelation of "an absolutely sanctioned public silence" on homosexuality.[81] If society proved unable to suppress queers—*raritos* or *jotos*—from using the baths to seek out sexual partners, then the next best thing that could be done was to place legal impediments to those practices that facilitated same-sex intimacy in bathhouses and swimming pools. Most interestingly the authorities' efforts to police the "dirty dealings" in the bathhouse led to the elaboration of a criminal discourse to contain the homosexual. Ironically, in doing so, they also constructed a new social category, which over time evolved into a distinct and thriving community of people. Historicizing the geography and practices of bathing thus sheds light on the degree to which employing masculinity as a unit of analysis helps us understand how the state's expansion of control over the body, its practices, and performances of gender occurred in a space that ironically facilitated the imagining of a community of same-sex-attracted individuals.

NOTES

1. I want to thank the International Development Fund and the College of Liberal Studies of the University of Wisconsin, La Crosse, for the research and travel funds that made this chapter possible.
2. Elías Nandino, *Juntando mis pasos* (Mexico City: Editorial Aldus, 2000), 12. Nandino used the word *pipí*—here translated into *peepee*. All translations, unless otherwise noted, are my own.
3. Nandino, *Juntando*, 19.
4. Nandino, *Juntando*, 33–35.
5. Nandino, *Juntando*, 39–40.
6. By "showcase" I refer to the concept of *vitrine identitaire* developed by French historians Brigitte and Joseph Krulic in their essay "Les lieux et la mémoire, la mémoire des lieux: L'Europe et ses lieux communs," in *Europe, lieux communs. Cafés, gares, jardins publics*, ed. Brigitte Krulic (Paris: Éditions Autrement, 2004), 7. The Krulics drew on the work of others, especially Jocelyne Bonnet, "La vitrine identitaire, une nouvelle source pour l'étude des recompositions identitaires," in *De l'Europe, Identités et Identité, mémoires et mémoire*, ed. Charles-Olivier Carbonell (Toulouse: Presses de l'Université des Sciences Sociales, 1996), 183–90.
7. "Los 41 bailarines," *La Patria*, November 22, 1901, cited in *The Famous 41: Sexuality and Social Control in Mexico, 1901*, ed. Robert McKee-Irwin, Edward J. McCaughan, and Michelle Rocío Nasser (New York: Palgrave Press, 2003), 37–38.
8. Consejo Superior de Salubridad, *Memorias del primer Congreso Higiénico-Pedagógico reunido en la ciudad de México el año de 1882* (Mexico City: Imprenta del Gobierno dirigida por Sabás A. y Munguía, 1883), 37–38 and 54–56; and Blas Escontrías, *Memoria presentada al H. Congreso del Estado de San Luis Potosí por el gobernador constitucional Ingeniero Blas Escontrías relativa a los actos administrativos correspondientes al periodo de 10 de septiembre de 1899 a 31 de agosto de 1901* (San Luis Potosí: Gobierno del Estado, 1901), unpaginated. In the *Memoria* of Escontrías, refer to the report by the new director of the Escuela Industrial Militar. The rare *Memoria* is located in the Colección de Memorias Administrativas, Fondo de la Secretaría General del Gobierno, Archivo Histórico del Estado de San Luis Potosí, San Luis Potosí, Mexico.
9. Mauricio Tenorio Trillo, *Mexico at the World's Fairs: Crafting a Modern Nation* (Berkeley: University of California Press, 1996).
10. Julio Guerrero, *La génesis del crímen en México* (Mexico City: Consejo Nacional para la Cultura y las Artes, 1996), 132–38.
11. Luis Sánchez Granjel, "Dos tratados de hidrología de Torres Villarroel," *Capítulos de la Medicina Española: Estudios de la historia de la Medicina Española* 3 (1971): 327–41; Félix Fermín Eguía y Harrieta, *Escrito phísico político: las utilidades y daños que trae la agua fria de nieve, á qué personas, y humanas dolencias conviene, y desconviene* (Madrid: Imprenta Real, 1749); and Jan Bazant, "El acueducto de

Ixtapan de la Sal, una obra hidráulica campesina del siglo XIX," *Historia Mexicana* 36, no. 1 (1986): 169–72.

12. Daniel Eisenberg, "Juan Ruiz's Heterosexual *Good Love*," in *Queer Iberia: Sexualities, Cultures, and Crossings from the Middle Ages to the Renaissance*, ed. Josiah Blackmore and Gregory S. Hutcheson (Durham, NC: Duke University Press, 1999), 259.
13. Artemio del Valle-Arizpe, *Calle vieja y calle nueva* (Mexico City: Editorial Jus, 1949), 446–47.
14. Moisés González Navarro, *Historia moderna de México. El Porfiriato. La Vida Social*, ed. Daniel Cosío Villegas (Mexico and Buenos Aires: Editorial Hermes, 1957), 90–91.
15. José Juan Tablada, *La Feria de la Vida* (Mexico City: Consejo Nacional para la Cultura y las Artes, 1991), 82–104.
16. Tablada, *Feria*, 194.
17. Jesús E. Valenzuela, *Mis recuerdos, Manojo de rimas* (Mexico City: Consejo Nacional para la Cultura y las Artes, 2001), 66–67.
18. Alain Corbin, *The Lure of the Sea: The Discovery of the Seaside in the Western World, 1750–1840*, trans. Jocelyn Phelps (Berkeley: University of California Press, 1994); and Peter Douglas Mackaman, *Leisure Settings: Bourgeois Culture, Medicine, and the Spa in Modern France* (Chicago: University of Chicago Press, 1998).
19. Corbin, *Lure of the Sea*, 57–63; and Sánchez Granjel, "Dos tratados de hidrología," 327–41.
20. Bazant, "El acueducto de Ixtapan de la Sal," 169–72.
21. Mackaman, *Leisure Settings*, 1–11.
22. Susan C. Anderson and Bruce H. Tabb, eds., *Water, Leisure and Culture: European Historical Perspectives* (Oxford and New York: Berg, 2002).
23. An example of state propaganda of the baths at Tehuacán is evident in the fifth volume of Antonio Peñafiel, *Ciudades coloniales y capitales de la República Mexicana*, 5 vols. (Mexico City: Imprenta y Fototípia de la Secretaría de Fomento, 1908–1914).
24. Edward H. Gibson, "Baths and Washhouses in the English Public Health Agitation, 1839–1848," *Journal of the History of Medicine and Allied Sciences* 9, no. 4 (1954): 391–406; and H. L. Malchow, "Public Gardens and Social Action in Late Victorian London," *Victorian Studies* 29, no. 1 (1985): 97–124.
25. Thierry Terret, "Hygienization: Civic Baths and Body Cleanliness in Late Nineteenth-Century France," *International Journal of the History of Sport* 10, no. 3 (1993): 396–408; and Brian K. Ladd, "Public Baths and Civic Improvement in Nineteenth-Century German Cities," *Journal of Urban History* 14, no. 3 (1988): 372–93.
26. Víctor M. Macías-González, "The *Lagartijo* at *The High Life*: Notes on Masculine Consumption, Race, Nation, and Homosexuality in Porfirian Mexico," in *The Famous 41: Sexuality and Social Control in Mexico, 1901*, ed. Robert McKee-Irwin,

Edward J. McCaughan, and Michelle Rocío Nasser (New York: Palgrave Press, 2003), 227–49.

27. On the evolution of elite residential patterns in the nineteenth century, consult Hugo Nutini, *The Wages of Conquest: The Mexican Aristocracy in the Context of Western Aristocracies* (Ann Arbor: University of Michigan Press, 1995).

28. María del Carmen Vázquez M., "Charros contra *gentlemen*: Un episodio de identidad en la historia de la tauromaquia mexicana *moderna*, 1886–1905," in *Modernidad, tradición, y alteridad. La ciudad de México en el cambio de siglo, XIX–XX*, ed. Claudia Agostoni and Elisa Speckman (Mexico City: UNAM, 2001), 161–93. On Payno's pursuits, see Guillermo Prieto, *Memorias de mis tiempos* (Mexico City: Consejo Nacional para la Cultura y las Artes, 1992), 93. On the decadence of Porfirian dandies, consult Macías-González, "Lagartijo."

29. Gabriel Rosenzweig, ed., *Un liberal español en el México porfiriano. Cartas de Telesforo García a Emilio Castelar, 1888–1899* (Mexico City: Consejo Nacional para la Cultura y las Artes, 2003), 153.

30. Víctor M. Macías-González, "Apuntes sobre la construcción de la masculinidad en México a través del arte decimonónico," in *Hacia otra historia del arte en México. Vol. 2: La amplitud del modernismo y la modernidad*, ed. Stacie Widdiefield and Esther Acevedo (Mexico City: Consejo Nacional para la Cultura y las Artes and CURARE/Centro Crítico para las Artes, 2004), 329–50. On the "strenuous life" consult Gail Bederman, *Manliness and Civilization: A Cultural History of Gender and Race in the United States, 1880–1917* (Chicago: University of Chicago Press, 1995).

31. Bederman, *Manliness and Civilization*, 120. Ilan Stavans quips, "In Golden Age Mexican films, showing stamina and force represented the masculine aspect of the collective Hispanic soul . . . to endure, to show determination, is the way in which the macho deals with doubt and insecurity." See Ilan Stavans, *The Hispanic Condition Reflections on Culture and Identity in America* (New York: Harper, 1996), 109–11.

32. Glenn Avent, "A Popular and Wholesome Resort: Gender, Class, and the YMCA in Porfirian Mexico" (master's thesis, University of British Columbia, 1996).

33. Anonymous, *El Hamm Am. Baños turco-romanos en la gran Alberca Pane. Hidroterapia completa. Guía del bañador* (Mexico City: Tipografia Berrueco Hermanos, 1887), 6–7, 38.

34. Macías-González, "Lagartijo," 228–30.

35. For further reflection on nudity, consult Richard Dyer, "The White Man's Muscles," in *The Masculinity Studies Reader*, ed. Rachel Adams and David Savran (Malden, MA: Blackwell, 2002), 262–73.

36. Guerrero, *La génesis del crímen*, 118.

37. Guerrero, *La génesis del crímen*, 132–33, 136–38.

38. Carlos Roumagnac, *Por los mundos del delito. Los criminales en México, ensayo de psicología criminal, seguido de dos casos de hermafrodismo observados por los*

señores doctores Ricardo Egea e Ignacio Ocampo (Mexico City: Tipografía "El Fénix," 1904).

39. Guerrero, *La génesis del crímen*, 140–41.
40. "Los Guardias de la Presidencia," *El Imparcial* 4, no. 1386 (July 6, 1900): 1.
41. José J. Rivas, *Código de urbanidad para uso de las escuelas de la República* (Mexico City: Imprenta del Gobierno en Palacio, á cargo de José María Sandoval, 1874), 89–91.
42. José Rosas, *Nuevo manual de urbanidad y buenas maneras escrito en verso para la infancia*, 30th ed. (Mexico City: Antigua Imprenta de Munguía, 1888), 8–11.
43. Guerrero, *La génesis del crímen*, 139.
44. Ibid., 110 and 144–47.
45. Ibid., 144.
46. Manuel Antonio Carreño, *Manual de Urbanidad y Buenas Costumbres para uso de la juventud de ambos sexos* (New York: D. Appleton y Compañía, 1880), 42–43.
47. Interview by the author of María Teresa Romero Rojas y Fajardo de González, Ciudad Juárez, Chihuahua, January 1994.
48. Tenorio-Trillo, *Mexico at the World's Fairs*, 144–57.
49. The director of the Consejo Superior de Salud, Dr. Eduardo Liceaga, mentions bathing facilities in his memoirs in great detail. See his *Mis recuerdos de otros tiempos* (Mexico City: Cooperativa Talleres Gráficos de la Nación, 1949). See also description of exhibits during the Centenario in Genaro García, ed., *Crónica oficial de las fiestas del primer centenario de la Independencia de México* (Mexico City: Talleres del Museo Nacional, 1911).
50. Liceaga, *Mis recuerdos de otros tiempos*, 152.
51. González Navarro, *Historia moderna de México*, 92–93; Manuel Marroquín y Rivera, *Memoria descriptiva de las obras de provisión de aguas potables para la ciudad de México* (Mexico City: Imprenta y Litografía de Müller Hnos., 1914); Ricardo Orozco Ríos, "El agua potable en la ciudad de México durante el Porfiriato," *Nuestra Historia La Gaceta del Centro de Estudios Históricos del Porfiriato* 36 (May 2000): 12–23; and Carlos Elizondo Alcaraz, *Horizontes del agua* (Toluca: Gobierno del Estado de México, 2000).
52. Refer to Terret's article cited in footnote 25 earlier.
53. Manuel F. Madrazo, Harms Hôtel Terminus, Cologne, Germany, July 26, 1914, to Toribio Esquivel Obregón, Brooklyn, New York, Box 29, Expediente 6, Archivo Toribio Esquivel Obregón, Universidad Iberoamericana, Mexico City.
54. A widely used Spanish book of etiquette for men did not mention a single comment on bathing! See *Nuevo manual de urbanidad, cortesía, decoro, y etiqueta, ó el Hombre Fino* (Madrid: Librería de los Hijos de D. J. Cuesta, 1889).
55. The first Spaniards in Anáhuac, accustomed to two or three baths per year, had been shocked to learn that the Aztecs, in the words of an early chronicler, "bathed much and often." Fray Toribio de Benavente noted in the sixteenth century that

the Indians were "very much in the habit of bathing frequently, whether well or ill, and continued to do so even when suffering from smallpox." See his account of "The Ten Plagues of Mexico," in Fray Toribio de Benavente Motolinía, *History of the Indians of New Spain* (Westport, CT: Greenwood Press, 1973), 38–43.

56. Isabel Pesado y de la Llave, duquesa de Mier, *Apuntes de viaje de México á Europa en los años de 1870–1871 y 1872* (Paris: Garnier Hermanos, Libreros-Editores, 1910), 61 and 76–77. The diary entry reads, "It was most difficult to even obtain a small basin with which to take a sponge-bath, as they said no one had ever requested even that."

57. Alicia Ortíz Rivera, *Juan Sánchez Navarro: Biografía de un testigo del México del siglo XX* (México: Editorial Grijalbo, 1997), 120.

58. Del Valle Arizpe, *Calle vieja y calle nueva*, 413–17; and anonymous, *El Hamm Am. Baños Turco-Romanos en la gran Alberca Pane. Hidroterapia completa. Guía del Bañador* (Mexico City: Tipografía Berrueco Hermanos, 1897), unpaginated. A copy can be found in the Felipe Teixidor Collection of the Rare Books Room of the Biblioteca México, Mexico City.

59. Anonymous, *El Hamm Am*, unpaginated.

60. J. Figueroa Doménech, *Guía general descriptivo de la República Mexicana. Historia, Geografía, Estadística, con triple directorio del Comercio y la Industria, Autoridades, Oficinas públicas, Abogados, Médicos, Hacendados, Correos, Telégrafos, y Ferrocarriles, vol. 1, El Distrito Federal* (Mexico City and Barcelona: Ramón de S. N. Araluce, ed., 1899), 283–87.

61. Serge Gruzinski, "Las cenizas del deseo. Homosexuales novohispanos a mediados del siglo XVII," *De la santidad a la perversión, o de por qué no se cumplía la ley de Dios en la sociedad novohispana*, ed. Sergio Ortega (Mexico City: Editorial Grijalbo, 1986), 255–81.

62. Causa formada con motivo de haberse encontrado hombres y mujeres en el baño que nombran del Padre Garrido, Año de 1793, Archivo Histórico de la ciudad de México (hereafter AHCM), Ramo Policias, Baños y Lavaderos, vol. 3621, exp. 5, ff 1–5.

63. José Álvarez Amézquita, Miguel E. Bustamante, Antonio López Picazos, and Francisco Fernández del Castillo, *Historia de la Salubridad y de la Asistencia en México*, 4 vols. (Mexico City: Secretaría de Salubridad y Asistencia, 1960), 2:400–10 and 4:132–45.

64. John Ibson, *Picturing Men: A Century of Male Relationships in Everyday American Photography* (Washington, D.C.: Smithsonian Institution Press, 2002).

65. Valenzuela, *Mis recuerdos*, 100 and 132.

66. Postcards—mostly French, German, and Russian—that found their way to Mexico, alongside the American magazine *Physical Culture*, had homoerotic images of nude or near-nude men. Their titles are listed in the descriptions of libraries of clubs like the YMCA and in the shopping lists and diaries of the period. See the list in the entry for Monday, August 29, 1904, in José Juan Tablada, *Obras IV: Diario, 1900–1944* (Mexico City: UNAM, 1992), 40.

67. Melchor Ocampo, "Don Primoroso, Sainete," in *Obras completas de Melchor Ocampo*, 3 vols., ed. Ángel Polá and Aurelio J. Venegas (Mexico City: F. Vázquez, 1900), 3:252–60.
68. José Tomás de Cuéllar, *La historia de Chucho el Ninfo* (Mexico City: Editorial Porrúa, 1975), 210–13.
69. José Rosas, *Nuevo manual de urbanidad y buenas maneras escrito en verso para la infancia*, 30th ed. (Mexico City: Antigua Librería de Murguía, 1888), 5.
70. Anonymous, *El Hamm Am*, 17–18.
71. Ibid., 18–19.
72. Ibid., 19–20.
73. On this matter, consult chapters 4 and 5 of my dissertation, "The Mexican Aristocracy and Porfirio Díaz, 1876–1911" (PhD diss., Texas Christian University, 1999). Refer also to Rob Buffington, "Los Jotos: Contested Visions of Homosexuality in Modern Mexico," *Sex and Sexuality in Latin America*, ed. Donna Guy and Daniel Balderston (New York: New York University Press, 1997), 118–32.
74. Rip Rip, "Lo que fué y lo que es," *El Imparcial*, September 16, 1898; Anonymous, "La generación nueva se pervierte," *Siglo XX: Semanario de Información Literatura y Variedades* (Ciudad Juárez), August 24, 1904; and Daniel Cabrera, "La aristocracia de Sodoma al servicio nacional," *El Hijo del Ahuizote*, November 24, 1901.
75. Rubén M. Campos, *El Bar: la vida literaria de México en 1900* (Mexico City: UNAM, 1996), 128.
76. The "41" was the principal one, but there was also a famous incident involving the staff of the Imperial German Legation. It happened when the German military attaché attended an official function so convincingly attired in feminine garb that he fooled an unsuspecting President Díaz into openly flirting with him. When the ruse was revealed, a much-embarrassed Díaz ordered the German's immediate expulsion from the country. See Victoriano Salado Álvarez, *Memorias, Tiempo Nuevo* (Mexico City: Edición y Distribución Ibero Americana de Publicaciones, 1946), 245.
77. Article 769 read, "Se impondrá la pena de arresto mayor y multa de cinco a quinientos pesos, al que ultraje la moral pública ó las buenas costumbres, ejecutando una acción impúdica en un lugar público. Se tendrá como impúdica toda acción que en el concepto público esté calificada de contraria al pudor." Crimes against decency, "atentados contra el pudor," were further defined in article 771, which made a passing reference to homosexuality in noting, "Se dá el nombre de atentado al pudor á todo acto impúdico que pueda ofenderlo, sin llegar á la copula carnal, y que se ejecuta en la persona de otro sin su voluntad, sea cual fuere su sexo." Its aim was clearly to penalize any unsolicited sexual advances and innuendos from individuals in public areas. See Estado de Chihuahua, *Código penal del Estado Libre y Soberano de Chihuahua* (Chihuahua City: Imprenta del Gobierno, 1905), 178–79.

78. See Pat Califia's comments on gay baths in *Public Sex: The Culture of Radical Sex*, 2nd ed. (San Francisco: Cleis Press, 2000), 6.
79. This was also part of the increased regulation of prostitution. See Katherine Elaine Bliss, *Compromised Positions: Prostitution, Public Health, and Gender Politics in Revolutionary Mexico City* (University Park: Pennsylvania State University Press, 2001).
80. Anonymous, *Ligeros apuntes históricos*, unpaginated.
81. Martin Nesvig claims that Mexicans understood homosexuality as morally unseemly but acceptable if left unspoken. See his article, "The Lure of the Perverse: Moral Negotiation of Pederasty in Porfirian Mexico," *Mexican Studies/Estudios Mexicanos* 16, no. 1 (Winter 2000): 1–37.

CHAPTER 2

Runaway Daughters

Women's Masculine Roles in Elopement Cases in Nineteenth-Century Mexico

KATHRYN A. SLOAN

EARLY ONE WEDNESDAY EVENING IN 1899, JOSEFA CALVO LEFT HER family home to meet her *novio* (boyfriend), Manuel Vivas, in the public garden of the Church of the Soledad in Oaxaca. Josefa, fourteen years old, a seamstress by trade like her mother, and Manuel, eighteen years old and a shawl maker, had been sweethearts for four months. The young couple wished to begin their lives together, but Josefa's mother stood in their way. Manuel had promised in a love letter that he would send his father to ask for her permission to marry. Josefa vehemently rejected his offer, stating that the "*mal vivir*" (bad home life) she already suffered would grow worse. Instead, in her letter, Josefa demanded that Manuel take her away from her mother immediately or she "may feel obligated to go away with someone else." Josefa then subsumed the active or male role in the elopement drama by subsequently setting the date, time, place, and plan of execution for their clandestine rendezvous. A few days later, she bundled up her clothes and other personal effects and left home to meet Manuel.[1]

The story of Josefa and Manuel leads us into the world of gender relations among young working-class individuals in Porfirian Mexico. Their story emerges from more than two hundred court records of *rapto* (abduction/seduction/elopement of a minor) proceedings housed in the municipal archive of Oaxaca de Juárez, Mexico, for the dates 1850–1920.[2] These cases are fascinating because within their pages unfold the various dramas of private lives made public by breaches of prevailing norms and laws. The various testimonies reveal how parents struggled with their children, lovers quarreled with each other, and all actors sparred with the state. Likewise, all participants transgressed established gender norms and traditional scripts of appropriate behavior. Take the case of Josefa, whose story introduces this essay. She set the date, time, and whereabouts of her own "abduction or seduction" and challenged Manuel's manhood if he did not consent to her plan. If he did not comply with her preparations, she would simply find another man who would. In effect, Josefa asserted her wants and desires and mobilized her resources to get her way. She wished to begin conjugal life with Manuel (or another man if he refused) and escape the torment and oppression of her mother. Noticeably, she acted masculine by engineering her own destiny to run away with her lover. In essence, she turned the tables and "seduced and abducted" her male sweetheart. Assertiveness, persuasion, cunning, and action were all traits associated with men but employed by Josefa in her plan to elope with Manuel.[3] Equally, Manuel admitted his passive role in his seduction, noting in his testimony that Josefa planned every detail of their escape and even raised the money to rent a room for the night. This chapter highlights some of the elopement dramas and evaluates how their participants performed various gender identities with creativity and purpose.

Mexican adolescents generally eloped as an opportunistic strategy. Why? It was understood that parents facing a daughter recently sullied often relented to allow the marriage of their minor children (less than twenty-one years of age). But other couples merely ran off together to form a trial marriage or consensual union and found themselves dragged into the courts to defend and justify their crime.[4] The process of rapto was deceptively straightforward. Having established a romantic relationship with a young man, the woman would leave her parents' home and go with her boyfriend to the house of a friend or relative. In some cases, the young man had saved money, planned for the "elopement," and might have a home or rented room of his own. Nonetheless, once free of parental surveillance, the couple would usually engage in sexual relations when the man would "take possession" of the young woman's virginity or honor. The couple would then set up conjugal life together and marry at some later date or maintain an *amaciato* (consensual union).

These young lovers, rejecting their parents' opposition and interference in spousal choice, followed the steps of seduction in effect to reorder power relations in families and by extension, the nation. After all, the goal of seduction was never sex for them; sex merely became the artifice that served as the means to an end. For example, Josefa and Manuel, impeded by her mother's objection to the union, followed the script of seduction and elopement as the means to their desired end: marriage. Armed with cultural understandings of honor, virginity, and gender roles, they played out their parts as seducer and seducee in order to achieve their aims. In an extraordinary twist, Josefa took on the role of seducer and her lover, Manuel, seducee. Hence, their case and the rest of the plebeian actors under study here provide an excellent arena in which to evaluate the landscape of plebeian moral codes that informed honor, marriage, and sexuality. In addition, these scenarios illustrate how individuals like Josefa transgressed gender norms by taking on the culturally understood attributes of Mexican masculinity to achieve her aims.

Rapto and Masculinity

Seduction (rapto) presented men the opportunity to display their virile manhood.[5] In fact, men often employed rapto in order to gain access to female sexuality to determine if their girlfriends were virgins. In effect, they coaxed young virgins into premarital sex to prove their purity, pledging that they would then make good on their promise of marriage. Likewise, when a man spoiled a woman's honor by removing her from her paternal home and then deflowering her, his actions denigrated the honor of her father and family, especially if it became public knowledge. While the seducer's honor and esteem rose in the community, the aggrieved father suffered a blow to his honor and reputation because he had failed to control and protect his female family member. When a seducer "abducted" and deflowered another man's daughter, the father was expected to act swiftly and publicly to restore his own honor and the honor of his family. He could confront the perpetrator and demand that he marry or monetarily compensate his daughter. For instance, one father, Juan, walked into his house late one night and found Arcadio with his pants in his hands and his daughter on her bed. He testified that he thought of getting his gun to defend his honor but that his daughter and her sisters wrapped their arms around his knees and pleaded with him to desist.[6] Refusing violence, Juan entered the courtroom to defend his honor. Likewise, a man that could boast of deflowering a virgin elevated his own masculine reputation among his peers. Moreover, a man who seduced and despoiled a young virgin but also wished to marry her could also elevate his honor by fulfilling the role of chivalrous redeemer who saves the young woman and her family from disgrace and ruin. Whether he abandoned or married her, the man saw his honor and reputation increased by his sexual prowess. For the most part when a man seduced and eloped with a young woman, he enhanced his own masculinity and in turn, emasculated her father. Likewise, it could be argued that men who employed rapto displayed a hypermasculinity by carrying out their plans for sexual access and/or marriage to their girlfriends even when an older male (the father) opposed him. For example, after seducing Primitiva, Francisco returned to her house and told her father in vulgar terms that "he had enjoyed his daughter and he took her because he was a man and he would not return her." He then taunted him to contact the police.[7]

On the surface, it seems that rapto simply perpetuated a patriarchal honor system that victimized women. But as we see with Josefa, some women took on the man's role in the drama of seduction and elopement. In effect, women like Josefa possessed agency by engendering and performing a masculine identity (seducer) to achieve their goals. This attests to the authenticity of masculinity not as a natural condition of men and their bodies, but as a performative element of gender that may also be executed by women. Indeed, Judith Halberstam argues that "it is inaccurate and indeed regressive to make masculinity into a general term for behavior associated with males."[8]

Some scholars have concluded that the practice of rapto was, in the end, a reproduction of male domination or at best a weak challenge to the dominant system. But looking at rapto as elopement among the working class gives us a far more complex and interesting picture of the practice. Raptos occurred not merely as a means to gain access to female sexuality but as a strategy to initiate family life. Sometimes young women ran off with their lovers as a prelude to marriage; other couples chose to live in free unions. The Oaxacan cases resemble Eileen Suárez Findlay's summary of rapto cases in nineteenth-century Puerto Rico. Oaxacan working-class women, like those of Findlay's study, "emerge from [the] judicial documents as sexual and social agents, struggling with their partners, parents, and wealthy judges over the terms of bodily and economic integrity as well as the meaning of marriage and respectability."[9] In the case of Oaxaca, many women participated actively in their own elopement either by orchestrating their "abduction" or challenging their boyfriends' manhood if they did not succumb to their demands. In essence, these forthright young women "behaved like men" by asserting an active sexuality, thus upsetting prevailing gender norms that expected passive femininity.

Rapto in the Eyes of the Court

This contravention of established gender norms presented serious problems for the Porfirian state. The elite believed that sexual differences that informed femininity and masculinity were a God-given fact, irrefutable and natural as the sun rising in the east and setting in the west. Women, whether they worked inside or outside the home, found their roles in society biologically determined. Their chief function as mothers took on political overtones as Porfirians emphasized their mission to reproduce and socialize new generations of hardworking Mexicans.[10] The elite disparaged women that acted outside proper gender roles by likening them to prostitutes. For instance, one defense lawyer criticized fourteen-year-old Petrona for sending her boyfriend a letter describing her ill treatment in the house where she served as a maid and her wish that he take her away. Sexualizing her and depicting her assertiveness as sexual treachery, the lawyer stated that when a "woman provoked, invited, or solicited the man to take her in his power, it was not seduction but an act of prostitution on the part of the woman to satisfy a lewd desire."[11]

Rapto as defined by the Mexican Penal Code of 1874 occurred when someone abducted a woman against her will by the use of physical or moral violence, deception, or seduction in order to have sexual relations or to get married.[12] If the woman was younger than sixteen years and accompanied her *raptor* (abductor/seducer) voluntarily, the perpetrator was charged nevertheless with the assumption that he must have employed seduction to get her to succumb to his nefarious motivations. If marriage resulted or the doctors determined that the woman had not been a virgin before the event, the case was dropped. The spirit of the law and others grouped under crimes against the family and public morality was to manage sexual behavior and promote civil marriages. In the eyes of the Porfirian elite, deviant sexual behavior jeopardized the order and stability of families and ultimately endangered the state's modernization project. However, rapto was a well-established social practice among Mexican working people by the nineteenth century.

In the eyes of the law, the man had stolen the young virgin's honor and must suffer imprisonment and/or payment of reparations for her lost virginity (honor). These reparations repaired family honor as well. In nineteenth-century Oaxaca, parents or guardians filed most complaints of rapto in the courts. Mothers of the working class filed the majority of petitions, but fathers also initiated a significant number of claims.[13] Some parents initiated complaints in order to force a marriage or a promise of one in the future. Other parents rejected the union and demanded a full enforcement of the law and the imprisonment and fining of the perpetrator.

In Porfirian Mexico, as in most other nations striving for modernity, the elite desired couples to contract a marriage through the secular courts. Consensual unions and concubinage, the elite believed, represented relics of a disorderly and traditional past that were further characterized by perverse sexuality and depravity. For the elite, civil marriage secured family networks and economic opportunities as parents and the state colluded to prevent unequal marriages. The elite in late-nineteenth-century Mexico penalized the crime of rapto and *estupro* (deflowering) to protect family and female honor but, more importantly, to maintain social order by directing the working class toward legal marriage.[14]

"¿Era niña o no era niña?": Judging Virginity in Porfirian Culture

Feminine honor was an important value in Porfirian society as it was in colonial Mexico. But feminine honor took on national importance during the Porfiriato as Mexicans linked female sexuality to the social health of the nation. As the Porfirian state embraced eugenics and scientific racism, they also tied the future of the nation to patriotic motherhood. In fact, mothers took on a greater social role as nurturers of future generations of patriotic and hardworking Mexicans.[15] Secular court officials set the parameters of sexual politics by punishing sexual crimes. Feminine honor in many cases was firmly defended as it was considered an important bastion of the family and by extension, the nation.[16] Therefore sexual crimes committed by or on women and social deviance presented grave threats not only to women and their family members but society as well. In a society determined to be civilized, its elite members attempted to control the presumed rapacious desires and actions of its commoners. While the penal code laid out the map of sexual crimes, its definitions of specific violations appeared poorly delineated. Thus, court officials had wide latitude in which to decipher and enforce these laws. Judges and lawyers had to interpret the law and gauge the honesty of the plaintiffs and defendants in the cases. First, the judge had to decide whether the young woman was a virgin before the crime or not. Definitions of "virgin" proved to be problematic because witnesses and the defendant could also challenge the young women's honesty. Ultimately, the young woman had to prove that she possessed honor (virginity) before the crime. In other words, the woman had to make the case that she was worth defending and protecting by asserting her reputation as a virgin. Once a case began, judging a woman's virginity presented numerous contradictions and interpretations.

If a judge found substantial merits and evidence to continue a rapto case, medical doctors performed a gynecological exam to determine the woman's virginity or lack thereof. Whereas in colonial times, midwives performed this exam and the presence of men could provoke a scandal, male medical doctors usurped this role during the Porfiriato.[17] Logically, trained medical personnel took over this function in Porfirian Mexico, an era that emphasized science and rationality. Generally, doctors looked for two things: signs of force or violence and evidence of deflowering. Physical evidence cited in the cases included the presence of blood on the body and clothes, swelling or lacerations, and a rupture of the hymen. The state of the hymen determined whether a woman had lost her virginity, and doctors ascertained whether it had occurred recently or at an earlier date. Clearly, the fate of some of these women rested on the doctors' judgments. For others, while having to suffer the humiliation of a gynecological exam, the fact that they had not recently lost their virginity mattered little to their boyfriends.[18] The case of Josefa and Manuel supports this conclusion. Doctors determined by physical exam that Josefa had lost her virginity sometime in the past, but Manuel still wanted to marry her. In another case, Cipriana charged Mariano with the abduction and seduction of her daughter, Petrona.[19] Petrona testified that she left the house where she worked as a domestic servant, and as she passed by Mariano's house, he met her and forced her with the threat of bodily harm to go with him to San Juanito. She claimed she went with him out of fear, had sex with him twice, did not have previous amorous relations with Mariano, and received from him neither gifts nor money. In contrast, Mariano testified that he had had amorous relations with Petrona for five months. Furthermore, she had sent him a letter describing the maltreatment she received at her employer's house. In that letter, she complained that her mother forced her to work as a maid and that she wanted to escape her dire conditions. Mariano then assured the judge that he did not coerce Petrona to go with him, and upon their sexual encounter, he discovered that she "*no era doncella*" (was not a virgin). Nevertheless, he testified that he wished to marry her anyway if she would have him. The judge then ordered a medical exam that determined that Petrona had been deflowered but not recently by Mariano. The judge dismissed the case. However, the fact that Mariano still desired Petrona as a wife proves that he held views of female honor and respectability that diverged from those of the elite. Mariano, Manuel, and other young men did not always hinge marriage choice on their lovers' virginity. Other factors certainly contributed to feminine honor and respectability.

Moral behavior also determined a woman's virginity or honor. Did she go out with more than one man? Did she walk alone in the streets at night? How did she spend her days? For the Oaxacan cases, there was little discussion of whether women walked in the streets without a chaperone. Feminine physical seclusion mattered little to the working class. Most of these women worked and had to move about outside the family home. They also had frequent contact with men, through their work as domestics, in shops, on market trips, in their neighborhoods, and at church. When a defendant or witness attempted to sully a woman's reputation, he spoke of rumors that she went out with other men or that they had heard that she had sex with a particular man. For the woman's part, she usually testified that she was a virgin (era doncella) before eloping and that she succumbed to her lover's sexual passions because she received a promise of marriage. Employing the classic language of the elite, the women swore to their honor (virginity) and denied having previous boyfriends, at least at first. In some cases, the women recanted their initial testimony and again, using mutually comprehensible language, told the judge that they had been deceived when they were young and were therefore not virginal when they were *raptada* (abducted/seduced).[20] Conscious of the dominant discourse governing honor and shame, women argued that men had "deceived" them, thus reinforcing the elite-defined notion of feminine vulnerability and passivity. By portraying themselves as victims of deception to their boyfriends and to judges, the young women manipulated prevailing stereotypes by asserting their passive sexuality that led to their defloration in the past. Likewise, even though some of them clearly possessed an active sexuality when they engineered their own rapto, they could switch roles if their interests demanded it. Clearly, sexual identity took on several faces depending upon the audience, situation, and ultimately the strategy of the young women.

Working-Class Honor

Notions of honor and shame have shaped women's lives from all classes.[21] While the elite may have believed that *only* they possessed honor, the popular classes accepted the honor code and fine-tuned and refashioned it for their purposes.[22] They were also very vocal and insistent about their possession of honor in their communication with each other. For instance, Enrique wrote in a love letter to Carmen about their impending elopement, "I don't want to overlook my obligations as a married man" and, "Darling, you also ask me if I will use you like all men use women. My love, I will never betray you, you very well know how much I love you and I would never use you."[23] His letter and testimony go on to claim that he always had honorable intentions in his love for Carmen. Additionally, fourteen-year-old laundress María testified that Francisco pursued her and attempted to talk to her several times. She informed the judge that whenever she met Francisco on the street and he attempted to sweet-talk her, she spurned him and pelted him with rocks to make him go away, in effect, staking her claim to honor.[24]

Even though the law dictated, however murkily, the distinction between dishonest and honest or prostitute and virgin, the discourse revealed in the testimonies of deflowered young women, their parents, and witnesses challenged the official version of female respectability and honor. In effect, the young women possessed their own sense of morality and honor that did not solely mimic the conceptualizations held by their boyfriends, parents, or court officials. To them (as well as to some of their boyfriends), the fact that they were not virgins before they ran off with their current lover did not diminish their personal sense of their honor or their marriageability. While the elite perceived them as dishonorable and therefore not protected under the laws governing the crime of rapto, the women asserted their worth through their comportment in daily life, work, and relationships. For example, Josefa claimed honor when she wrote in a love letter to Manuel that even though she was poor and had to go out in the street, she maintained her good reputation by her modest conduct.[25] As a result, new or alternative constructions of moral behavior emerged that in effect muted distinctions between virgin and whore. In this scenario, women could have been deflowered but still possess honor in their own eyes and the eyes of their sweethearts and families. Young women could also display masculine traits such as brazenness and cunning and not suffer the censure of their peers. Hence, the popular classes asserted their own version of morality and social norms that sometimes paralleled, and at other times diverged from, the elite's rendition.[26]

The fact that the poor brought cases of seduction and deflowering to the courts proves this point. The popular classes respected the concept of honor and virginity and knew how to use the courts to achieve a desired outcome. However, they did not unconditionally accept the dominant honor code. The working class creatively maneuvered through the court proceedings, using their own honor code that was conditioned by traditional notions but something uniquely their own as well. They also used the courts to regulate, in part, their compatriots' sexual behavior even when their notions of appropriate behavior differed from the elite. Parents initiated rapto petitions because they wanted to expedite a marriage or at least secure a man's promise to take care of their daughter. At other times, they simply rejected their daughter's suitor even when she had been deflowered. Josefa's mother, in particular, never accepted Manuel as an acceptable partner for her daughter. She charged him with being a vagrant, which could have meant several things but probably denoted his inferior status in her eyes.[27] Parents also may have been concerned about social mores that promoted marriage over consensual unions, but more likely they were concerned about the relative youth of the couple and their economic prospects for making a home. For the single mothers of Petrona and Josefa, it also seemed that they did not want to lose the income the daughters contributed to the household or the helping hand they provided around the home. Single mothers, in effect, acted like fathers (took on masculine roles) by repudiating their daughter's spousal choices and deciding that it was more important for the family to maintain their daughter's labor and presence in the household or that she make a more acceptable match. In these cases, practical and economic reasons for forbidding the marriage superseded concerns about individual or family honor.

The Treachery of Words: Wielding the Language of Honor

The loss of virginity occurred as a meaningful event in a woman's life, but it could be an occurrence that was not always private. In the eyes of the elite, when it occurred without a promise of marriage or when a promise was not fulfilled in reasonable time (another subjective perspective), the woman became "dishonored" or "disgraced." Most of the women from the court cases understood that proving their virginity to their boyfriends was a prerequisite for marriage, albeit a risky undertaking considering their vulnerability to deception. In almost all the cases, the women, whether prompted by the police or their family, stated that they had engaged in sexual relations because they believed their deflowerers would marry them. In most cases, even when the women initiated their own "abduction," they argued that their subsequent participation in the sexual encounter was passive or neutral as they recounted it to the court. Things were done to them, not by them. Why? Perhaps the court or police recorders guided the women in their telling of the crime, but women also were not expected to take an active sexual role and their testimonies reflected this norm. They expertly played the role of passive victim, albeit coached by their director (court official). In essence, women could sometimes display masculine characteristics and fall back on feminine attributes as they played out their role of seduced victim in the courtroom. Nevertheless, it is clear that virginity was an important benchmark for all actors involved, but it was not a sole determinant of a woman's social worth as a marriage partner. Indeed, the language used by the particular actors in the case warrants attention. In describing the consummation of the union, the couple used formulaic language such as, "We committed the carnal act," or, "I was deflowered after we had carnal relations." Parents who initiated the petition also employed established phrases such as, "He violated the honor of my home," or the perpetrator "corrupted my home," and, "I come before this very respectable court with a matter against the order of families." Clearly the plaintiffs, defendants, and witnesses had not only internalized the language of the elite culture but also used it to make them convincing to the courts and to mobilize the state's punitive power in their favor. In effect, the women (both mothers and daughters) exploited juridical language and normative concepts to claim male authority. Young women worked the courts and wielded the language of the jurists to exert their sense of honor and self-worth vis-à-vis the dominant culture.

The young men, or defendants in the cases, usually admitted that they had had sex with the young woman, but some attempted to prove her dishonest or promiscuous before their sexual contact. In some of the Oaxacan cases, the defendants testified that they had heard that the women had sexual relations with men previously, and thus they were not virginal and honest. In virtually every case, the young men stated that they had engaged in sexual relations, and the girl had agreed to it in order to prove her virginity. The unspoken rule in these cases was that proving female virginity through premarital sex was in fact a condition for marriage. Even in the cases where the young man wished to marry the girl, he sometimes attempted to dishonor her reputation in the courtroom. Perhaps court officials coached the defendants' testimony to not only nullify the case but also damage the women's public reputations. Nevertheless, Manuel and others found their girlfriends were not virgins upon their initial sexual encounter, but they still wished to marry them. What does this say about the nature of female honor as a component of male honor? Clearly, Manuel and others did not care enough about the state of their girlfriends' hymens to back out of their betrothal. Perhaps for them, a love match superseded norms that required worthy wives to be virgins.

Multiple and situational gender identities and sexualities emerge from the documents. Young women acted masculine by orchestrating their own abduction, but they also presented themselves as virginal and honorable to the court. In essence, they behaved assertively in orchestrating or influencing their elopement but also acted demurely, honorably, and passively in their testimonies before the judges. In effect the women appeared to be fully cognizant of the traditional expectations of being a respectable woman but were not so constrained by them that they could not creatively exert their own identities. In essence, the assertive young women of these cases took drastic steps to control their destinies. Moreover, the young women (and men) displayed situational identities. They could behave one way to each other and another way before court officials.

Courtship and Elopement in Oaxaca: Four Dramas

Josefa and Manuel

Let us return to the case of Josefa and Manuel. She chose the archway of the Templo de la Soledad for their rendezvous. Josefa, accompanied by her best friend, thirteen-year-old Teresa Hernández, arrived at 7:00 p.m. After Josefa stashed a small bundle of clothes and other personal effects under some rocks in the garden, they searched for Manuel. The three found each other and made plans to find a safe place to stay the night where Josefa and Manuel could consummate their union. Josefa tried to retrieve her belongings, but the three were accosted by the gardener and a police officer who accused them of stealing the clothes and then hiding them. Imagine the anxiety and fear of the three as the police interrogated them at the station. Eventually, the police decided that Josefa told the truth and believing that the three were siblings, freed them. The trio then proceeded to Xochimilco, a barrio north of the city limits where they posed again as siblings to rent a room. In this rented room, the sweethearts engaged in sexual intercourse. The next morning, Josefa's mother appeared accompanied by a police officer. Manuel was incarcerated, and a criminal complaint was subsequently filed.[28]

Juana Pérez, the mother and plaintiff in the case, told the magistrate that it would be easy to ask for the marriage of the couple but that her daughter was only fourteen, and Manuel had neither resources nor anything else to prove him a responsible man. Furthermore, she charged the young man with vagrancy and asked for full prosecution of the law. Her daughter's virginity had been taken; dishonor rained down upon her home, but still Josefa's mother did not wish for marriage. In fact, she opposed their relationship from the outset. We can never know the reasons, but we can surmise that the dominant honor code (that required marriage or money to repair honor) was not as important as wishing that her daughter be taken care of or losing a helping hand around the house. Charging vagrancy also revealed the mother's motivations. If the law would not penalize him on the charge of rapto, he could be incarcerated for vagrancy. Or alternatively, labeling him a "vagrant" may have also denoted his inferior position within the hierarchy of honor for Josefa's peer group.

In several Oaxacan cases, including the example of Josefa and Manuel, the young woman testified that she was a virgin before their night together while the man attested that upon committing the act, he discovered that his girlfriend "no era niña" (was not a virgin). Manuel interrogated Josefa on this point. She told him she had been deceived as a young girl and that even though he had heard rumors that she had slept with an Alfredo, they were untrue. Per usual procedure, doctors from the General Hospital examined Josefa in order to assess her virginity or honor by judging the integrity of her hymen and looking for signs of violence or force. The physicians found no signs of violence. She had engaged in coitus, but because she possessed what they termed "an elastic hymen" she had not been "deflowered." Even though Manuel professed that she was not a virgin as he expected (because she showed no blood), he testified that he desired to marry her anyway. It is possible that Manuel accused Josefa of being dishonorable in order to void the court proceeding. He also may have been influenced by the lawyer or by traditional norms and gave a formulaic defense that men sometimes used to sully women's reputations and place themselves higher in the hierarchy of honor and credibility. Nevertheless, Manuel wanted to marry Josefa, believing her worthy of marriage, a fact that throws new light on notions of female respectability among working-class people. While virginity was highly valued by all levels of Mexican society, working-class people may have been more flexible than the elite in defining female respectability solely on the basis of virginity. Other bases for female respectability may have included the ability to work hard and earn money, make a home, and raise children.

Five love letters from Josefa to Manuel provided evidence that they had an ongoing relationship and that Josefa orchestrated the elopement. In them, she professed her love for Manuel and her desire to move out of her mother's home to begin life anew with him. She passed them through her friend, Teresa, because her mother threatened to kill her if she carried on her relationship with Manuel. She desired to marry Manuel most of all, but because she lacked her mother's approval, she chose elopement. Her masculine behavior characterized by action and assertion and her outright defiance of her mother upset prevailing prescriptions of how young modest female minors were supposed to act. In the official script, women behaved demurely and exhibited a passive sexuality. Children respected and obeyed their parents. Men seduced inexperienced virgins. Josefa diverged from these scripts by symbolically seducing her sweetheart and laying out the parameters of their escape. Josefa also thought herself worthy of marriage. But knowing that her mother did not approve of Manuel, she either initiated her own rapto to have the courts force a marriage in lieu of her mother's response, or she accepted a consensual union as an appropriate alternative.

Carmen and Enrique

In another case, sixteen-year-old Carmen arranged to run away with her boyfriend of three years, Enrique. She testified that her mother hit her at times and even attacked Enrique in order to terminate their relationship. Consequently, she took her belongings and left home alone. Carmen met Enrique on the corner and told him to take her away. María, her mother, testified that Enrique must have seduced Carmen and she wanted him imprisoned and the 125 pesos that they allegedly stole from her returned. She further testified that they had been carrying on for two years and she had witnessed the disgrace of Enrique laying his hands on her daughter. María produced two love letters from Enrique as evidence of their relationship, but she still did not want a marriage between the two. In effect, Carmen's mother took on a father's prerogative in her physical attacks on Enrique but also in her very active and assertive dealings with the court. Enrique, twenty-three years old and a carpenter, swore that he rescued Carmen from her mother's abuse and that he had, as his letters professed, promised marriage to Carmen. He stated that Carmen met him on a corner near her house and asked to go away with him. He complied with her wishes and that night took Carmen's virginity.[29]

In contrast, Carmen testified that Enrique met her at her house, she gathered some personal effects, and she left home a virgin and remained a virgin, because they did not have sexual relations. The judge determined that there was indeed a promise of marriage but that Carmen's parents objected. Three witnesses vouched for Enrique's good character. It appears that the judge never ordered a gynecological examination of Carmen to determine whether Enrique had deflowered her. However, the case exhibits a twist as Enrique, Carmen, and her parents agreed that the couple would marry in the near future.[30] Yet, almost three weeks later, Carmen revoked her consent to marry Enrique. She explained that since her previous declaration, she had received vile knowledge about his conduct and way of life and could not marry him. Unfortunately, her testimony lacks specific details of why she had spurned Enrique, but she clearly criticized his character and reputation (honor). In essence, Carmen employed hearsay, perhaps gossip, to undermine Enrique's honor and establish her moral and social superiority. In contrast to the other cases, where the young men invoked gossip to tarnish their sweetheart's reputation, or declared that the women were not virgins to weaken the case, Carmen wielded the same strategy to shame Enrique and release herself from the commitment to marry him. While she maintained an affectionate relationship with him for at least two years and then chose to run away with him, in the end, she controlled her own life by refusing to marry her "abductor." Perhaps suffering the shame of a scandal provoked by the criminal case and accusations of her deflowering proved less grave than a marriage to a man Carmen judged unworthy and dishonorable. Both female actors, Carmen and her mother, asserted their rights through masculine means. Carmen publicly spurned her lover and in essence abandoned him while her mother asserted her rights and honor as head of the household to protect Carmen and the family's reputation.

Néstora

Néstora, fifteen years old, approached the same court on her own and accused Francisco of various crimes including rapto, *calumnia*, estupro, and *separación de su virginidad* (abduction, slander, deflowering, and separation of her virginity). According to her testimony, Francisco had taken her from her home with a promise of marriage. She remained "intact" (a virgin) for three days, but when she wanted to leave, Francisco brought her wine, made a bed, put on his sleeping clothes, and took her virginity. She remained with him for five months fulfilling her conjugal contract by making tortillas in the morning, washing and ironing the clothes of the family, preparing *moles*, and fulfilling other duties expected of a wife. Néstora appeared before the courts because Francisco asked another woman to marry him. His fiancée's mother visited Néstora, accused her of being a whore, and insisted that she sell her the ring given to her by Francisco for fifteen pesos. Subsequently, Francisco threw Néstora into the streets, and she appeared before the courts asking for her clothing, bedding, a black *rebozo* (shawl), and one hundred pesos for her lost virginity. For his part, Francisco denied that he ever promised marriage and that they simply had lived as *amasios* (lovers).[31] The case unfortunately ends there, but several conclusions can be drawn from the limited testimonies. While we do not know the outcome of Néstora's situation, the point is that women did not hesitate to use the courts on their own to seek reparations for their loss of honor, virginity, or security. Francisco did in fact victimize Néstora, but to simply depict her as a victim of male desire denies her agency in the matter. In fact she appealed her case to the court, alone and without a patriarchal figure such as a father, brother, or uncle. She adopted the masculine role of avenging honor in her claim for compensation against the lover who deflowered and abandoned her.

In her testimony, she used notions of a conjugal contract where men and women fulfill their duties without undue abuse or negligence. The conjugal contract implied that husbands be faithful and provide economic support to the household. For their half of the reciprocal agreement, wives promised fidelity and to uphold the honor of their husbands and household. Women tolerated some abuse of the conjugal contract (adultery, physical abuse) but appealed to the courts when husbands abandoned the household either physically or economically.[32] Even though they did not have a legal marriage, Néstora believed they had a bargain where she performed wifely duties and that when Francisco abandoned her, she possessed the honor and legal right to seek reparations and justice through the court. In her original petition, she not only charged Francisco with taking her virginity but also with slander and defaming of her reputation. Probably incensed by the accusations of his future mother-in-law and her abandonment by her conjugal partner, Néstora thought herself worthy of legal defense. She also needed to repair her good reputation in the community by receiving a monetary payment for her lost virtue (virginity). In addition, by citing her fulfillment of her wifely duties of keeping a home, Néstora identified herself as "wife" and thus honorable in civil society. Interestingly, she used masculine methods to defend her status as a wife worthy of justice.

Luz and Manuel

While most of the rapto cases reported involved working-class families, middle- and upper-class parents also appealed to the courts to remedy the "abduction" of their daughters. Luz Esther left her home to go to piano lessons during the afternoon of June 22, 1899. When she did not come home as usual, her mother, Señora Valle, took to the streets to investigate. In her letter to the authorities, she stated that she came before the court with "grave and delicate matters, a matter against the order of families." She charged Manuel Canseco with "forcing" her nineteen-year-old daughter at his store on Oaxaca's central plaza. She also stated that she had contacted the police and confronted Manuel at this place of business. Her husband was suspiciously absent from the complaint, and it was clearly the agency of the mother who physically looked for Luz Esther. She left her traditional sphere, the home, and proceeded alone to the shop to accuse Canseco of dishonoring her daughter. Perhaps mothers sometimes took a more active role in rapto accusations because their occurrence intimated that fathers had lost control of the family. In this formulation, fathers had more to lose than mothers, and their less overt response may have been an attempt to avoid attention to their slippery grasp on family honor. In effect, Luz Esther's mother (this time for the middle class) carried out a patriarchal duty to defend not only her daughter's reputation and well-being, but the honor of the family as well.[33] Nevertheless, court officials summoned all parties into court for depositions, and the case evolved into a litany of claims, countercharges, and finally a dismissal.[34]

Luz Esther testified that she had had amorous relations with Manuel for eleven months and a promise of marriage. She also testified that she had been in Mexico City in the previous month and Manuel had asked her to prove to him that she was not a "*mujer común*" (promiscuous woman) upon her return to Oaxaca. Moreover, on the day in question, Luz Esther went to his shop to discuss their marriage arrangements. They talked, and it became clear to her that Manuel wanted to make her his lover (*amasia*).[35] She protested, but he beseeched her with many offers to take her to a hotel in "*un coche bien cerrado*" (a private carriage) while he made marriage arrangements. She refused all his offers and they quarreled. Manuel grabbed her arms and told her to wait in his office while he finished some business outside the store. Luz Esther then claimed that his brother, Agustín, came to the store, offered her wine, and told her to wait for Manuel while he watched the store. She also testified that she sent one of the store employees to alert her mother to her abduction.

For his part, Manuel testified that he had not maintained relations beyond shopkeeper and customer with Luz Esther and that while she had bought items in his shop, he never promised marriage to her. He also accused Luz Esther and her mother of forging the eight love letters included in the legal complaint as evidence of a betrothal. Specifically, he said he was out of the store on the day in question until he returned after closing and discovered that an "*escandalito*" (small scandal) had occurred during his absence. Moreover, he professed to be mortified by the charges of the young woman and her mother. Agustín testified next, stating that he never offered Luz Esther wine and that Manuel never contracted marriage with the plaintiff.

Witnesses testified next. A young couple had taken refuge under the portal in front of Manuel's shop during a rainstorm. They saw Luz Esther run out of the rain and into the store. They decided to shop, and when they entered the store they noticed Manuel and Luz Esther talking at his desk in raised voices. After a few minutes, they saw Manuel leave the store while Luz Esther stayed behind. Agustín testified again that his brother was not in the store that afternoon. Also, another witness stated that he met Canseco and they had some beers together at a tavern and left each other around 4:30 p.m. A worker at the store then vouched that Manuel had left to drink with a friend, leaving Agustín in charge of the store. The worker also stated that Manuel did not return to the store until ten o'clock that night. He claimed that Luz Esther had entered the store and talked excitedly with Agustín. Unhappy with their conversation, she jumped over the sales counter, passed into the backroom, and refused to leave the store until Manuel talked with her! The worker then stated that Luz Esther's mother arrived, summoned Luz Esther, and they both left the store soon after.

With the various testimonies in hand, the judge ruled on the case. While he stated that all the witness statements possessed merit (even though they contradicted each other), he ruled that the charge of rapto could not be proven because Luz Esther voluntarily went to his store to discuss their alleged marriage plans. Moreover, because she was nineteen years old, a rapto charge of seduction was also invalid (she was over fifteen years old). He dismissed the case and their story ended there. While Luz Esther certainly did not achieve her aim of marrying Manuel (or did they marry later?), her testimony reveals traditional aspects of elite honor that contrast with the previous cases with Josefa, Carmen, and Néstora. Luz Esther acted boldly by going alone to Manuel's shop and either talking with Agustín or Manuel (depending upon the account). Perhaps to cover her impropriety, she testified that she refused both an offer to become Manuel's lover and the wine proffered by his brother.

Or conversely, she may have gone to meet Manuel who then plotted to undermine her credibility before the court. After all, he was a businessman and likely thought her a foolish young woman. Luz Esther also played on feminine vulnerability and masculine power by describing how Manuel forcefully grabbed her arms and ordered her to await his return. In Luz Esther's testimony and alleged behavior, she acted in ways that fit traditional gender roles—superior morality (her shock at his request to make her his lover), chastity, and victimization. She refused to be his lover outside of marriage, turned down a glass of wine, and depicted herself as a prisoner in the store until her mother rescued her. Yet, her foes, the shopworkers Agustín and Manuel, portrayed her behavior as argumentative, dramatic (jumping over the counter and refusing to leave), and treacherous (forging love letters from Manuel). Manuel insisted that he never wrote the letters (which would have proven an engagement between the couple) and that Luz Esther and her mother (two women) conspired to trick him into marriage. Both sides wielded mutually comprehensible language that manipulated notions of traditional female and male attributes in hopes of furthering their case. Luz Esther emerged the loser in the case as she undoubtedly suffered the shame of public humiliation, although her virginity was never questioned.

In fact, in the few rapto cases brought by middle-class families, medical examinations never occurred to determine whether the young women had been virgins or not. While it is difficult to assess the exigencies that may have excused a medical evaluation, probably middle- and upper-class families could avoid the embarrassment and humiliation of having their daughters examined by male doctors. If the young women were found not to be virgins, the families had much to lose in terms of honor and cultural power. Conversely, judges may have believed that a working-class girl was more sexually active and pursued a medical evaluation even when the young boy wished to marry her. To prove that the poor girl was not a virgin when the "abduction" occurred would quickly bring the court proceedings to an end. Perhaps it was not culturally appropriate to have middle- and upper-class daughters subjected to a gynecological exam. What if doctors found that she had lost her virginity long ago? What damage would that wreak on Oaxaca's elite families?

Lessons from the Dramas

There are several issues that jump out from the stories. First, as a caveat, my aim is not to conjure up women's masculine power out of a set of documents. The reality is that vis-à-vis men, women held the short straw when it came to politics and public life. Undeniably, the bargaining power between lovers in the process of courtship and rapto was anything but even. Women gave up their virginity in return for the man's commitment to marriage or a consensual union. They had more to lose if their suitors had a change of heart and left them alone and deflowered or worse still, pregnant. Yet, scholars have overemphasized virginity as the main determinant of female honor, especially for the working class. In fact, as the cases from Oaxaca attest, female honor and respectability were not always monopolized by sexual purity. Likewise, I am not refuting the existence of patriarchy or glossing over the fact that many women suffered abuse at the hands of men and/or the social system. However, as Steve Stern and others have argued, men and women negotiated and renegotiated the patriarchal contract.[36] The word *contract* is important because the two parties in the case, man and woman, each had responsibilities to fulfill. Many women sought legal redress if their husbands abandoned or abused them, reasoning that the men had not fulfilled their duties as a husband and/or father. Women did hold power in these cases and worked the courts often in their favor. The term *contract* is also crucial because these actors, no matter how lowly in the eyes of the elite, considered themselves a part of the social contract or body politic and thus creatively maneuvered through the world of laws and politics to achieve their goals and exercise their rights as citizens.

Regarding the rapto cases, if the woman was a virgin before the elopement she had little trouble in the courts. If doctors found that she was not a virgin or witnesses slandered her reputation, she had little recourse but to endure her public shame. However, these scenarios are two sides of the extreme. For Oaxaca, young couples such as Josefa and Manuel and Carmen and Enrique eloped to initiate family life together. The mothers of Josefa and Carmen contacted the court because they disapproved of their daughters' choice in partners or decried that they were too young to marry. Other parents wished to force a quick marriage presumably to restore their family honor. Josefa's mother rejected Manuel because she thought him a vagrant, a man incapable of maintaining a household. Carmen's parents disapproved of Enrique, and ultimately, Carmen rejected him as well when she learned of his bad reputation. Clearly, that working-class people used the courts to manipulate their destinies illustrates the fact that they thought themselves honorable and worthy. Working people selectively internalized the honor system, as several studies have pointed out.[37] They also adeptly and shrewdly wielded the classic language of the dominant culture when speaking of threats to family order and stains on their honor.

The daughters and mothers in these cases possessed masculine agency in the rapto dramas. Josefa directed her own elopement, going as far as naming the day, time, and meeting place for her escape. She also made it clear to her sweetheart that she would find another man if he did not comply with her plan. Carmen behaved assertively by gathering her belongings and leaving willingly with Enrique to escape the abuse of her mother. She took action to flee her alleged maltreatment at home but then also flouted proper gender norms by ultimately rejecting her lover even after she was dishonored in public. Néstora, abandoned and then thrown into the street by her lover, appeared at the court alone (a role usually associated with a male protector) to defend her honor and behavior and demand compensation for her lost virginity from Francisco. Señora Valle, Luz Esther's mother, took to the streets to confront her daughter's alleged seducer and demanded her return and his fulfillment of a marriage promise. Señora Valle simply acted like a father with masculine rights to uphold family honor.

Moreover, some of the young women of these rapto dramas directed their own elopements because they lacked parental approval to marry their sweethearts and/or to escape mistreatment at home. They ran away and had sex to initiate family life with their boyfriends but also as an act of defiance toward their parents and the state. These couples asserted their own notions of courtship and sexual behavior, suggesting that an alternative code of honor and sexuality may have existed for them. Likewise, their notions of female respectability and honor proved to be flexible. In fact, all of the women voluntarily left with their sweethearts and testified that they had not been deceived by them. Moreover, some of the women in essence behaved like men by asserting an active sexuality and a forceful strategy of eloping with their lovers. In many ways, they acted like men by masterminding their elopement and persuading (seducing) their lovers to run away with them. This is evident in the love letters written to their men and their testimony of how particular events unfolded. Yet, before the courts they also displayed a passive, traditional femininity and attempted to prove their honor by appealing to traditional notions of female respectability. When it came to describing the actual sexual act(s), they related their participation in passive terms, possibly scripted by the lawyer or their traditional consciousness of female sexual roles. They could act within the parameters of appropriate female behavior and transgress these very norms by displaying masculine traits to steer their own destinies.

If we return to the story of Josefa that began this chapter, we might say that she and Manuel, as well as many other working-class Mexicans, performed multiple gender identities to defend and regain their honor and rights. The many faces of Josefa show that she, like her compatriots, displayed masculine and feminine traits that neither conformed to nor simply deviated from the dominant honor complex that laid out gender norms. This alternative structure displayed through the rapto cases shows that masculinity and femininity did not rest on binary poles. In fact, in the time and place of the preceding stories, female agency was masculine.

NOTES

1. Contra Manuel Vivas por rapto en la jóven, Josefa Calvo, Oaxaca, 1899, Juzgado Primero de lo Capital, Archivo Histórico Municipal de la Ciudad de Oaxaca, (AHMCO).
2. While the term *rapto* translates into English as "abduction," in the cases under review for this project, the process more closely resembles elopement because the women left voluntarily with their boyfriends but without the permission of their parent(s). Viewing these cases as "elopement" is also appropriate because for the majority of the participants, the ultimate goal was marriage. In general, this study was based on more than 209 cases of elopement between 1841 and 1920.
3. I found only one case where a woman was charged with rapto. In this case, a mother was charged with "abducting" a young woman for her son. Unfortunately the documents only include the original complaint with no supporting depositions. See Contra Faustina Medina por atentados contra el pudor y rapto en Francisca Martínez, Oaxaca, 1896, Juzgado Primero Criminal, AHMCO.
4. Eileen J. Suárez Findlay also surmises that plebeian *ponceños* often chose serial monogamy over marriage. See her *Imposing Decency: The Politics of Sexuality and Race in Puerto Rico, 1870–1920* (Durham, NC: Duke University Press, 1999), 40.
5. Ramón Gutiérrez, *When Jesus Came, the Corn Mothers Went Away: Marriage, Sexuality, and Power in New Mexico, 1500–1846* (Stanford, CA: Stanford University Press, 1991), 221.
6. Contra Arcadio Ortega acusada de fuerza en Anastacia Delgado, Oaxaca, 1875, Juzgado Tercero de lo Capital, AHMCO.
7. Contra Francisco Mimiago por rapto de seducción en Primitiva Franco, Oaxaca, 1886, Juzgado Primero Criminal, AHMCO.
8. Judith Halberstam, *Female Masculinity* (Durham, NC: Duke University Press, 1998), 241.
9. Suárez Findlay, *Imposing Decency*, 42.
10. For Porfirian attitudes toward natural gender roles, see Verena Radkau, *"Por la debilidad de nuestro ser": Mujeres del pueblo en la paz porfiriana* (Mexico City: Centro de Investigaciones y Estudios Superiores en Antropología Social, Secretaria de Educación Pública, 1987); Andrés Molina Enríquez, *Los grandes problemas nacionales (1909)* (Mexico City: ERA, 1981); Carmen Ramos Escandón, "Señoritas porfirianas: Mujer e ideología en el México progresista, 1880–1910," in *Presencia y transparencia: La mujer en la historia de México*, ed. Carmen Ramos Escandón (Mexico City: El Colegio de México, 1987); and William E. French, "Prostitutes and Guardian Angels: Women, Work, and the Family in Porfirian Mexico," *Hispanic American Historical Review* 72, no. 4 (November 1992): 529–55.
11. Contra Mariano Cruz por rapto de seducción en Petrona Vásquez, Oaxaca, 1886, Juzgado Primero de lo Criminal, AHMCO.

12. William E. French, "Rapto and Estupro in Porfirian and Revolutionary Chihuahua," paper presented in session, "El Espacio y el Peligro en México, 1750–1930," IX Reunion of Mexican and North American Historians, October 2, 1994.
13. From 1880 to 1910, 105 cases of rapto or rapto and estupro were filed by family members or guardians. Of those that include documentation, single mothers initiated fourteen cases, widowed mothers eleven, and married mothers seven. Fathers initiated twenty-seven cases during the same period. Ten cases were initiated by the young women themselves while other family members filed six cases.
14. Sonya Lipsett-Rivera in her study of rape in early national Mexico found that rape was associated with marriage and encouraged either marriage between perpetrator and victim or monetary reparations when the victim was a virgin. Marriage and dowries served as an acceptable solution to repairing family honor but also as a means to restore the social peace and order. See Sonya Lipsett-Rivera, "The Intersection of Rape and Marriage in Late-Colonial and Early National Mexico," *Colonial Latin American Historical Review* 6, no. 4 (Fall 1997): 559–90.
15. French, "Prostitutes and Guardian Angels," 529–54.
16. Donna Guy's work, *Sex and Danger in Buenos Aires: Prostitution, Family, and Nation in Argentina* (Lincoln: University of Nebraska Press, 1991), eloquently links female honor to the family and nation.
17. See Gutiérrez, *When Jesus Came, the Corn Mothers Went Away*, 224–25, for a discussion of an upper-class woman who had a male notary present during her exam to prove her honorable status. The judge in the case accused the notary of depraved and dishonest behavior while the woman was accused of being a common woman for allowing herself to be examined in such a manner.
18. In at least one case, doctors could not determine whether a young woman had lost her virginity because she had what they termed an "elastic hymen." The court dismissed that case because deflowering could not be proven. See Contra Manuel Vivas por rapto en la jóven, Josefa Calvo, Oaxaca, 1899, Juzgado Primero de lo Capital, AHMCO.
19. Contra Mariano Cruz por rapto de seducción en Petrona Vásquez, Oaxaca, 1886, Juzgado Primero de lo Criminal, AHMCO.
20. For example, see Contra Mariano Cruz por rapto de seducción en Petrona Vásquez, Oaxaca, 1886, Juzgado Primero de lo Criminal, AHMCO; Contra José García por rapto y estupro en Narcisa Rafaela Cortés, Oaxaca, 1886, Juzgado Primero de lo Criminal, AHMCO; and Contra Enrique Martínez por rapto, Oaxaca, 1892, Juzgado Primero de lo Capital, AHMCO.
21. Colonial Latin Americanists have contributed the most extensive research on the honor/shame complex as it patterned gender roles over time. See especially, Asunción Lavrin, ed., *Sexuality and Marriage in Colonial Latin America* (Lincoln: University of Nebraska Press, 1989); Lyman L. Johnson and Sonya Lipsett-Rivera, *The Faces of Honor: Sex, Shame, and Violence in Colonial Latin America* (Albuquerque: University of New Mexico Press, 1998).

22. Several scholars substantiate that the working class believed that they possessed honor and regularly defended it. See for examples the collections cited in the previous footnote and Nancy E. van Deusen, "Determining the Boundaries of Virtue: The Discourse on *Recogimiento* Among Women in Seventeenth-Century Lima," *Journal of Family History* 22, no. 4 (October 1997): 373–89.
23. Love letters contained in the case file Contra Enrique Martínez por rapto en la jóven Carmen Llaguno, Oaxaca, 1892, Juzgado Primero de lo Capital, AHMCO. Whether Enrique penned the letter himself, I cannot determine with certainty. Some lovers used scribes or friends who could write. Enrique was literate enough to sign his name to his deposition.
24. Contra Francisco Lorza por rapto y violación en María de los Santos González, Oaxaca, 1884, Juzgado Primero de la Capital, AHMCO. With a more recent take on this, Jaime Luis Daza found in his contemporary field research in Bolivia that rock throwing was akin to flirting with a potential lover or a step in courtship where the girl encouraged the boy's overtures through hurling a rock at him. See "The Cultural Context of Courtship and Betrothal in a Quechua Community of Cochabamba, Bolivia" (PhD diss., UCLA, 1983).
25. Love letter contained as evidence in Contra Manuel Vivas por rapto en la jóven, Josefa Calvo, Oaxaca, 1899, Juzgado Primero de lo Capital, AHMCO.
26. Studies by Martha Esteves and Sueann Caulfield substantiate this point. In their study of sexual politics in judicial and popular discourse in Brazil, they find that while the legal and popular interpretations of appropriate sexual behavior differed, there were also key points of commonality. See "Fifty Years of Virginity in Rio de Janeiro: Sexual Politics and Gender Roles in Juridical and Popular Discourse, 1890–1940," *Luso-Brazilian Review* 30, no. 1 (1993): 47–72.
27. Scholars have shown that a hierarchy of honor existed within the working class. See Lyman L. Johnson, "Dangerous Words, Provocative Gestures, and Violent Acts," 127–50; and Richard Boyer, "Honor Among Plebeians," in Johnson and Lipsett-Rivera, *The Faces of Honor*, 152–75.
28. Contra Manuel Vivas por rapto en la jóven, Josefa Calvo, Oaxaca, 1899, Juzgado Primero de lo Capital, AHMCO.
29. Contra Enrique Martínez por rapto, Oaxaca, 1892, Juzgado Segundo, AHMCO.
30. Ibid.
31. Contra Francisco Cruz acusado por Néstora Cruz de los delitos de injurias, difamación, calumnias, atentado contra el pudor, rapto de seducción, estupro no violento y separación de su virginidad, Oaxaca, 1893, Primero Juzgado Criminal, AHMCO.
32. Much has been written on the conjugal and patriarchal contract between husband and wife. See for example, Nancy E. van Deusen,"Determining the Boundaries of Virtue"; and Steve J. Stern, *The Secret History of Gender: Women, Men, and Power in Late Colonial Mexico* (Chapel Hill: University of North Carolina Press, 1995).

33. Other mothers took on active masculine or fatherly roles. Angela accompanied Aniceto to the river, and about the time he attempted to have sex with her, Angela's mother appeared wielding a knife to fight off her daughter's seducer. See Contra Aniceto Ramos por el delito de rapto hecho en Angela Gabriela Ramírez, Oaxaca, 1852, Juzgado Criminal Segundo, AHMCO.
34. Contra Manuel Canseco por conatos de rapto de seducción de que lo acusa Adela Valle, Oaxaca, 1899, Juzgado Primero de lo Capital, AHMCO.
35. For middle- and upper-class Mexicans, *amasiatos* were looked at with disdain. They were conjugal relationships maintained by poor Mexicans, not the elite. Hence, Luz Esther professed to be outraged that Manuel would suggest she be his amasia. For more discussion of this, see Pablo Piccato, *City of Suspects: Crime in Mexico City, 1900–1931* (Durham, NC: Duke University Press, 2001), 114–15.
36. Steve J. Stern, *The Secret History of Gender.*
37. See especially Asunción Lavrin, ed., *Marriage and Sexuality in Colonial Latin America* (Lincoln: University of Nebraska Press, 1989); and Johnson and Lipsett-Rivera, *The Faces of Honor*.

CHAPTER 3

Dominance and Submission in Don Porfirio's Belle Époque

The Case of Luis and Piedad

JAMES A. GARZA

THE YOUNG WOMAN STAGGERED INTO THE LATE-MORNING SUNLIGHT, clutching a knife wound as two men ran from the dark confines of the Mexico City *pulquería* where they had confronted the victim. As the men fled, the victim, Francisca Escorcia, fell dead on the street. Police managed to quickly capture the assailants, Inocencio "El Gendarme" González and his comrade Salvador "El Chino" Guerra, thanks to the timely efforts of Virginia Villalobos, who had been drinking with Escorcia at the time of the stabbing. Fearless, Villalobos chased the men and managed to flag down the police. Investigators later determined that González and Escorcia had lived together for a month, during which time they had argued endlessly, thanks in part to Escorcia's friendship with Villalobos, a woman González detested. On the day of the murder, González apparently ran into his girlfriend on the street and asked her where she was going. Escorcia replied that she was on her way to a local bathhouse. She was lying. After Escorcia left, González followed her at a distance and spied her entering a pulquería in the notorious Lagunilla neighborhood. She was not alone. With her were four other persons, including Villalobos. Barely controlling his anger, González went to look for his friend Guerra, and after meeting him, both men walked to the Tepito neighborhood where González bought a knife and told his friend, "Let's go find her." However, both men meandered around for a few hours as González fingered the blade, perhaps having second thoughts. He soon worked up his nerve and decided to put an end to his lover's disobedience, especially her visits to pulquerias, traditional places of masculine refuge where female honor was sometimes questioned. In the end, González enforced, or reinforced, his authority and killed the woman he felt most threatened by—not Villalobos but Escorcia because she was the easier target.[1]

González, as he meandered across the dangerous terrain of Porfirian Mexico City, was performing a gender role prescribed for men of his place and time, that of a man protecting his property—in this case Escorcia. However, Escorcia crossed the boundary between behavior appropriate for women and actions ordinarily reserved for men by disobeying her lover and choosing her friends. Escorcia subverted traditional masculine authority, and González may have felt his own authority as a man threatened as he witnessed Escorcia's challenges to feminine propriety. Unsure about what to do until the very end, González finally fulfilled his role by stabbing his lover in public.

On October 13, 1890, another public murder also brought to light challenges to traditional Mexican masculinity. On that day, Luis Yzaguirre, a twenty-five-year-old clerk employed by the National Treasury, shot his lover María Piedad Ontiveros inside a rented coach parked in front of a house of prostitution in Mexico City. Ontiveros, a young woman of nineteen years and reported to be of delicate beauty, died soon after. The case captivated Mexico City society, for it had all the markings of a crime of passion: illicit love, secretive encounters, a shocking discovery, and increasing violence—all culminating in a final release of blood and anguish. Enthralled readers soon learned about how the young and amorous Yzaguirre had carried on an affair with Ontiveros and had demanded that she leave her older lover, Carlos Rodríguez. The details were too scandalous to be ignored and hinted at intimate questions. What elements drove this young clerk to murder his girlfriend? What role, if any, did the young woman's other lover play in this deadly love triangle? And finally, what did a secretive cache of love letters reveal about the personal lives of the trio, especially about Yzaguirre? These questions and others help illuminate the daily lives of middle-class men who sought to dominate personal and social situations amid rapid change in the capital of Porfirian Mexico.

Yzaguirre, as the letters preserved in the court records reveal, struggled to make sense of his ever-changing relationship with Ontiveros even as he was descending into a private hell of drinking and violence. But Ontiveros's other lover, Rodríguez, left no traces in the documentation. His silence questions common perceptions of Latin American honor, especially the image of a wronged man out for blood. Both men, in essence, stood on opposing poles, one taking a dominant position reinforced by masculine bonds of friendship and carousing, while the other played a silent, submissive role. This essay probes deeply into the issues of masculinity and gender in Porfirian Mexico City. What emerges is a complex portrait of three people shaped by the happenstances of their intimate lives but also by powerful cultural and social forces.

Setting the Stage

Yzaguirre and Rodríguez were connected by each man's relationship with María Piedad Ontiveros. What we know about her is pieced together from personal correspondence, newspaper reports, and the judicial file. The eldest of several children, Ontiveros came from a dishonored family. Her father was Colonel Pedro Ontiveros, a supporter of Emperor Maximilian during the French Intervention of 1862–1867. The decision to side with the invaders of Mexico doomed the Ontiveros family to destitution. Judging from newspaper accounts, Ontiveros was rescued by Carlos Rodríguez and soon developed an intimate relationship with him.[2]

That relationship began in 1886 when Ontiveros met Rodríguez, a paymaster with the Mexican army and an upper-level clerk with the National Treasury. The exact nature of their initial meeting is unknown, but one can speculate that the younger Ontiveros, who was fifteen at the time, fell in love with the older, dashing thirty-one-year-old Rodríguez, who held a secure position in the Porfirian bureaucracy. To a financially troubled woman, Rodríguez may have appeared to be a godsend. In any case, the paymaster was also equally enamored, so much so that he soon began paying the housing and living expenses of Ontiveros and her family. Despite the amorous nature of his relationship with Ontiveros, however, Rodríguez was more of a father figure to her, as she suggested in her correspondence.[3]

Rodríguez also had a quasi-parental relationship to the third figure in this narrative, Luis Yzaguirre. Born in Mexico City, Yzaguirre was twenty-five years old at the time of the incident and was employed as a clerk in the treasury, under Rodríguez's supervision. However, the men's relationship went deeper. Yzaguirre and Rodríguez were childhood friends, their fathers having been close. Yzaguirre not may have considered Rodríguez a friend, precisely, but thought of him instead as a sort of patron. Unlike the Ontiveros family, Yzaguirre's family had been on the Liberal side during the War of the Reform and the French Intervention, which Luis Yzaguirre may have hoped would ease his ascent as a bureaucrat. Rodríguez and Yzaguirre also were linked by their enjoyment of theater performances. This led to Rodríguez's ill-fated decision to invite Yzaguirre to join him and Ontiveros while at the theater one evening in January 1889.[4]

On that evening Rodríguez and Ontiveros attended a performance at the Teatro Principal, a theater favored by the Porfirian middle class. Carlos Rodríguez spotted Luis Yzaguirre there on this particular evening. Rodríguez immediately invited his younger coworker for drinks at his house and introduced him to his companion, Ontiveros. The trio then retired to Rodríguez's residence, where they conversed and where, by all accounts, Yzaguirre and Ontiveros fell madly in love with each other. A few days after their meeting, on February 4, they met again on a street corner and proceeded to a house of assignation, where the couple consummated their newfound love. After this first encounter they regularly met in other inexpensive hotels. Yzaguirre, apparently emboldened by his secret affair, invited Ontiveros on several occasions to dinner, to the theater, and on Sunday and holiday picnics. They were sometimes accompanied by Rodríguez, who did not at first suspect anything. Yzaguirre was so eager to see his new lover that he would even pay Rodríguez's expenses when the three of them went out to the theater. The combination of open and secret meetings was apparently too much for Ontiveros, who felt increasing shame. Yzaguirre attempted to lessen her growing remorse by giving her small gifts such as inexpensive jewelry. Ontiveros, however, began to cool, especially since most of her meetings with Yzaguirre were taking place in houses of assignation known as *casas de citas*.[5]

An integral part of Mexico City's sexual underworld, casas de citas (literally, appointment houses) were boarding houses where prostitutes went with their customers but where no girls actually lived. Other couples intent on consummating their love also used casas de citas. Regulated on paper but ignored by authorities, these casas were usually situated on out-of-the-way streets, perfect places for secretive meetings. They functioned, in essence, as sanctuaries where Porfirian propriety did not apply. Couples belonging to the middle class and, for that matter, any person who had the money could use these places to escape the prying eyes of neighbors and family friends or find refuge from restrictive social rules. Ontiveros knew the owner of one house on number 8 San Jerónimo Street, María Refugio Pulido, and preferred her hotel to all others. Ontiveros's growing doubts did not stop her, though, from regularly meeting Yzaguirre at prearranged street corners, where he picked her up in his rented coach and then took her to a room. On occasions, however, when Rodríguez was away on business, Ontiveros welcomed Yzaguirre into her house, much to her later regret.[6]

Information about Yzaguirre and Ontiveros's relationship has survived thanks to a series of letters the couple exchanged, letters that reveal as well the hopes and fears of aspiring members of the middle class and their ideas about sexuality, honor, and love. Ontiveros's letters were the most revealing and were directed not only toward Yzaguirre but also to her longtime companion, Rodríguez. The character of this personal correspondence changed with the passage of time. The first letters were personal notes passed between Ontiveros and Yzaguirre to arrange meeting times and dates. These letters reflected the beginning of their romantic involvement, before any problems surfaced. Later the letters took on a more ominous tone and were almost all from Ontiveros to Yzaguirre. In this set, the couple's troubles are visible, troubles caused by Ontiveros's continued relationship with Rodríguez and Yzaguirre's growing displeasure with the situation. Ontiveros's later correspondence also included a letter directed at Rodríguez in which she declares her true love to be Yzaguirre. In all of these letters, Ontiveros is seemingly struck by an ominous foreboding. Her tone and words reflect an almost fatalistic acceptance of the patriarchal authority Mexican society prescribed. Yet her letters also reflect Yzaguirre's dominant and aggressive behavior as well as his constant bullying of Ontiveros and Rodríguez. In fact, he demonstrated his hostility by committing several acts of violence toward his lover, such as firing a pistol at Ontiveros's bedroom wall, with no apparent legal consequences.[7]

At the beginning, Yzaguirre and Ontiveros were intent on developing their relationship, but they were aware of the potential consequences. On one occasion, Ontiveros told Yzaguirre that she was possibly pregnant, but in another letter she told him that she had begun her menstrual cycle.

> My Luis,
>
> Yesterday at 8:30 I became an honorable woman again. Now I am going to go through with my promise and not go anymore to

> any bad house, and also not have friends that you do not like, and see you with a clean body and heart. I am also going to love you very much and be yours. Now I expect you to do the same, fulfilling your promise to me. Until we meet again, remember me.
>
> From you know who[8]

This revealing letter reflects Ontiveros's growing guilt about the affair, which may have been shaped by notions of female honor and cleanliness. The reference to "any bad house" obviously refers to the inexpensive hotels where the couple met. The letter implies that Yzaguirre felt threatened by Ontiveros's continued friendship with other women, including Pulido, the owner of Ontiveros's favorite hotel. Yzaguirre seems to have been more committed to the idea of a monogamous relationship than Ontiveros was, and so he pressured Ontiveros to leave Rodríguez.[9]

Yzaguirre's views reflect male anxieties, common in Porfirian Mexico, about "loose" women who challenged male dominance in sexual relationships. Like Escorcia, Ontiveros subverted Yzaguirre's authority and carried out relationships with persons her secret lover found objectionable. By the late nineteenth century, Porfirian reformers, dubbed *científicos*, had not only formulated national programs to modernize Mexico along the lines of the United States and Western Europe, they also attempted to educate Mexicans to follow gender-scripted roles. Men were supposed to be sober and hardworking, while women were to be compliant and submissive, transforming both into *gente decente*, people who lived and acted decently, members of Mexico's nascent urban middle class. Both Yzaguirre and Ontiveros seem to have aspired to be successful members of the gente decente, but their behaviors contradicted their aspirations, making them seem more like the "immoral" persons from the "gente del pueblo" that the Porfirian elite linked with Mexico City's imagined criminal underworld.[10]

As the relationship between Yzaguirre and Ontiveros expanded, the correspondence changed from letters that arranged for secret meetings to notes that hinted at a deepening financial relationship between the pair. In one letter Ontiveros asks Yzaguirre about some money he owes her:

> Luis my beautiful child,
>
> I am sorry to bother you but the money I gave to the Italian is for the expense. It is five pesos, plus four more from my mother. I hope it is not a bother, but please drop it off with your mother and

> I will send Paco for it. Soon you will finish paying the account. In fact, figure out your account since September 16 to today's date and subtract the nine pesos from it. I send you my thoughts.

The identity of the Italian is never explained in any of the other letters, so we are left with speculation. It appears that Yzaguirre had borrowed money from Ontiveros's family for some unnamed expense. Yzaguirre had stepped out of the traditional role of the male provider; Ontiveros once again was in a relatively powerful position that undermined the role of the Mexican male. Ontiveros, despite her gender, practiced a certain amount of influence over the men in her lives. She also clearly was willing and able to negotiate with Yzaguirre, as seen in another letter:

> *Mi flaco lindo,*
>
> I would like it better that you came to my house, which is yours, at the regular time, but if you do not want to, then I will be waiting for you on Lerdo Street at three; please be there since I will also be there.
>
> From the one who is always yours, Piedad Ontiveros[11]

The secretive nature of the relationship led to further clandestine meetings, with letters often delivered via other messengers (such as Paco, one of Ontiveros's younger brothers) and with notes written by Pulido, Ontiveros's closest female confidant. It seems that the hidden nature of the relationship began to weigh heavily on Yzaguirre, who grew increasingly anxious to see his lover and would meet her in public and even make up some sort of pretense to visit her home. However, in December 1889 Yzaguirre had to make changes to his strategy when his secret was found out.

During that month Rodríguez found out about the affair when his maid went to Ontiveros's house, ostensibly to deliver some food, and saw Yzaguirre there. She dutifully informed her employer, who then confronted Yzaguirre. The meeting must have been explosive, for angry words were exchanged between both men, but especially by Rodríguez, who reportedly cursed at Yzaguirre. We can only guess what the maid saw. In any case, Rodríguez already suspected something was going on, since in his statement to the police he mentioned an argument he had with Ontiveros about her close friendship with Yzaguirre on the day before the maid's visit. Rodríguez admitted jealousy on his part. Ontiveros's response to his complaints had been to storm out of the meeting, leaving Rodríguez to ponder the situation and, of course, setting up the incident the next day with the maid, who may have been sent to not only deliver the food as an apology, but perhaps also to spy on Ontiveros.

Rodríguez's angry confrontation with his friend seemed to be the only time the man showed any backbone, although one newspaper reported that he dragged Ontiveros back to his house. The incident must have been serious since Yzaguirre stopped seeing Ontiveros, but in April 1890 Ontiveros convinced Rodríguez that nothing had happened between her and Yzaguirre and that Yzaguirre was very sad about the falling out. Rodríguez believed Ontiveros, had a change of heart, and sent his estranged friend a letter on Good Friday, pleading with him to visit Ontiveros, because, in her words, she needed him. Rodríguez was apparently willing to forgive his friends' betrayal, if only to make Ontiveros happy. Of course, Yzaguirre eagerly took Rodríguez up on his offer. Soon after, Yzaguirre and Ontiveros resumed their affair and even began to attend the theater again, sometimes with Rodríguez in tow. Their meetings were infrequent enough, though, for Yzaguirre to complain in the following letter, composed shortly after Easter:

> Alma mía,
>
> When I checked into the hotel I found your precious letter. I am also not satisfied with watching you at your house as I pass by, and if you tell me where and when we could meet to talk, then you would make me happy. In regards to my photograph, you will have it soon and you will give me yours, right my love? What are you telling me? My love, are you afraid I am going to tell you that it would be better that I will not see you anymore? But you know, beautiful child, that to stop seeing you would be to stop living; do you not believe that I love you, Piedad of my life? I think of you always and even though I am far from your eyes, I am always with you in my thoughts. Answer me soon, telling me where and when we can see each other. May your coral lips receive a kiss of love from the person who loves you more than life itself.[12]

The letter hints at a deepening obsession on the part of Yzaguirre that threatened to leave Rodríguez behind. Yzaguirre, eager to continue seeing Ontiveros but also aware that the situation could not continue as before, prepared a complex strategy manipulating the gendered discourses of morality, propriety, and honor to permanently remove his rival. In July 1890 he launched his plan when he told Rodríguez that Ontiveros was being unfaithful to him with another man and that if Rodríguez did not stop seeing Ontiveros, Yzaguirre would be forced to end his friendship with Rodríguez. Yzaguirre hoped that Rodríguez would realize that to knowingly consent to be Ontiveros's cuckold would dishonor not only him but also by extension Yzaguirre. Yzaguirre's able manipulation of the morality and honor of his friend was aimed at removing him from the triangle, but the plan failed. Rodríguez refused to break up with Ontiveros, leaving Yzaguirre no other option but to carry out his threat and stop speaking to his friend.

Descent into the Underworld

The summer of 1890 was a watershed moment and marked the beginning of an increasingly violent relationship among the three. Yzaguirre, perhaps realizing that his threats had effectively cut him off from open access to Ontiveros, turned desperate and violent, demanding that she leave Rodríguez and go live with him instead. For example, he showed up at Pulido's house, apparently having followed Ontiveros there. Using the false pretense that he had a box of perfumes for Pulido's daughter Juana, Yzaguirre gained entry to the house, where he confronted and threatened Ontiveros. Pulido interceded, though, and pulled out a gun. She aimed it at the interloper and told him not to threaten the family. Yzaguirre immediately backed down, telling Pulido that he would leave, while Ontiveros came out of a back room to talk to her estranged lover, who left shortly afterward. Two weeks later, in another incident, Yzaguirre showed up at Ontiveros's house and demanded sex, but Ontiveros refused. Angered, Yzaguirre fired his pistol at a wall, causing some damage that Ontiveros had to quickly fix so that Rodríguez could not find out. Yet despite the violence, Ontiveros did not approach the police, perhaps fearful of revealing the secret relationship.[13]

By this point the relationship had devolved into an ongoing series of threats of violence by Yzaguirre. Despite the confrontation at Pulido's house, Yzaguirre refused to back down. In a subsequent incident, Yzaguirre assaulted Ontiveros with the handle of a knife. He also threatened to kill both Ontiveros and Rodríguez. Ontiveros confessed her growing fear of Yzaguirre to her friend Pulido, telling her that she was afraid Yzaguirre would eventually kill her. Pulido counseled her to stop seeing Yzaguirre, but

Ontiveros was resigned to the inevitable. In the following letter, she writes to Rodríguez, addressing him not as a lover but as a father figure or patron:

> My father,
>
> I know I have made you suffer much but you have always been good to me. Once again, for a thousandth time I ask for your forgiveness with all my heart. I would rather die than hurt you again. You did not know what was going to happen when you brought Luis to the house, and I did not know my destiny and did not control my heart when I fell in love with him, a powerful passion that is my first and shall never die. I will not leave you angry at me, not you or him, so I would rather die, a punishment I happily receive for making you suffer so much. Because I have decided not to go with him, I am going to die in my best years, but God knows that if I had another chance I would not be with him. Now, instead of Heaven awaiting us we will see each other in Hell. My feelings will not leave me in peace since you have never given me problems and you have always loved me with kindness. I confess all this to you since he has decided to kill me. Since in life you never refused me, I expect you to follow my last wish, that of never abandoning my beloved mother or my brothers. Please do what you think is best and give them a good education. Make a man out of Paco, and do not let him fall like I have. For Tomasito and Alejandro I also expect you not to abandon them. I also ask you to hold the wake at my house, and to have a tomb where they can go visit me. Don't believe that I am afraid of death. You, my second father, my beloved mother, my loving brothers will not remember me, but Luis will remember me and be happy once he sees me in the coffin. This is my destiny. Only you and my family know that he [Luis] was the one who killed me, and if he does not come to justice, it is better since there is no remedy for my death. In closing, goodbye my good father, my brother, my good angel; do not forget my last wishes and I die happy if you forgive me. Goodbye and may the maker of the universe forgive me. Goodbye Carlos.[14]

This letter reveals much about the nature of the relationship between Ontiveros and Rodríguez. In spite of his financial benevolence or possibly because of it, Rodríguez had been transformed, in Ontiveros's rhetoric, into a second father, while she wrote of Yzaguirre, on the other hand, as an exciting young man. Further, the importance of patriarchal relationships emerges from the letter's discourse. Ontiveros had been a father substitute to her younger brothers and was worried, if Yzaguirre was successful in carrying out his threat, they would also "fall" like her.

Several styles of masculinity played an important part in this story, as they did in many kinds of interpersonal relationships in Porfirian Mexico. On one hand, Rodriguez enacted a mature, moral form of masculinity, seeking to dominate others through control of resources. On the other hand, a less mature but much more sexually exciting form of masculinity emerges in the figure of the younger male—whom Ontiveros refers to in the endearing term of "my child." And unlike the rational older male, he is emotional, chaotic, and cannot control his violence. It is also interesting to note that Ontiveros's prediction of her fate implied, on her part, an acceptance of the Porfirian role of the submissive woman. At no point in this letter did Ontiveros defend herself to Yzaguirre. Generally she relied on others for protection, including Carlos Rodríguez—another man—and Refugio Pulido, an older woman who happened to run a hotel for prostitutes and was accustomed to confronting unruly men (as evidenced by her reaction to Yzaguirre). In addition, Ontiveros and her family never approached the police for help, reflecting perhaps resignation on the part of women that a certain degree of domestic violence was part of every relationship. In essence, Ontiveros's public voice was silenced; instead she found an outlet in private forms of expression, namely though love letters and female-to-female relationships. It would seem, in this case, that Ontiveros embraced *marianismo*—a gender ideology that takes the Virgin Mary's absolute self-abnegation and acceptance of suffering as the model for acceptable feminine behavior while also assuming the moral and spiritual superiority of women—and accepted her fate, reinforcing the existing hierarchy that placed males in a position of power.[15]

But Ontiveros's silence was short-lived, for she soon delivered a scathing diatribe against Yzaguirre, asking for forgiveness and at the same time assailing him for treating her with scorn and ridicule. In the following excerpt from Ontiveros's personal correspondence a picture of an increasingly distant and angry Yzaguirre emerges, portraying a man bent on dominating the situation and at the same time preparing to discard his lover:

> Luis!
>
> The suffering of my disgraced heart is reflected in your sad eyes. Forgive me. The truth is full of pain and my soul suffers for you. I

> have approached you to see if your love would respond and lower itself into my grave. You, however, have hurled hatred and abandon at me without mercy. You have given me sour nourishment and I have drunk it all, thus killing my heart. A ray of pain has entrapped my heart, making it necessary for me to forget you.[16]

At one point Ontiveros labels Yzaguirre's existence as empty and reminds him that his life had no meaning until he came into her "port" of salvation. Yet despite her spirited voice, Ontiveros accepts a "fatal" destiny and ultimately begs Yzaguirre for forgiveness if her harsh words have hurt his feelings.

Ontiveros's personal correspondence indicates that the affair, at least in its last stages, was increasingly one-sided and had begun to cool off. Yzaguirre's behavior also contributed to a sense of fatalism that becomes evident, once again, in this letter:

> Luis,
>
> It would be criminal if I did not take a pen in hand and tell you about my life. Luis, we are children of a fate that follows us. I am one of those beings that was born predestined to be a toy of evil fortune. I inhabit this world and live a miserable life without finding anyone that can understand my ideas and beliefs. Since I was a child I have looked for happiness and did not find it in my parents and in my friends. As a woman I looked for a man to make me happy and I have only found those that would take advantage of me. Remember that I love you with all my soul the way you love someone only once in your life. Aware of how human nature is I have abandoned you and have resigned myself to suffer with the hope that one day you will remember me. I believe that you have good sentiments and remember about past judgments so do not insult me; I do not deserve it since the only fault I have is loving you. You remember what was the cause of our problems. But do not believe that I am trying to evade blame since you are always able to see reasonably. You are such a good person despite my sins that were the cause of our fight.[17]

Ontiveros hoped that Yzaguirre would not hate her and have any bad memories of her, suggesting her acceptance of the role of the fallen woman.

By the fall of 1890, Yzaguirre had also silenced his competitor Rodríguez, cowing him with threats of violence directed against Ontiveros. As for Ontiveros, she had accepted the inevitable collision and confessed so to her mother and friends. It was only a matter of time when the right conditions would come together and produce the dreaded result.

Black Monday

On Sunday, October 12, 1890, Pulido fell ill. Ontiveros went to visit her and promised to return the next day, which she did, arriving sometime during the morning but leaving around 2:00 p.m. She had an appointment to keep with Yzaguirre. Meanwhile, Yzaguirre had begun the week by reporting to work as scheduled. Sometime late in the morning, however, he accompanied his close friend Carlos Sheridan to the dentist. After the visit, both men went to a cantina to get some water since Sheridan was bleeding. Before they got there, though, they ran into Manuel Esquerro, a mutual friend and a paymaster with the military. Yzaguirre considered Esquerro to be an intimate friend, whose relationship to the clerk was strengthened by shared visits to cantinas. On that day, Esquerro suggested to Yzaguirre that perhaps Sheridan's pain might be lessened by a few glasses of strong liquor. The trio therefore proceeded down bustling Cinco de Mayo Street, past restaurants and shops to the cantina "Nueva Orléans," located below the Hotel Comonfort. Once there, each man drank several glasses of brandy. This meandering soon continued at another watering hole, "El Aseo," located near the Alameda, where they each drank three glasses of tequila.[18]

Yzaguirre and his friends valued their time in cantinas and did not believe that visiting these places labeled them as drunks. To them, cantinas provided a refuge from the pressures of daily life in the big city and a social gathering place where moral constraints could be loosened and masculine bonds of friendship strengthened. By about 1:00 p.m., Yzaguirre's bonds to his friends were indeed improved; he was very drunk. Soon after, the trio left the bar and parted ways. Esquerro returned to his job. However, Sheridan noticed that Yzaguirre was too inebriated to return to work, so he decided to take him to eat at a *fonda* (small restaurant) on the corner of Cinco de Mayo Street and Santa Clara Street. The two men ate but also drank good amounts of pulque, a common alcoholic beverage, with the afternoon meal. Sheridan noticed that Yzaguirre was in good spirits (in more ways than one), and they both left at around 3:00 p.m.; Sheridan returned to work but not Yzaguirre, who left for his home.[19]

It remains unclear if Yzaguirre began the day with the intention of settling the issue with Ontiveros, but by midafternoon he had determined to end the matter once and for all. He set out to find her, arriving first at his home in a rented coach where he asked the doorman to get his gun. Yzaguirre, after his arrest, told police that since he worked for the National Treasury, it was customary for him to be armed. He also added that he was afraid of a confrontation with Carlos Rodríguez and thus had to be ready to defend himself. Yzaguirre's rationale would not serve him during his subsequent trial, since the jury believed that his crime had been premeditated. Certainly his path after leaving his home indicated so. After obtaining his weapon, Yzaguirre ordered the coachman to proceed to Jesus Street, where he failed to find Ontiveros, and then to the intersection of Don Juan Manuel Street and Monterilla Street, where he waited and eventually opened the door as Piedad Ontiveros entered the coach.[20]

Yzaguirre and Ontiveros then went for a ride on Paseo de la Reforma, one of the main thoroughfares where Porfirians went to see and be seen. Yzaguirre then ordered the driver to proceed to number 8 San Jerónimo Street, the house of assignation owned by Refugio Pulido. Upon arriving there, Yzaguirre asked the driver to bring Pulido to the coach. The driver went to the house, but instead of the matron the driver returned with Cleotilde Ávila, a friend of Ontiveros. Ávila informed Yzaguirre that Pulido was ill and could not speak to him. Yzaguirre exploded in anger and demanded that Ávila board the coach or if not, "she was not a woman." However, Ávila ignored the insult and walked away. Sensing danger, Ontiveros tried to exit the coach and enter Pulido's house, but Yzaguirre prevented her from doing so, saying that he did not want her to visit that type of place. He then began arguing with her, demanding that she leave Rodríguez and live with him, growing enraged at her refusal to do so. Yzaguirre ordered the driver to leave. As they started moving, he took out his pistol and fired five shots at Ontiveros at point-blank range.[21]

Influenced by alcohol and angered by challenges to his dominance not only from Ontiveros but also from her female friends, Yzaguirre decided to put an end to his ongoing battle with Ontiveros and Rodríguez. The final spark came when Ontiveros attempted to enter the Pulido house, a place that signified, for Yzaguirre, sexuality outside of masculine control. Yzaguirre wished to cleanse Ontiveros of associations he found offensive to masculine honor, especially Rodríguez's inability to control the woman in his life. Yzaguirre wanted to control Ontiveros completely. Failing to do so, he resorted to violence. If he could not have her, no one else could, including Rodríguez, Pulido, and Ontiveros herself. For Yzaguirre, violence and death would prove to be his ultimate recourse.

Whether Yzaguirre experienced any satisfaction is unknowable. He later testified that some unknown force had forced him to shoot Ontiveros. However, the authorities would not be satisfied with that answer. After he fired the shots, the coach sped down the streets, alerting a couple of police officers that something was amiss. Officer Pedro Ruiz later testified that as the coach passed him, he looked inside and saw a woman grimacing and moving in pain. After some difficulty he managed to stop the coach and, along with another officer, José María Carrillo, looked inside and saw a man and a woman. Ontiveros had her left arm and chest covered in blood and was crying the words "I am dying" while Yzaguirre sat silent. Officer Ruiz asked the woman who had wounded her, and she motioned with her eyes toward Yzaguirre. Ruiz spotted the gun, a .38 caliber double-action revolver, lying beside the girl, and detained Yzaguirre, ordering the other officer to arrest the driver. The officers took the trio to the fifth precinct headquarters for a full declaration. With some difficulty, they lowered Ontiveros from the coach and took her to the medical section. The attending physician, Dr. Salvador Alvarado, treated Ontiveros's wounds as her mother arrived. Given the severity of the wounds, though, Alvarado ordered her transferred to Juárez Hospital, where after a brief farewell to her mother, Piedad Ontiveros died at approximately 7:00 p.m.[22]

As the evening chill descended on the Mexican capital, news about the incident spread quickly. Carlos Rodríguez had been unaware of the shooting until one of Ontiveros's brothers went to his office and notified him that Piedad was wounded and at the fifth precinct police station. Rodríguez left his office at around 5:30 p.m. and went to locate Ontiveros's personal physician, a certain Dr. Macías, but unable to find him, went instead to fetch his friend Juan Domínguez, an apothecarist. When he finally arrived at the station, though, he was told that Ontiveros had been taken to the hospital where she had passed away. Rodríguez made the arrangements for her burial the next day. However, before the day was out, he went to Ontiveros's home and found a letter written to him, addressing him as "father." It was the same letter quoted earlier in which she declared her undying passion for Yzaguirre and asked for forgiveness from the man she considered not her lover but her father.

Because of Her Sex

Given the overwhelming evidence against him, the state had no problems bringing Yzaguirre to trial on charges of premeditated murder early in 1891. The prosecution alleged that Yzaguirre shot Ontiveros five times and that two of the wounds had caused her death. Prosecutors also charged the coach driver, Sabino Domínguez, with acting as an accomplice. The prosecutors based their accusation on Domínguez's actions after the shooting, specifically his refusal to stop the coach when ordered to do so by the police. Domínguez, who was illiterate, testified that he had no advance knowledge of the crime but had merely been hired by Yzaguirre that day and had only done as his customer had ordered. Domínguez added that when he heard the shots he actually stopped the coach and looked inside. He saw Ontiveros and she looked pale, but he found no other clue indicating that she had been shot. Still suspicious though, the driver got back on the coach and decided to look for the officer he had just passed when another officer showed up and ordered him not to proceed. By this time Yzaguirre was upset and demanded to know why they had stopped. Domínguez did not reply and merely stood by while the police investigated. Authorities believed his story eventually and finally dropped charges against him by May 1891.

The trial formally began on June 4, 1891, and was heavily attended by Mexicans from all walks of life. The prosecution's allegation that Yzaguirre had plotted all along to kill Ontiveros was countered with the defense assertion that the shooting had been accidental. The young clerk's case was helped by his political connections. His advocates, José María Pavón and don Guillermo Prieto, called in several midlevel government officials, including General Marcos Carrillo, chief of the first military zone, as character witnesses. Yzaguirre's close friends also testified. Manuel Esquerro told the court that although Yzaguirre had indeed drunk heavily the day he shot Ontiveros, he was not a drunk. Esquerro's defense of his friend reflected the Profirian gente decente class's perception of drunkenness as an exclusive working-class phenomenon. Esquerro, Sheridan, and Yzaguirre all shared gente decente ideals about drinking and sexual behavior. Their own private social network, rooted in the office but extended in the cantinas, stood in marked contrast to the pulquería-centered social patterns of the poor. Carlos Sheridan's own statement of concern for his friend, who had clearly drank so much that he had to go eat something, reflected a certain disapproval of public drunkenness. However, Sheridan vouched for his friend. Despite the shared concerns about drinking, though, all three men pursued privacy in terms of their personal lives. There is no indication in the trial records that Yzaguirre ever told his friends about his personal problems with Ontiveros. However, given the fact that Carlos Rodríguez worked in the same government circles as Yzaguirre's friend, some gossip must have spread.[23]

Ontiveros's confessional letters to her friends and family proved especially damaging to Yzaguirre's case, but the young clerk had some information of his own that proved equally explosive. On the stand, several witnesses, including Pulido, repeated that it was common knowledge that Yzaguirre had threatened to kill his lover. Curiously, Carlos Rodríguez did not reveal any damaging testimony against his former friend, opting instead to give a full account of the three-sided relationship, corroborating some of Yzaguirre's own statements. However, Yzaguirre, in an effort to take the moral high ground, testified that he began his affair with Ontiveros only after he found out she was not married to Rodríguez, who had originally claimed that she was his wife. He sought to justify the affair with the claim that there was no moral shame in pursuing a single woman who did not even live with Rodríguez. Rather, the shame he felt was based on her refusal to leave Rodríguez, defying his wishes. Yzaguirre added that Rodríguez knew that he had been carrying on an affair with Ontiveros for some time before their falling out but chose not to do anything. Rodriguez, of course, denied Yzaguirre's statements, but the damage was done. By accusing his rival of moral laxity, Yzaguirre's masculinity superceded that of Rodríguez, who was transformed into a source of pity. Further, Rodríguez's own statement declaring that Yzaguirre had taken advantage of his friendship made the paymaster look weak. Finally, Ontiveros's own choice of friends, especially Pulido, made her look less like a respectable woman and more like a prostitute, which she was not. For instance, when Pulido took the stand, the audience snickered. Although destined for prison, Yzaguirre appeared to have won the battle for the moral high ground, at least until Piedad Ontiveros's own words, in the form of the love letters, were read, revealing her fears about Yzaguirre, the violence he directed against her, and her belief that he would eventually kill her.[24]

The police were not aware of the existence of the love letters until they interviewed Rodríguez, who had several in his possession. They then discovered more letters that Yzaguirre had stashed in his house. Miguel Cabrera, second-in-command of the Comisiones de Seguridad, Mexico City's plainclothes detective force, escorted Yzaguirre to his residence, where he retrieved a box containing all the personal correspondence between Luis and Piedad. Prosecutor Antonio Ramos Pedrueza made good use of the information in the letters, arguing that they proved Yzaguirre's actions were premeditated. Yzaguirre's attorneys mounted a decent defense, calling the shooting accidental. Yzaguirre's own testimony about his alleged sobriety (disproved by Esquerro) and reasons for carrying a weapon (not believed by the prosecutors) did not help him. Further, Yzaguirre claimed that he did not remember firing the gun and then changed his story, telling the jury that the gun was on his belt and must have gone off accidentally when he touched it. How Yzaguirre could have fired five shots accidentally with such ferocity that investigators had to pry some of the bullets from the coach's rear seat was not adequately explained by the former clerk.

On June 5, 1891, a jury composed of eleven members found Luis Yzaguirre guilty of murder. The prosecution's charges numbered twenty-five and ranged from the simple question of premeditation to whether or not Yzaguirre was drunk at the time of the incident. The jury determined that he was not totally inebriated and further concluded that he was never in physical danger from Ontiveros. This last matter was crucial in criminal trials since it could determine if the defendant acted in self-defense. In this case, it was clear that Ontiveros was helpless at the time of the shooting. The jury found Yzaguirre guilty and Judge Salvador Medina y Ormaechea immediately pronounced a sentence of capital punishment. Prieto and Pavón began the usual appeal process immediately thereafter, but on November 5 of the same year, the Supreme Court confirmed the death sentence.

The defense had one last card left to play: they appealed the case directly to President Porfirio Díaz. Ordinarily, death sentences were reserved for soldiers who killed senior officers, or for hardened criminals, but there was no set pattern. Díaz regularly commuted death sentences in an effort to look magnanimous. Most probably, a successful stay of execution and a commutation to prison time depended on the strength of the appeal and on the publicity of the case. Yzaguirre was in luck. On June 10, 1892, Díaz commuted Yzaguirre's sentence to twenty years in the island prison fortress of San Juan de Ulúa, located in Veracruz harbor. Spared from death (and from the torment of Belén Prison, where he had been held), Yzaguirre found himself on a train transport to the Gulf Coast shortly after his successful appeal. Nevertheless, the thought of twenty years in San Juan de Ulúa must have terrified the former office clerk to the bone. The truth was that few, if any, prisoners survived their twenty years in the humid prison, and if they managed to obtain an early release, the deleterious aftereffects of the tropics would eventually claim them. These thoughts must have provided little comfort to Yzaguirre as he speeded to the coast, accompanied by three other prisoners, one of them Francisco Guerrero, alias El Chalequero, the serial murderer whose trial took place in the same time span as his. Indeed, Yzaguirre must have felt a certain chill as the train left the mountain valley of Anáhuac for the torrid lowlands of the coast.[25]

Beauty and Strength

Six days after Piedad Ontiveros's murder, the Mexico City newspaper *La Patria* commented on the crime, saying that it did not want to report on the "sensationalistic episode," but since the entire city was talking about the case, it had no choice but to include some information. Interestingly, it chose to focus on the memory of Piedad Ontiveros, noting her beauty and reaffirming her ideal role in Porfirian society:

> She was young, very young, delicate and tender. Her soul was sweet and passionate and did not know fury, or vengeance, or hatred. She had been born to happily love and obey, and was destined to silently welcome death, without complaint.[26]

The newspaper invented an image for Ontiveros that differed from earlier portrayals in the press. *La Patria* presented her as a morally ambiguous woman and portrayed her as a victim, an unthreatening member of the middle class. But Ontiveros, despite her apparent passivity, did challenge traditional masculinity. She was not the ideal Porfirian woman, chaste and pure, but instead a sexually provocative figure. Despite her unorthodox personal relationship with two men, she was not criticized in the press. She was appropriated instead, turned into gente decente, and enlisted after her death to reinforce Mexican masculine identity.

In its praise of Ontiveros, the paper also elaborated on what she was not—a vicious creature. Indeed, these words were a thinly veiled criticism of her assassin, Yzaguirre, whose masculinity *La Patria* rejected. Yzaguirre was everything she was not: hateful, vengeful, a bringer of death. Yzaguirre had, in the process of domination, completely stepped out of the bounds of Porfirian moral decency and committed the unthinkable: he murdered a woman, thus having no consideration for her sex. In the relevant Mexican legal system, consideration for the female sex was paramount. In fact, these words were incorporated into the legal wording of the charges against Yzaguirre. Was he respectful of her sex? Apparently not. Yzaguirre had undermined Porfirian masculinity in the pursuit of his own.[27]

This essay has explored the intricate world of masculinity and gender relationships in Porfirian Mexico City through the window of criminality. Criminal cases, far from being simple narratives, can actually speak volumes about relationships and communal values. In this case, court documentation reveals a hidden world of masculine friendships and codes of conduct, reinforced by homosocial networking. Luis Yzaguirre and Carlos Rodríguez, middle-class participants in the ongoing process of urban modernity, represented opposites in an ongoing struggle against some of the more disruptive elements of modernity. For Yzaguirre, fear of the influence of Mexico City's sexual underworld translated into violence as he sought to dominate his lover, Ontiveros. For Rodríguez, a male friendship became the vehicle for his submission to a stronger masculinity. As Porfirian Mexico entered its gilded age, its citizens welcomed the force of modernity but at the cost of their personal honor and, in this case, their bonds of brotherhood.

NOTES

1. *El Imparcial*, February 16, 1909; pulquerías were drinking establishments where *pulque*, a fermented drink made from the sap of the maguey cactus, was served; see Jeffrey Pilcher, *¡Que vivan los tamales! Food and the Making of Mexican National Identity* (Albuquerque: University of New Mexico Press, 1998), 12, 51–52.
2. "Luis Yzaguirre y Sabino Domínguez por la muerte de Piedad Ontiveros," Expediente 196498, Juzgado 5 de lo Criminal, October 14, 1890–June 10, 1892, Caja 17/6852 1890, Tribunal Superior Justicia Distrito Federal, Archivo General de la Nación; hereafter cited as Expediente 196498, TSJDF/AGN; *El Monitor Republicano*, June 6, 1891; *El Tiempo*, October 16, 1890.
3. Expediente 196498, TSJDF/AGN.
4. Ibid.; *El Partido Liberal*, June 6, 1891.
5. Expediente 196498, TSJDF/AGN.
6. Catherine Elaine Bliss, *Compromised Positions: Prostitution, Public Health and Gender Politics in Revolutionary Mexico City* (University Park: Pennsylvania University Press, 2001), 31; Luis Lara y Pardo, *La Prostitución en México* (Mexico City: Librería de la Vda. de Ch. Bouret, 1908), 17; Expediente 196498, TSJDF/AGN; "Reglamento de la policía de costumbres (Reglamento regulando la prostitución)," Sección s/n, 1887, Gobierno del Distrito Federal, Ramo Gobernación, AGN.
7. Expediente 196498, TSJDF/AGN.
8. Ibid.
9. For a historical analysis of women and menstrual cycles, see Elaine and English Showalter, "Victorian Women and Menstruation," in *Suffer and Be Still: Women in the Victorian Age*, ed. Martha Vicinus (Bloomington: Indiana University Press, 1972), 38–44.
10. Expediente 196498, TSJDF/AGN; for the Porfirian ideal family, see William E. French, *A Peaceful and Working People: Manners, Morals and Class Formation in Northern Mexico* (Albuquerque: University of New Mexico Press, 1996); for the criminal underworld, see James A. Garza, *The Imagined Underworld: Sex, Crime, and Vice in Porfirian Mexico City* (Lincoln: University of Nebraska Press, 2008); for a discussion of women's roles in Porfirian society, see, for example, Carmen Ramos Escandón, "Señoritas Porfirianas: Mujeres e Ideología en el México Progresista, 1880–1910," in *Presencia y Transparencia: La Mujer en la historia de Mexico*, ed. Carmen Ramos Escandón (Mexico City: El Colegio de México, 1987), 143–61; see also Julia Tuñón Pablos, *Mujeres en Mexico: una Historia Olvidada* (Mexico City: Grupo Editorial Planeta, 1987); and Vivian M. Vallens, *Working Women in Mexico During the Porfiriato, 1880–1910* (San Francisco: R&E Research, 1978).
11. *Flaco lindo* is a term that describes someone's physical qualities in an endearing fashion; in this case literally as "my thin sweet man." Expediente 196498, TSJDF/AGN.
12. Expediente 196498, TSJDF/AGN.

13. Ibid.
14. Ibid.
15. Expediente 196498, TSJDF/AGN; for *marianismo*, see Evelyn P. Stevens, "Marianismo: The Other Face of Machismo" in *Confronting Change, Challenging Tradition: Women in Latin American History*, ed. Gertrude M. Yeager (Wilmington, DE: Scholarly Resources, 1994), 3.
16. Expediente 196498, TSJDF/AGN.
17. Ibid.
18. Ibid.; *El Monitor Republicano*, June 5, 1891.
19. The afternoon comida was the largest meal of the day and usually took place between 1:00 and 4:00 p.m. See Pilcher, *¡Que vivan los tamales!*, 53–54, for a discussion of the urban practice of meandering that often preceded a crime; see Piccato, "Urbanistas, Ambulantes and Mendigos: The Dispute for Urban Space in Mexico City, 1890–1930," in *Reconstructing Criminality in Latin America*, ed. Carlos A. Aguirre and Robert Buffington (Wilmington, DE: Scholarly Resources, 2000), 113–48; Expediente 196498, TSJDF/AGN.
20. Expediente 196498, TSJDF/AGN; *El Tiempo*, October 15, 1890.
21. Expediente 196498, TSJDF/AGN; *El Mundo*, October 15, 1890; *El Nacional*, October 15, 1890.
22. Expediente 196498, TSJDF/AGN; *El Monitor Republicano*, June 5, 1891; *El Tiempo*, October 15, 1890.
23. Expediente 196498, TSJDF/AGN; *El Monitor Republicano*, June 5, 1891; *El Monitor Republicano*, June 6, 1891.
24. Expediente 196498, TSJDF/AGN; *El Monitor Republicano*, June 5, 1891.
25. Expediente 196498, TSJDF/AGN; "Relativo al pago de los gastos de traslación de los reos Francisco Guerrero, Luis Yzaguirre, Pioquinto Zaldívar, y Ignacio García," Sección 1a, 1892, Estados de la República, Presos, Relaciones con los estados, gastos en los presos de alimentación, traslados, y estancias, Legajo 892, Ramo Gobernación, AGN; for the uses of capital punishment, see Patrick Weldon Lowery-Timmons, "The Politics of Punishment and War: Law's Violence during the Mexican Reform, circa 1840 to 1870," (PhD diss., University of Texas at Austin, 2004).
26. *La Patria*, October 18, 1890.
27. Ibid.

CHAPTER 4

Meretricious Mexicali

Exalted Masculinities and the Crafting of Male Desire in a Border Red-Light District, 1908–1925

ERIC SCHANTZ

RUDOLPH VALENTINO AND HIS SOON-TO-BE SECOND WIFE, NATACHA Rambova, boarded an automobile in the spring of 1922 with friends and headed south for Mexicali, Baja California, to get married on the other side of the international border, beyond any interference from American courts.[1] Hollywood film stars popularized the border marriage as a form of tourism that brought Americans to indulge in Mexico's notoriously permissive border zone. Valentino had been granted a divorce from his first wife, actress Jean Acker, but it would not be effective until March 4, 1923. Hollywood's first Latin lover and Rambova impetuously followed the example of their industry friends, director Frank Mayo and actress Dagmar Godowsky, who had tied the knot earlier that year in Tijuana.[2] But Valentino and Rambova chose to go to Mexicali, a youthfully exuberant border city that became the capital of northern Baja California in 1915, while Mexico's dueling Revolutionary factions struggled for national power.

Attempting to declare Baja California neutral from the internecine conflict that was consuming Mexico, Governor Colonel Esteban Cantú rose to power and held on to it largely by establishing the territory as a safe haven for foreign investment in commercial agriculture. Before being driven from power in 1920, Colonel Cantú ruled the military and political affairs of Baja California for over five years. During his stint Mexicali developed economically, financed by commercial agriculture (especially cotton, driven by Los Angeles real estate money and Chinese immigrant labor) and tourism (especially a piping-hot red-light trade that catered to local workers and increasingly long-distance sightseers). Both these forms of development took advantage of the economic conditions created by U.S. participation in the First World War. Colonel Cantú understood the nuances of the Victorian double standard and race segregation and knew how to impose a carefully constructed sense of order that appealed to the Euro-American bourgeoisie. He reformed the vice trade and made a strategic alliance with a group of American "sporting" investors called the ABW Syndicate. This effectively transformed the border from notoriously dangerous and disreputable to increasingly respectable and central to sightseeing itineraries of wealthy tourists like Rambova and Valentino. But Colonel Cantú modernized Baja California without overly sanitizing the masculine elements of fantasy and performance.

Male tourists, whether middle-American Babbitts or bon vivants such as Valentino, were responsible for disseminating images and news of Mexicali as a "wide-open" city specializing in masculine "sporting attractions" that rivaled Laredo or Juárez. Mexicali's sex trade certainly surpassed Tijuana's.[3] Mexicali offers a unique example of what I will call transculturative masculinities. That is, its brilliant "red-light reputation" was based on Mexican models of male privilege and *macho* leisure yet highly influenced by transnational models of red-light commerce. At the heart of wide-open geographies was the Chinese ghetto, or Chinatown. Mexicali had its own segregated Chinese community and neighborhood (*chinesca*, or "Chinatown"), concentrated in a narrowly confined area that overlapped with the red-light zone (*zona de tolerancia*), a common pattern in urban centers of the nineteenth-century United States. Chinatowns from Vancouver to Salina Cruz were notoriously red-hot sites for transgressive male fantasies. Terms like *wide open* and *chinesca* encouraged Mexicans and foreigners to associate Mexicali with red-light leisure and illicit diversion for men.[4] Also, by adopting segregationist patterns exhibited in the chinesca, local settlers and Mexican officials resembled their U.S. counterparts by marginalizing and demonizing the immigrant Chinese community.[5] What is clear from the following pages, and in Valentino's mock marriage to Rambova, is that examples of men behaving poorly, exercising their libidinal license with gusto, went hand in hand with international images of Mexican masculinities. Nowhere was this more obvious than the border vice trade that developed in Mexicali between 1905 and 1925. Other than its reputation for ribaldry and manufactured hedonism, why did the Valentino wedding party choose Mexicali over its better-known coastal cousin, Tijuana? Certainly Mexicali's controversial mayor (*presidente municipal*) Otto Moller had something to do with Valentino and Rambova's decision. Moller served as witness to the civil matrimonial proceedings and hosted the wedding party at his house. The gala affair was "wonderful," Rambova recalled, even though it "caused many heartaches and worries later."[6] A stringed orchestra lent the wedding party a touch of cosmopolitan elegance for which the "entire town turned out."[7] The couple's presence drew throngs of fans and curious spectators filling the streets, a consumer-driven buzz created by Hollywood's star factory common enough to Tijuana but relatively new to Mexicali.

Valentino (born Rodolfo V. Guglichieni) performed in roles of exalted masculinity.[8] His fans—mostly women—saw in him the authentic symbol of Latin romance and passion in screen roles such as the daring *torero* Juan Gallardo in the Hollywood adaptation of bullfighting's most famous novel, *Blood and Sand*.[9] Willing to assume the exoticized role of Spanish matador, Valentino—who was gay—also performed exaggeratedly heterosexual roles as a diversionary tactic to calm studio jitters.[10] Valentino's trip to Mexicali included both of his male lovers, Paul Ivano and Douglas Gerrard, as well as MGM star and Rambova's lover, Alla Nazimova.[11]

Like Valentino's stage performances, the border tourism industry fed off of Mexico's reputation for macho adventure. Mexico appealed to a popular notion of masculinity in the United States that reflected the gendered contours of the moral reform that was supposed to be sweeping organized vice and sin from the American cityscape. Colonel Jack Atkins, a greyhound racing promoter preparing for Tijuana's inaugural season, articulated this point through the notion of unfettered male liberty.

> We are a class of folks who do enjoy liberty in connection with the use of our stomach and like a smile with a foot on the rail with no violation of law and no sneaking, but open to the eyes of God and man as a righteous, decent and honorable privilege regardless of what the longhaired sisters in both trouser and skirts may or may not think.[12]

Valentino's wedding trip illustrates how the growth of automobile-fueled tourism to Mexico's border challenged puritanical bourgeois social values while underlining the power of the novel leisure industry. The Valentino-Rambova wedding party traveled along the advancing network of roads and highways that connected Los Angeles with popular desert oases such as Palm Springs and, later, El Centro's "historic" Barbara Worth Hotel.[13] Like the development of rail travel, the extension of drivable roads through the infernal deserts of the Southwest, built on the backs of convict labor, played an important role in making the western United States and the border region accessible to travelers, adding to its allure while reducing the risks of the journey. Initially, sex tourism fueled a disorderly trade in red-light diversions that gradually forced the adoption of marking mechanisms that organized space around Mexicali's border zone into discrete spheres of institutional architecture and the Chinatown zona de tolerancia.

The Frontal Assault on Public Morality, 1909–1914: Vice Commerce and the Immigration of Alien Prostitutes

Sex commerce may be the Mexican border's most resilient vice attraction. Whether in viewing a bawdy revue, dancing, or paying for sex, men knew that they could find sexual titillation and gratification across the border in "Old Mexico." The infamy of Mexico's red-light border drew criticism from within and abroad throughout the twentieth century. This criticism has ranged from the Victorian view of prostitution as a necessary evil best confined to a special district, to the Progressive-feminist rejection of the double standard and the health danger posed by venereal diseases. Unregulated, uncontrolled, and unrepentant, sex commerce flooded Mexicali between 1908 and 1914. The advent of a regulated prostitution program and the parallel construction of the Owl's mega-brothel in 1916 temporarily stifled the most vitriolic complaints.[14] But stepping across the border into Mexico triggered anxieties over public and community health. Moralists feared that boys and men who were tempted by the red diversions across the line were not only in danger of contracting a sexually transmitted disease, but were draining community wealth and morale. They were effectively becoming emasculated through an overly permissive consumerism. And while Mexico was often imagined as macho, the consensual culture that reinforced male privilege undermined the embryonic masculinity that had risen abruptly from the sands of the Colorado Desert.

Prostitution threatened the safety of honorable families with disease and dishonor. As border cities still in their infancy, the *Chronicle* sounded the alarm: "Calexico should do everything to discourage the degenerate white girl traffic that is taking possession of Mexicali."[15] The johns (consumers of prostitution) were not just single, working-class men. Wealthy men could send their wives and children from the infernal desert summer to San Diego's temperate littoral. Temporary bachelorhood led to temptations. "Some men are liars, and others say they are lonesome while their wife is at the coast on her vacation" a Calexico newspaper reported.[16]

Protest texts used two historical narratives to explain the rampant growth of vice services in Mexicali: one story about penetration and another about vagination.[17] These narratives explained the sudden growth of prostitution, gaming, and cantina culture in Mexicali by either the forceful introduction of foreign capital, workers, and consumers from the United States, or by way of Mexico's permissive laws and the officials who profited from vice penetration. The penetration narrative privileges the corrupting power of foreign vice capital and the lowly cultural status of the saloon milieu, comprised by social pariahs and parasites. The vagination narrative emphasizes the enabling role of corrupt officials who facilitated a permissive red-light geography that systematically drew in vulnerable males to Mexicali. Most of the following texts used in the petitions and protests that the trans-border community sent to Mexican and U.S. authorities between 1909 and 1914 relied on a combination of both penetration and vagination stories to explain the moral distortions and disfigured development afflicting the young border city.

Echoing the turn-of-the-century cultural critique of hygiene reformers, who saw powerful underworld forces corrupting urban centers, a protest letter sent by the Imperial Valley Chamber of Commerce in 1909 to Mexico's aging president Porfirio Díaz lamented that American men of "dissolute and disreputable character" were exploiting the border's "peculiar conditions." This petition, republished by the Calexico *Chronicle* for local readership, featured a prefatory editorial note by Otis B. Tout in which he referred to the letter as an "arraignment of the white men in business [in Mexicali]." Diseased capitalists penetrating Mexico's border membrane rebounded as a health concern for the hygienic-minded citizenry of California. The letter referred to a dance hall owner who was afflicted by an "unmentionable disease" who was undermining "public morality" on both sides of the border: "the town of Mexicali, . . . its twin sister, the City of Calexico and indeed the entire Imperial Valley."[18] The authors carefully reassured Díaz that Mexicans "compared most favorably with American citizens so far as morality and the observance of the law." Driven from "their criminal haunts in San Francisco and New York," these were the very same "thieving fraternity" that descended upon poor Mexicali according to an editorial entitled "Somebody Dreamed About Old Mexicali." Instead of preying on "small schoolboys," the author of "Somebody Dreamed" imagined the jubilant day when the social parasites of Mexicali would find Christianity, temperance, and "devote [their] genius to the betterment of Mexicali."[19] *Chronicle* editor Otis B. Tout offered a more direct if not repressive solution: call the "moral lepers" of Mexicali "vags and run [them] up the railroad."[20] Indeed, this was precisely how law enforcement dealt with radicals like the Wobblies, and later with communist organizers of the Depression era.[21]

Another version of the penetration narrative attributed the spread of red-light commerce to the long phallus of foreign capital. A group of leading merchants from Mexicali and the municipal tax collector rebutted the sharp criticism of their livelihood and moral position. They said that the social distortions afflicting the border city were not due to the saloon business culture but rather were the direct result of three foreign firms stunting Mexicali's development through their monopolistic positions in real estate, utilities, and water markets.[22] Calling themselves the "Merchants of Mexicali," they were mostly small-time, foreign saloon operators whose attack on "big business" reflected skewed property relations in the Imperial Valley and different views over what constituted appropriate forms of male business. After all, Harry T. Cory, president of the Imperial Valley Chamber of Commerce and cosigner of its petition, was also the land sales executive and engineer of the Sociedad de Irrigación y Terrenos, a Southern Pacific subsidiary and one of the Mexicali Valley's early irrigation companies.[23]

Just as foreign capital was a penetrating force on Mexicali, the local population disagreed with the central government on whether to accommodate and retain this class of investment. The highest federal official in Baja California, prefect (*jefe político*) colonel Celso Vega, administered the affairs of the territory from Ensenada but incurred the wrath of the upstanding citizens (*gente decente*) on both sides of the border for his active participation in Mexicali's red-light trade. Owner of Mexicali's Hotel Emporio, Celso Vega used his deputy (*subprefecto*) in Mexicali and the federal immigration inspectors to collect a percentage of the "wages of sin."[24] Since the Colorado River flood had washed out Mexicali's first settlement in 1907, the construction frenzy to rebuild Mexicali and rapid growth of the surrounding agricultural area drew in working men and, of course, women. The number of prostitutes increased, especially after El Centro became a stop along the Southern Pacific's Los Angeles-Yuma-El Paso line in 1911. Imperial Valley's protest petitioners hoped to mobilize local politicians to exercise greater control over the sex industry. The Imperial Valley Chamber of Commerce concluded their stern petition by wishing Díaz a happy Mexican Independence Day, qualified with a sober reminder that bad relations could result from the persistence of "said moral conditions and depravity between Mexican and American peoples."[25] Widespread disorder in the border zone captured by the local press as knife-fighting prostitutes, doped-up addicts, and drunken Indians in bloody fisticuffs underlined the daily realities of violence that often spilled across the border line. Although petty, these were the incidents that could certainly lead to an international incident.[26]

Mexicali's "Fathers and Family Heads" also petitioned Díaz, denouncing the threat that the vice trade posed to community and national health.[27] Not only was this unbecoming to the fatherland, it was also a threat to the patriarchal order. The Fathers' petition characterized Mexicali as a "frightful center of vice," objecting to the disproportionate number of saloons concentrated around the highly transited border port. The location of cantinas and hotels catering to the sex trade made it unpleasant for families. Proper fathers objected to the stain and insinuation that followed upstanding women and girls as they walked through the area. Moreover, the Fathers' petition made sure that Díaz understood that Mexico's recently passed immigration statutes were being violated on a daily basis.

A disorganized vice trade disgraced the fatherland but also underscored for the "Fathers of Mexicali" what seemed to be dubious priorities of the district government regarding education. Bad government and unequal development forced Mexicali's children who wanted an education to seek their educational nourishment (*pan intelectual*) in Calexico. The Colorado River flood of 1907 destroyed Mexicali's only school, and despite promises from Colonel Vega, it had not been rebuilt. Mexicali's Fathers warned President Díaz that they would even take the drastic step of leaving for the United States in order for their children to receive an education and a healthy environment for the family. The vice business also thwarted "middle-class" tourism. Honorable families from the Imperial Valley no longer engaged in border shopping or tourism.[28] Echoing the social logic of municipal planners and urban planners of vice districts across the hemisphere, they requested that federal authorities relocate Mexicali's de facto red-light district far from the gaze of the town's children.[29]

Five years later, after initial attempts to reform and regulate the vice trade were defeated, Baja California suffered from a series of territorial governments who were even more ensconced in the red-light trade. In their cavalier attitude regarding their involvement in the vice business, these military governments exhibited what Woodrow Wilson called a "studied contempt" for American institutions.[30] They provoked community protests, triggered by scandals arising from bad government, the threat of violence on the part of the military, and the immigration of undocumented prostitutes. (The leader of one such protest in Mexicali was Major Captain Esteban Cantú, who soon after rose to power over the entire state.) But the constant coming and going of sex workers to Mexicali rankled the transborder gente decente.

Expectations of change and reform rose with Madero guiding the Mexican Revolution. His representative in Baja California Norte, General Manuel Gordillo Escudero, assumed the position of jefe político in 1911 with similar reformist zeal. Gordillo Escudero tried to restructure fiscal and immigration policies relating to prostitutes and associated businesses, as well as impose a nationalist language requirement to halt the spread of English, American cultural influence, and what might be called the *texanization* of Baja California.[31] As an outsider with few ties to the territorial political scene, Gordillo Escudero's policies triggered a protracted dispute between municipal (*ayuntamiento*) and federal territorial governments.[32] In any case Madero's regime soon was replaced with military officials whose involvement in vice tourism even went further in antagonizing and displeasing the border's gente decente. Baja California's federal officials seized control of Mexicali's vice trade, extracting tribute from prostitutes, madams, and pimps. They resorted to violence when they sensed a threat to their political authority, whether it was posed by Revolutionaries or by meddlesome individuals seeking to rid if not alter the border red-light trade.

Mexico's Secretariat of the Interior (Gobernación) issued a memo during the Porfiriato setting the tenor of formal immigration policy: immigration inspectors should only authorize desirable or productive immigration and dissuade the entrance of elements whose presence could pose a threat to the health of the nation.[33] But with appreciable sums of money to be made by key officials and the strategic sensitivity of transit across national borders, the execution of antiprostitution immigration policy generated heated struggles for power between the jefe político's deputy prefects and immigration officials. Federally appointed officials seeking to reform corrupt practices disturbed Mexicali's red-light business. They often ended up in jail or simply decided to move on when intimidation tactics grew severe. Mexico's judicial authorities also jailed officials who violated personal rights of foreigners and nationals alike.[34]

Although mitigated by the distance between Mexico City and Baja California, Gobernación attempted to increase its vigilance over what had been a neglected border port between 1912 and 1914. Immigration officials attempted to restrict the immigration of prostitutes, madams, pimps, professional gamblers, and ailing Chinese "coolies" (laborers). Deportation data highlight Mexicali's unique standing among Baja California's border towns. The deportation of foreign prostitutes from Mexicali far surpassed those deported from Tijuana or Ensenada. This border port witnessed sixty of sixty-four deportations of undesirable foreigners from Baja California's Norte ports of entry from 1912 to 1914. The deportation of one "prostitute" from Ensenada and three foreign gamblers from Tijuana pales in comparison to Mexicali: fifty-one prostitutes, four pimps, and three Chinese deported; while interestingly, authorities granted work-residency permission to seventeen prostitutes and two madams.[35] But just who got to stay, and who was given the boot?

The outcomes of deportation cases between 1912 and 1914 suggest that the practical objective of immigration authorities was to nationalize sex work by expelling those foreign prostitutes, pimps, and madams without proper residency or citizenship. As the Memphis-born prostitute Le Ray Fensley stated before an immigration court, "Foreigners, who have resided in this Republic for more than three years, will be considered equally as Mexicans before the law." Fensley provided witnesses in a special hearing by Mexicali's Immigration Tribunal to testify that she had resided in Mexicali for over four years. But she had absented herself from Mexicali in the midst of the Revolutionary upheaval between 1911 and 1912, so Gobernación decided to uphold the deportation order. However, she eventually returned during the government of Esteban Cantú to ply her trade at the border's most successful and distinguished resort for masculine diversions: Mexicali's premiere casino, theater, and brothel, the Owl Café.[36]

Sex commerce deepened the relations between the border cities. As regulated prostitution advanced, Mexican officials provided registries of prostitutes working in Mexicali to immigration authorities from both countries.[37] These registries theoretically made it easier for officials to identify and deport clandestine prostitutes. How did the immigration official discern the prostitute from other workers? Fragmentary evidence suggests that immigration officials could not always distinguish prostitutes from other unchaperoned women. For example, in 1912 Immigration Inspector Javier Velasco tried to deport Elena Warren for practicing clandestine prostitution. Accompanied by a witness, she argued that she was a *cook*, not a prostitute, and Gobernación reprimanded Velasco for carelessly accusing "honest" women of prostitution.[38] The memo also admonished Velasco to consult the prostitution registry that Mexican officials had shared with their U.S. counterparts to avoid embarrassing encounters with honorable female immigrants.

A week later El Centro resident John Carrison complained to Gobernación that Velasco had offended his wife—"a model mother of her home"—and daughter by accusing them of being prostitutes. Velasco was responsible for the sudden influx of foreign women, he added, "especially black prostitutes." Velasco could not recall the incident Carrison mentioned, but he showed a surprising interest in refuting the allegation about black prostitutes. He sent Gobernación the latest prostitution registry where he emphasized that white prostitutes outnumbered blacks.[39] Velasco's stint as immigration inspector came to an abrupt end after he was found at a notorious assignation house, undressed, thoroughly inebriated, pistol free of its holster, trying to negotiate with a prostitute named Sadie Barnet.[40]

Controversies over immigration increased during the Huerta government (1913–1914) and ultimately led to the arrest of Velasco's successor, José Eraso Ituarte. Eraso was jailed for taking his job too seriously. He proved to be the busiest immigration inspector during the Madero-Huerta period, deporting thirty-three prostitutes. In a lengthy report to Gobernación, Eraso expressed indignation at the corruption and immorality that Mexicali's red-light sector fostered, especially among Mexicali's prefect authorities.[41] Eraso's main ally was Major Cantú, and both mobilized a community campaign against the Huerta government and the widespread malfeasance of his officials in Baja California. Adding to the long list of ills and danger courted by the disorderly border commerce, Cantú and Eraso identified another immigration problem that threatened their jobs more than any sex worker did: the immigration of revolutionaries. As they understood the problem, these professional troublemakers mixed freely among the increasing throngs of tourists who visited Mexicali (which they calculated to reach 1,500 on weekdays and 2,500 on the weekends).[42]

For many, the military execution of Encarnación Sánchez on New Year's Day 1914 expressed what was abhorrent in Mexicali and with the Huerta regime.[43] A naturalized citizen of the United States and resident of Los Angeles, Sánchez traveled to Mexicali in search of his missing daughter who, he alleged, had been abducted and forced to work as a prostitute in Mexicali.[44] In Calexico, Sánchez enlisted his friend Pablo Flores to help in the rescue of his daughter, and they were joined by José Valenzuela. As the three men crossed the border, Immigration Inspector Adolfo Pecina detained and arrested them on the charge of being *revolucionarios*. On the orders of Mexicali subprefect colonel Agustín Llaguno, soldiers marched them to the Río Nuevo channel and administered the military punishment called *la ley fuga*, whereby prisoners are shot in the back after being instructed to run away, in order to subsequently demonstrate that they were shot attempting to escape capture.[45] Sánchez and Valenzuela died, while Flores was "left for dead," in the words of U.S. secretary of state William Jennings Bryan. Surviving with a slight wound to the head, Flores played "opossum" before crawling back to the border. He informed U.S. border officials of the incident and later guided a team of investigators to the spot where the bodies lay.[46] Print media and governmental officials expressed concern over the execution of U.S. citizens and the behavior of Mexico's military officials, but they never mentioned the fate of Sánchez's daughter. Perhaps she was a prisoner in some grisly sex factory—"an inmate of a Mexicali sporting house," as the Calexico *Chronicle* phrased it—or perhaps she had merely run off with a suitor.[47]

The Sánchez case produced immediate repercussions among federal officials and a swift response by Gobernación.[48] The repeated scandals witnessed in the administration of Mexicali's red-light sector prompted Mexico's secretary of foreign relations to send a special investigator to report on the "anomalous situation." The special report criticized the federal government's failure to appreciate the region's strategic importance. Mexicali was integrated into one of the "richest agricultural regions in the United States," one that generated an annual surplus of $40 million while employing ten thousand Mexicans. This particular situation created a never-ending demand for prostitution services that Mexican officials, in collaboration with vice entrepreneurs, systematically exploited. The Sánchez execution was just one example, albeit a notorious one, of this collusion between political authority and the prostitution business.[49] Finally, the report criticized immigration officials for their obsessive concern in controlling female immigrants, especially "those who went to exercise prostitution" in Mexicali. Instead, federal authorities were advised to focus more on dangerous agitators and revolutionaries who threatened Mexico's security. The report concluded that public security would benefit if revolutionaries and professional criminals could be contained in the red-light zone where police could monitor them. Family men of honorable reputation in the community, those "who will serve loyally, and not end up disgracing their country," should occupy the strategically sensitive federal positions.[50] One such family man was Esteban Cantú, promoted to colonel for distinguished military service against Sonoran Revolutionaries.

In the wake of the overthrow of Huerta, a mutinous rebellion broke out against the shaky *convencionista* government in Baja California, giving Colonel Cantú the opportunity to rise from his power base in Mexicali and establish the territorial government there. After declaring himself military commander and civil governor of Baja California, he rigged municipal elections in Ensenada and declared Mexicali an independent municipality. With military and political control established, Colonel Cantú set out to perfect a political-economic strategy that post-Revolutionary governments have found irresistible: stimulating the agricultural and industrial economy while closely regulating the vice tourism trade. He focused his campaign in Ensenada, Tijuana, and especially Mexicali, where his municipal officials imposed regulatory mechanisms that effectively sequestered prostitutes in the brothels. They threw the social outcasts out while initiating an aggressive publicity campaign to reassure border residents in Southern California. Cantú was responsible for making the border's attractions safe again for family men and their female companions, enabling a resurgence of middle-class tourism.

Red-Light Reform: Making the Border Safe for Bourgeois Debauchery

Before Baja California's vice attractions could draw a wider clientele, the border required red-light reforms and an effective public relations promotion to reassure anxious foreigners that they would be safe from the delinquencies and violence of "Barbarous Mexico."[51] Colonel Esteban Cantú's government set in motion reforms designed to effectively appeal to the tastes of a mobile, largely white class of sightseers from north of the border. Cantú understood that gaining the approval of critics in the United States and drawing a more affluent type of sightseer required the taming of Mexicali's vice tourism trade.

Cantú's government set out to moralize Mexicali. Cantú's federal officials and Mexicali's newly formed city council set about to achieve this by three means. First, they directed a new fiscal policy of prohibitive taxation at the red-light sector. Second, they rounded up hustlers, slackers, drug dealers, petty thieves, and other undesirables periodically. Third, they subjected prostitutes to a regulated, hygienist program that was designed to contain the red-light trade's most blatant symptoms of disorder. When questioned about his tolerance of the opium, casino, and brothel economy, Cantú would instead claim to have given the once chaotic border trade a stable and orderly administration. He was also proud of the advances in education, road building, and street paving that were financed by taxes on vice. Whereas the rest of Mexico was consumed by revolution and civil war, Cantú hewed to the Porfirian mantra of progress, order, peace, and prosperity.

At midnight on January 1, 1915, Governor Cantú imposed a new fiscal policy that immediately (but temporarily) closed down the red-light sector. Employing taxation as a moral weapon, this maneuver sought to force vice interests and tourism concessionaires to pay increased amounts for taxes and licenses. Cantú often mused that high taxation was merely the cost of doing business during Mexico's Revolutionary upheaval. Furthermore, it was easier to tax the vice trade rather than foreign-owned agribusiness. Prohibitive taxation, according to the *Chronicle*, would initiate Mexicali's "final regeneration" by economically eliminating the "disreputable saloons" and "cheap places," thereby improving Mexicali's "moral tone." Instead of the "vile alcohol disguised as whiskey being sold to the pauper class" patrons could select the "very best liquors obtainable."[52]

Coercive policies such as de-facto extradition and forced repatriation of socially marginal foreigners contributed to the image of order and discipline that the Cantú administration imposed. Operating in Baja California, generally free from Revolutionary entanglements and alliances, Cantú was able to broadcast a message of law and order to the audience that mattered most, the border communities and states across the border. His racialized ideas about morality and decency found an especially sympathetic audience in the Dixie-minded border communities that abutted Mexico. "Mexicali Scum Dumped into Calexico," read a Calexico *Chronicle* headline. The "Mexicali Scum" were mainly "immigrants," "dusky-hued [men who] . . . walk with a shuffle."

> The Ethiopians were not alone in their abdication of the Mexicali joy palaces, being accompanied by several Asiatics, among whom figured Chinese and Hindus. Among the polyglot crew was found

> a Hungarian who had got lost in the shuffle. The negroes were all cooks out of a job. They all hailed from the sunny south.[53]

Upon arriving in the United States, local police escorted the men to work details: they would be forced to build and repair roads. Only one year before the Automobile Club of Southern California had declared its support for the "institution of convict labor" to construct roads.[54] Imprisoned workers made it cheap to construct difficult stretches of highway. Mexicali's offcasts helped make long-distance tourism in automobiles a reality.[55]

In contrast, class and race protected a certain Father O'Hara when he mistakenly hit his automobile's accelerator and crashed into the U.S. border station. Although the drunken priest was accompanied by a Spanish violinist from a "resort" in Mexico (implying that he had met a companion at a casino or brothel), O'Hara received notably cushy treatment. Customs officials persuaded him to go with officers to the city recorder's house. After rousting the slumbering judge, Father O'Hara paid a ten-dollar fine and then was released.[56]

Roundups of undesirables associated with cross-border tourism and vice industries occurred regularly. Pressured by U.S. military intelligence concerned about a rumored German espionage unit in Baja California during the First World War, Cantú agreed to monitor slackers, trouble makers, drug runners, and slavers. The antivagrancy directive he sent to municipal governments and law enforcement required police to identify and apprehend suspicious and armed individuals, or those engaged in dishonest pursuits. Cantú's order used the term *vago* (vagabond) to identify all these individuals.[57] The vagos, too, were sent to perform road work, helping construct the National Highway connecting Mexicali to Tecate and Tijuana.[58]

Regulated Prostitution and the Segregated Vice District

The Cantú government hoped to end disorder and scandal in Mexicali by regularizing the administration of sex commerce. The sex trade had been located embarrassingly close to the border station and the border avenue Porfirio Díaz. As the morality protests of 1909 declared, border residents of the Imperial Valley wanted public officials to relocate brothels and related establishments to the back streets.[59] Mexicali's authorities permitted the vice business, but (as the Calexico paper reported) at least they would "keep [those objectionable things] back and not plant them up right under our noses on the border."[60] Officials responded by segregating Mexicali's "zone of tolerance" to the back streets of Chinatown.

Simultaneously Mexicali's newly elected municipal officials implemented regulations that forced sex workers to report for weekly venereal examinations with the city doctor. When a sex worker exhibited signs of infection, municipal health authorities consigned her to a quarantined hospital cot until external symptoms cycled clear.[61] However draconian the new program was for Mexicali's sex workers, women continued to immigrate in large numbers to work in Mexicali's red-light district.[62] The segregated vice district and the brothel regime appealed to urban professionals and civic planners who felt that the best way to combat the evils of the sex trade was to control and sequester prostitution to a clearly demarcated district. The architectural descriptions of Mexicali's new "restricted area" reiterate the notion of control and containment. As the flagship of the "restricted district," a new brothel named the Tecolote (the Owl) was "entirely fenced in. Planners had the foresight to install a 'string of lights' that guided visitors from the Mexican customs house across the once forbidding and darkened plaza to the 'new restricted' district."[63] The lighting guided the tourists to the new red-light district and led the way back to the security of the border crossing. These spatial reforms—dependable roads, modern lighting, and clearly differentiated commercial urban geography—were novel in that they were designed to draw in middle-class tourists.

The principal "sporting influence" behind the new restricted vice zone was Carl Withington, whose firsthand experience gained from the oil and agricultural boomtown of Bakersfield reflected these concerns. Withington and his partners had reportedly fled Bakersfield after antivice reformers drove the "sporting" men from town in 1913. The concession contract that Withington signed with Colonel Cantú in 1916 stated the district government's intention to create a special zone along the banks of the Rio Nuevo for houses of assignation and *games of chance*.[64] That gaming was included points to another novel development envisioned for the Owl Café by Withington and his partners, Marvin Allen and Frank "Booze" Byers: the Owl would not be a business that exclusively dealt in prostitution services but rather a multiservice emporium for risqué entertainment and popular leisure. After moving from Porfirio Díaz Avenue to the back streets of Chinatown in 1916, Mexicali's zona de tolerancia overlapped quite nicely with its chinesca.[65] The Owl's success paved the way for the expansion to neighboring border cities such as Tijuana and Matamoros to capture the swelling demand for gambling operations. The power of Allen, Byers, and Withington over the border vice trade became such that they were collectively referred to as the ABW Syndicate until Owl principal Withington's death in 1925.[66]

The construction of a long-awaited secondary school on Porfirio Díaz Avenue, where the vice trade once had flourished, advanced Cantú's modernizing project.[67] Newly relocated to the back streets of the Chinese quarter, the shameful spectacle of vice commerce would no longer tarnish the symbolic foreground of the borderline:[68]

> Desirous of seeing this class of business entirely removed from the main street and kept as completely out of sight as possible . . . , Col. Cantú will have all such concessions isolated and away from the children who will attend the new school building . . . and which will house Mexican children from all over Lower California.[69]

Soon, Mexican children were transferring out of American schools in Calexico and crossing the border to attend the new Escuela Cuauhtémoc.[70] A major alteration in migratory patterns achieved, prostitutes now faced a defacto demobilization of sorts while quartered at the Owl. The unevenness and haphazard nature of these reforms, however, always created unexpected or unintended results. Before completion, Escuela Cuauhtémoc's classroom capacity was so limited that students were forced to share space with municipal treasury officials. The constant coming and going of prostitutes coming to pay taxes created an embarrassing situation, according to Baja California's school inspector. Until the situation could be resolved, the inspector urged police to ensure that Owl prostitutes (*meretrices*) dressed less meretriciously when in public.[71]

Race, Gender, and Class Considerations at the Owl: Performance Space and Appropriate Masculinities

The new rulers of Baja California imposed their gendered project of modernization for Mexicali by segregating prostitution to Chinatown and confining it to the Owl. The Owl's managers tried to control the brothel's internal space, the workers who created the attractions, and the clients who consumed them: the Owl's design carefully contained prostitutes and people of color in such a way as to accommodate commercial sex without repelling bourgeois sensibilities. Both of these efforts were intended to create a commercial playground for men of differing ethnic and racial backgrounds. In combination, they crafted a social architecture that made the Owl one of the most popular tourist attractions of Mexico and the United States.

Described as the biggest casino on the continent by the *Los Angeles Times*, El Tecolote was often characterized as a massive, lumbering building that sprawled across one city block.[72] Jack Tenney, composer of "Mexicali Rose" and musical director at the Owl at various times during the 1920s, called it "rough" and "unattractive," like the mining towns of Nevada. Still, the "profuse display of large potted imitation palms" not only made the Owl "culturally distinctive" but also offered a "preview of what would happen one day in Las Vegas."[73] The Owl entertained visitors with vaudeville, silent movies, and a dance floor animated by raucous jazz dance bands and *ficheras* or "percentage girls."[74] Ten bartenders served liquor at a lengthy bar. Hop Lee's restaurant dished up Chinese food; a barbershop offered hot-towel shaves and haircuts. The management of the Owl boasted that the house was never closed and advertised, "both night and day, across the way, you will never find closed, the Owl Cafe."[75]

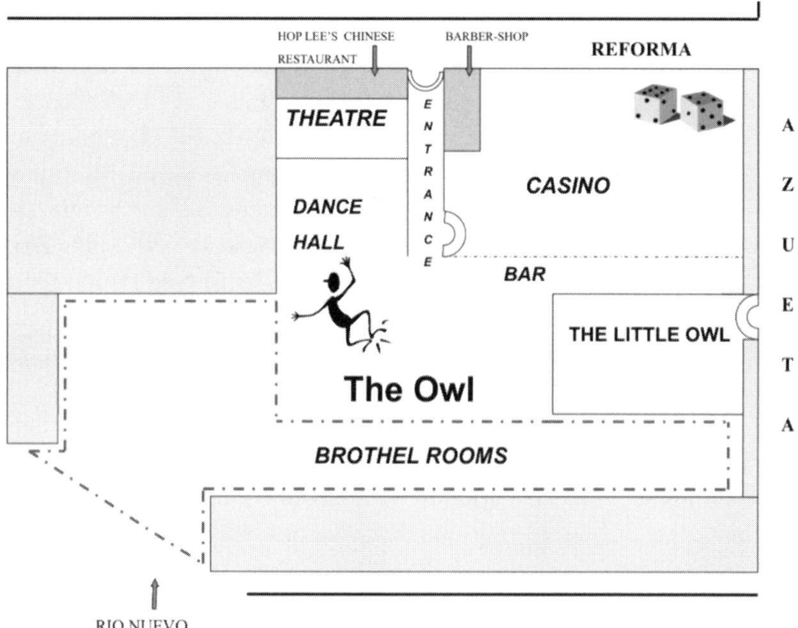

Figure 4.1. Map of "The Owl," Tijuana. By the author.

After 1915, slumming in Mexicali's chinesca became a predictable if not acceptable pastime for American bourgeois sightseers. No other establishment along Mexico's border epitomized the creation of a specially crafted red-light attraction that both catered to local workers and affluent tourists as did the Owl. In 1919, the *Los Angeles Times* reported that a "gallery, used exclusively for 'slumming parties' was rarely empty as tourists from the American side of the line were always present."[76] A promotional advertisement for Mexicali's nightlife in 1922 reassured the *Chronicle*'s reading public that honorable Americans could indulge their curiosity and desire from a safe distance:

> The Owl is of special interest to those who desire to go slumming. A [separate] entrance for private parties is afforded and booths are arranged along the side of the dance floor, which give seclusion to those who merely wish to look in.[77]

The Owl's attention to thus guaranteeing anonymity made red-light diversion palatable to white bourgeois tourists.

The Owl's large-scale brothel operation requires a moment of elaboration to grasp just how massive the commercial sex operations had grown.[78] A brothel like the Owl profited from diversity, catering to clients' desires for women sex workers of different races and ethnicities. The Owl's concession contract left little ambiguity about its prostitution business. Withington specified that the Owl would feature seventy-five rooms for the prostitutes and could be expanded if needed.[79] Demand had increased, and by 1918, the Owl expanded to 104 rooms.[80] The entry of the United States into the First World War brought with it wartime restrictions that slowed cross-border movement of tourists and business in general. Before the slowdown "the gambling concession was open at its widest extent, more than sixty girls appeared nightly in the dance hall and among the tables."[81]

The deceleration of cross-border movement and freeze of Mexico's border tourism lasted until the United States lifted restrictions in 1920. The timing was uncanny considering the onset of Prohibition. Estimates claimed that the Owl was drawing over one thousand customers, and the number of prostitutes had grown to one hundred. But as Prohibition rekindled Mexicali's red-light tourism, a fire on February 9, 1920, practically destroyed the entire building, sparing only the Little Owl—that section of the Owl zoned for nonwhites.[82]

The Owl's adaptation of U.S.-style Jim Crow policies featured a specially reserved cantina and casino for nonwhite customers. A designated entrance led blacks and others who might be described as "people of color" (*gente de color*) from Azueta Street to the Little Owl.[83] The diverse racial and ethnic backgrounds exhibited by Owl sex workers did not mark a radical departure from the past. What was unique about the Owl was that it housed working women of different ethnicities and races under the same roof. No longer did patrons have to shop for women at different bars and assignation houses, which were divided by their menu of first-, second-, and third-class prostitutes. At the Owl, men could choose among different kinds of prostitutes without leaving the premises, even though Mexicali's municipal health and tax policies continued to divide prostitutes by color, and the spaces in the Owl that the male clientele did not enter continued in that division.[84] For example, first-class prostitutes were examined by Dr. Jáuregui or Dr. Roel, the municipal hygienists, in their own waiting room.[85]

Colonel Cantú added only one social stipulation to the Owl's concession contract: the Owl should admit only "whites (raza blanca) and the games they are accustomed to."[86] Fluid practice trumped static legal text, however, as other evidence contradicts the notion of "whites only." When wartime border restrictions slowed the arrival of Euro-American tourists, press reports indicate that Mexican and Chinese patrons frequented the Owl. Nothing was said about where they fell along the color bar.[87] Chinese men continued patronizing the Owl after the war ended. Cantú was ousted from power on August 20, 1920, and shortly thereafter, Mexico's new interim president (Adolfo de la Huerta) ordered the Owl closed. Newspapers covering the story reported that the astonished Chinese patrons "couldn't believe their ears" but "stampeded wildly through all the wide doorways and ran for the Chinese quarter."[88]

When the Owl closed, its employees began working elsewhere—including on the streets. Not surprisingly, Mexican and U.S. officials parroted the imperative for strict surveillance and control over prostitutes. Many of the women crossed the border, prompting Calexico's city marshal to order the Owl women "to leave town" in an orderly fashion. "Women habitués" had been "turned loose on the town and the hotels . . . literally spread all over the place."[89] Conrado Silver, the federal agent sent to oversee the transition in Mexicali, informed the U.S. press that the Owl's prostitutes would be "segregate[d]" and expected that a new establishment would reopen with "several women placed under strict police supervision."[90]

In fact, the Owl was rebuilt across the street from its original location, despite a flurry of protests by Mexican labor organizers and U.S. reform groups. A second fire destroyed the new Owl, creating yet another zoning challenge for city planners. Once again, the problem of social disorder created by the invasion of city streets by "public women" became a primary concern for district and municipal governments. Having lost spaces like the Owl where disreputable commerce could safely and lucratively be conducted, Mexicali's red-light business reverted to its scandal-plagued past.

During Mayor Otto Moller's tenure, Mexicali's city council renewed declarations about the need to strictly confine sex workers to the zona de tolerancia. In the fall of 1922 Grace Bartlet and Juanita Deal, two veteran prostitutes of Mexicali, requested permission from city officials to go shopping and attend a boxing match in Mexicali.[91] A handwritten note by Mexicali's mayor, Otto Moller, granted the women a three-day recreation pass allowing them to leave their work and living quarters at the Hotel Mexicali. And while Mexican officials preferred to hide the vice trade, they could not as easily cover up the economic advantages that came with controlling border vice markets. After an internal investigation exposed his administration for peculation of municipal funds and accusations of extortion by sex workers from the Hotel Mexicali, a recall campaign effectively removed Moller from power.[92] Without the dominant force of Cantú, Baja California would have to wait for another military governor whose business and cultural exposure combined with excellent relations with President Plutarco Elías Calles and the experience of the Northwest Army (unit commanded by General Obregón).

In step with the moralizing reforms that Sonoran Constitutionalists imposed in 1920 to dampen the types of scandals associated with the Moller government, the principal Owl investors renamed their establishment the ABW Club in 1924. Carl Withington died in 1924, marking the end of the ABW Syndicate's domination of the border vice racket. Increasingly, businesses in Mexicali and Tijuana were ones like the Foreign Club and the Agua Caliente Casino, examples of mixed investment involving foreign entrepreneurs like Wirt Bowman of Nogales and Baja California's governor, General Abelardo L. Rodríguez, who was in turn backed by President Plutarco Elías Calles. Brothels and casinos at the border began operating under the guise of a social club, a members-only space that was supposed to protect the public, especially the vulnerable working class, from the ravages of red-light consumption. At the original Owl, socially marginal groups such as Asians,

Mexicans, and blacks entered as consumers and workers. But the revamped ABW Club reverted to a wealthier, whiter clientele: exercise of masculine privilege now required higher class and race status. Border sightseeing continued to grow until 1933 when the combination of prohibition's repeal and the deepening economic depression slowly diminished the volume of red-light tourism to Baja California. At the same time, President Lázaro Cárdenas banned casino gaming in an effort to clip Calles and Rodríguez, or at least reduce their income.

Baja California's reputation for exalted masculinities and libidinal license experienced a dramatic rebirth between the Second World War and Vietnam. Once again, the militarization of the U.S. Southwest was met by a new source of sex workers. No longer so overwhelmingly foreign, the prostitutes of Tijuana and Mexicali after the Depression were increasingly regional products of the failure of Mexico's agrarian reforms in the Northwest and Bajío. Such a collision produced similar protests against vice as those that took place in Mexicali between 1909 and 1914. Similarly, initial vice eradication campaigns gave way to renewed regulatory programs that had a way of reenacting the rationale of gendered masculinities: men were animalistic and relentless in their search for sexual outlets, and the tide of foreign sex tourists to Tijuana and Mexicali between the Second World War and Vietnam literally overwhelmed any attempts to impede the vice trade.

NOTES

In citing works and sources in the notes, short titles have generally been used. Works frequently cited have been identified by the following abbreviations:

AGN: Archivo General de la Nación (Mexico City, Mexico)
AGN-IIH: Instituto de Investigaciones Históricas (Universidad Autónoma de Baja California, Tijuana, Baja California); includes microfilmed collections from AGN
AFT-APEC: Archivo Fernando Torreblanca/Plutarco Elías Calles (Mexico City, Mexico)
AHE: Archivo Histórico del Estado (Mexicali, Baja California, Mexico)
AHM: Archivo Histórico del Municipio (Mexicali, Baja California, Mexico)
ARPP: Archivo del Registro Público de la Propiedad (Ensenada and Mexicali, Baja California, Mexico)
CIH: Centro de Investigaciones Históricas (Universidad de Baja California, Mexicali, Baja California)
Chronicle: The Calexico *Chronicle* (Calexico, California)
NE: Notarías del Estado (Mexicali, Baja California, Mexico)
SDHS: San Diego Historical Society (San Diego, California, United Status)

1. Confusion clouds Rambova's real name. Her marriage act in Mexicali is signed *Winifred de Wolfe*. See AHM Mexicali, Registro Civil #16, May 13, 1922. However, according to David Bret in *Valentino: A Dream of Desire* (London: Robson Books, 1998), 49 and 82–84, she was born *Winifred Shaugnessy*. Her mother, Winifred Kimball, remarried a number of times. Winifred would consequently take up her stepfathers' last names, becoming known as Winifred Hudnut and later as Winifred de Wolfe.
2. "Frank Mayo in Marital Mess," *Los Angeles Times*, October 19, 1922, II:1. The wedding inspiration is described in Natacha Rambova, *Rudy: An Intimate Portrait of Rudolph Valentino by his Wife Natacha Rambova* (London: Hutchinson, 1926), 50.
3. Eric M. Schantz, "All Night at the Owl: The Social and Political Relations of Mexicali's Red-Light District, 1913–1925," *Journal of the Southwest* 43, no. 1 (Winter 2001): 549–642. This special edition dedicated to border cities and culture was reprinted in book form as *On the Border: Society and Culture Between the United States and Mexico*, ed. Andrew Grant Wood (Wilmington, DE: Scholarly Resources, 2004), 91–144. Hereafter I will cite the book version. As my work illustrates, the phenomenon of babbitry in the border was well established by 1915. See Sinclair Lewis, *Babbitt*, 2nd ed. (New York: Harcourt, Brace and World, 1950). I am indebted to Kerwin Klein's magnificent master's thesis on the development of tourism in Arizona. See "The Last Resort: Tourism, Growth, and Values in Twentieth-Century Arizona" (master's thesis, University of Arizona, 1990).
4. Schantz, "All Night at the Owl," 114–18.

5. Work on the Chinese immigrant community has grown in the following years. The following works are representative of the best scholarship on the Chinese diaspora in Mexico and the borderlands: Charles C. Cumberland, "The Sonora Chinese and the Mexican Revolution," *Hispanic American Historical Review* 40, no. 2 (May 1960): 191–211; Evelyn Hu-DeHart, "The Chinese of Baja California Norte, 1910–1934," *Proceedings of the Pacific Coast Council on Latin American Studies* 12 (1985–1986) and "Immigrants to a Developing Society: The Chinese in Northern Mexico, 1875–1932," *Journal of Arizona History*, 21 (Autumn 1980): 49–86; Robert Chao Romero, "The Dragon in Big Lusong: Chinese Immigration and Settlement in Mexico, 1882–1940," (PhD diss., University of California at Los Angeles, 2003) and "Transnational Chinese Immigrant Smuggling to the United States via Mexico and Cuba, 1882–1916," *Amerasia Journal: UCLA Journal of Asian American Studies* 30 (2004/2005): 3; Yong Chen, *Chinese San Francisco, 1850–1943* (Stanford, CA: Stanford University Press, 2000); Erika Lee, "Orientalisms in the Americas: A Hemispheric Approach to Asian American History," *Journal of Asian American Studies* 8 (October 2005): 235–56; and Grace Delgado, "In the Age of Exclusion: Race, Region, and Chinese Identity in the Making of the Arizona-Sonora Borderlands, 1863–1943" (PhD diss., University of California at Los Angeles, 2000) and "At Exclusion's Gate: Changing Categories of Race and Class among Chinese *Fronterizos*, 1890–1900," in *Continental Crossroads: Remapping U.S.-Mexican Borderlands History*, ed. Samuel Truett and Elliott Young (Durham, NC: Duke University Press, 2004).
6. Rambova, *Rudy*, 50–51.
7. Bret, *Valentino*, 82.
8. Rambova understood her relationship with the sex symbol in mystical and artistic terms. Bret, *Valentino*, 48–64.
9. Vicente Blasco Ibañez, *Sangre y arena* (Mexico City: El Imparcial, 1909). It was Valentino's performance as bullfighter Juan Gallardo, according to Rambova, that appealed to him the most. He grew his sideburns, learned to walk like a *torero*, and even ate like one. If ever a character had come to life, it was Gallardo as he was lived by Rudy. See Rambova, *Rudy*, 49.
10. Bret, *Valentino*, 67 and 77. Valentino's homosexuality was an open secret, as was that of both of his wives, Acker and Rambova. Valentino fancied himself a robust, masculine type—a boxer, bullfighter, and athlete—rejecting the popular ridicule of gay men as effeminate pansies.
11. Ibid., 82.
12. "Kennel Man Sees Great Things Ahead Hereabout," *The Rounder* (n.d., ca. 1927), SDHS, Tom L. Atkins Collection.
13. The Barbara Worth originally serviced travelers and rail tourism from the Midwest going to the Southwest with final destination to Los Angeles. "New Sunset Trains Beautiful," *Chronicle*, October 7, 1911. For luxury travel, affluent sightseers could ride the Southern Pacific's "Sunset Train," with Pullman service

as early as 1911. Promotions for the new line highlighted a shortened travel time (from four to three days) as well as exclusivity and the latest luxuries for ladies, such as a manicurist and a personal maid.

14. Macías-González and Anne Rubenstein, introduction to this volume.
15. *Chronicle*, September 2, 1909.
16. *Chronicle*, June 3, 1909.
17. "Denuncias e informes de vecinos y autoridades sobre la existencia de cantinas y burdeles en Mexicali, Baja California. Varios Vecinos de Mexicali manifiestan que el expresado lugar es un centro de depravación y vicio," Enrique de la Sierra to Secretary of Gobernación, Mexico City, August 31, 1909, AGN-IIH, 1909.41 [40.41], Gobernación, Exp. 10, 1909–1910, August 30, 1909, Mexicali; Otis B. Tout and anonymous prophet, "Somebody Dreamed About Old Mexicali," *Chronicle*, September 9, 1909; and H. T. Cory and H. H. Griswold (Imperial Valley county supervisors) "Letter Sent to President Díaz," *Chronicle*, September 30, 1909.
18. Cory and Griswold, "Letter Sent to President Díaz," *Chronicle*, September 30, 1909.
19. Otis B. Tout and anonymous prophet, "Somebody Dreamed About Old Mexicali," *Chronicle*, September 9, 1909.
20. Ibid.
21. For a similar instance of reporting and constructing the hobo or vagabond, see "IWWs Moving Southward in Droves," *Chronicle*, December 5, 1913. For vigilante repression against labor activists recalling Steinbeck's Central Valley, see William McCarey, *Factories in the Field* (Santa Barbara, CA: Peregrine, 1971).
22. "Los Comerciantes de Mexicali a Gobernación," AGN-IIH, 1909.41 [40.41].
23. Otis B. Tout, *The First Thirty Years, Being An Account of the Principal Events in the History of Imperial Valley, Southern California, U.S.A.* (San Diego: Otis B. Tout, 1931), 103–9; for background on biographic details for Cory, see NE, Protocolo del Juzgado de Primera Instancia de Mexicali, Baja California, Libro I, Volúmen de instrumentos públicos en general.
24. Otis B. Tout and anonymous prophet, "Somebody Dreamed About Old Mexicali," *Chronicle*, September 9, 1909. Even after Celso Vega left following his embarrassing defeat at the hands of the PLM-IWW rebels of 1911, and subsequent peace arrangement by Maderista-Federal forces, he continued to own the property as late as 1918. "Catastro," 1917–1918, Lote #9, Celso Vega #111, 113, El Hotel Emporio, AHE, Gobierno del Distrito Norte, Sección Hacienda del Distrito, Serie Tesorería General, unnumbered Exp.
25. Cory and Griswold, "Letter Sent to President Díaz," *Chronicle*, September 30, 1909.
26. Schantz, *On the Border*, 96–97; Consul Sierra phrased it succinctly as problems with "wine, women, and gambling." These were not idle warnings. See Eugene Keith Chamberlin, "The Japanese Scare at Magdalena Bay," *Pacific Historical Review* 24 (November 1955): 345–59. For other discussions of annexationist plans, see Michael C. Meyer, "Albert Bacon Fall's Mexican Papers: A Preliminary Investigation," *New Mexico Historical Review* 40, no. 2 (April 1965): 165–74; and

Joseph Werne, "Esteban Cantú y la soberanía Mexicana en Baja California," *Historia Mexicana* 30, no. 1 (July–September 1980): 1–32.

27. "Denuncias e informes de vecinos y autoridades sobre la existencia de cantinas y burdeles en Mexicali, Baja California. Varios vecinos de Mexicali manifiestan que el expresado lugar es un centro de depravación y vicio," AGN-IIH, 1909.41 [40.41]; Gobernación, Exp. 10, 1909–1910, Baja California Distrito Norte, August 30, 1909, Mexicali.
28. For a similar argument expounded by Chinese merchants, see Ivan Light, "From Vice District to Tourist Attraction: The Moral Career of American Chinatowns, 1880–1940," *Pacific Historical Review* 43 (1973): 367–94; and Dean MacCannell, *The Tourist: A New Theory of the Leisure Class*, 3rd ed. (Berkeley: University of California Press, 1999), 31–36.
29. "Denuncias e informes de vecinos y autoridades sobre la existencia de cantinas y burdeles en Mexicali," AGN-IIH, 1909.41 [40.41]; Jorge Trujillo Bretón, "La prostitución en Guadalajara durante la crisis del porfiriato 1894–1911" (licenciatura de historia thesis, Universidad de Guadalajara, 1994), 93; Katherine Elaine Bliss, "The Science of Redemption: Syphilis, Sexual Promiscuity, and Reformism in Revolutionary Mexico City," *Hispanic American Historical Review* 79, no. 1 (February 1999): 1–40; William French, "Prostitutes and Guardian Angels: Women, Work, and the Family in Porfirian Mexico," *Hispanic American Historical Review* 72, no. 4 (1992): 529–53; Andrew Grant Wood, "Viva La Revolución Social! Postrevolutionary Tenant Protest and State Housing Reform in Veracruz, Mexico," in *Cities of Hope: People, Protests, and Progress in Urbanizing Latin America, 1870–1930*, ed. Ronn Pineo and James A. Baer (Boulder, CO: Westview Press, 1998), 88–128; Donna Guy, *Sex and Danger in Buenos Aires: Prostitution, Family, and Nation in Argentina* (Lincoln: University of Nebraska, 1991), 12 and 86–95; David McCreery, "'This Life of Misery and Shame': Female Prostitution in Guatemala City, 1880–1920," *Journal of Latin American Studies* 18, no. 2 (November 1986): 333–53; and Neil Larry Shumsky, "Tacit Acceptance: Respectable Americans and Segregated Prostitution, 1870–1910," *Journal of Social History* 19, no. 4 (Summer 1986): 665–79.
30. Quoted in Alan Knight, *The Mexican Revolution: Porfirians, Liberals, and Peasants* (Lincoln: University of Nebraska Press, 1986), 2:152.
31. Manuel Gordillo Escudero to Secretario de Gobernación, March 7, 1912; Circular of Manuel Gordillo Escudero (Jefatura Política del Distrito Norte, Baja California), February 15, 1912; and Secretario de Gobernación J. Flores Magón to jefe político, March 27, 1912, AGN-IIH, Gobernación, 1912.2 [14.49], Caja 36, Exp. 7; "Propuesta de Manuel Vizcarra, Comisario de Policía de Tecate, Baja California, para que se elimine la prohibición de venta de licores en el lugar por Manuel Gordillo Escudero," AGN-IIH, 1911.3, Gobernación, Caja 97, Exp. 37; "Jefe Político to el Presidente del H. Ayuntamiento," document excerpts from inspection made by C. Visitador Judicial del Territorio, August 16, 1911; "Solicitud de informes sobre los establecimientos

que explotan ene ese distrito juegos permitidos por la ley" and "General Manuel Gordillo Escudero al Subprefecto Político de Mexicali," September 6, 1911, AHE, Fondo Gobierno del Distrito Norte, Sección Ayuntamiento, Serie Subprefectura/ Gobernación, 1916–1928, Exp. 228, September 23, 1911.

32. Ensenada's Ayuntamiento argued its case against Gordillo Escudero in *Periódico Oficial*, Sección Oficial, May 31, 1913; Ayuntamiento de Ensenada, July 12, 1912; "El Sub-Colector de Mexicali dejar de cobrar las cuotas correspondientes a bailes públicos por el mes de Noviembre del próximo pasado," AHE, Fondo Distrito del Norte, Sección Ayuntamiento, Serie Tesorería, Exp. 31, Ensenada, January 18, 1913; "Se queja el Ayuntamiento de Ensenada contra el Jefe Político de ese Distrito por los impuestos establecidos en Mexicali a las cantinas y mujeres públicas," Ayuntamiento de Ensenada to Secretario de Gobernación, July 15, 1912; and "Cortes menusales de caja de la sub-colectoria municipal de Mexicali, Baja California," Julio de 1911 a mayo de 1912, AGN-IIH, Gobernación 1912.44.

33. Secretary of Gobernación to Dr. B. Peterson, Delegado Sanitario, Ensenada, July 1908–June 1909, "Instrucciones dadas . . . para que se encargue del registro de inmigrantes por dicho puerto," AGN-IIH, Porfiriato, Gobernación Vol. IV, 1908.8 4ª sección, Volúmen Migración, Exp. 1/1, folder 1; "Instrucciones para nombrar médico de la inspección sanitaria de los inmigrantes en Mexicali," AGN-IIH, 1912.60; and "El Inspector de Inmigración en Mexicali comunica la introducción de Chinos al Distrito Norte," AGN-IIH, 1912.110.

34. Jailed deputy prefects included Julio Ramírez (1912), Luis Álvarez Gayou and Tejedor Pedrozo (1913), and Agustín Llaguno (1914). Jailed immigration officials included José Eraso González Ituarte (1913), and Javier Velasco and Adolfo Pecina (1913). See "Queja el Subprefecto de Mexicali contra uno de los dueños de casas de asignación," November 14, 1912; "El Sr. Quong Wing de Calexico se queja de ser objeto de persecuciones por parte del Subprefecto Alvaro Gayou," February 1, 1913; and "Aprehensión de Luis Alvaro Gayous," AGN-IIH, 1913.16 [5.20] and 1913.21 [5.25], Ramo Gobernación, Periodo Revolucionario, Caja 65, Exp. 76 and 81, 1912.123 [3.43], and Caja 98, Exp. 71.

35. "El Subinspector de Inmigración en Mexicali . . . informa sobre incidente en la deportación de la norte-americana Elena Warren, y lista de prostitutas radicadas en la localidad," "El Subinspector de Inmigración de Mexicali envía las actas con motivo de la expulsión de algunas prostitutas . . . ," "Instrucciones para nombrar médico de la inspección sanitaria de los inmigrantes en Mexicali, B.C.," and "El Inspector de Inmigración en Mexicali comunica la introducción de Chinos al Distrito Norte," AGN-IIH, 1912.11, 1913.85, 1912.110, and 1912.60.

36. Clara Wallace is another example of a deported prostitute who returned to work in Mexicali, citing articles 6 and 7 of 1908 Immigration Law. See "La Señora Le Ray Fensley se queja del Subinspector de Inmigración en Mexicali . . . ," AGN-IIH, 1913 [5.17]; Ramo Gobernación, Periodo Revolucionario, Caja 96, Exp. 57, January 27, 1913.

37. This type of binational cooperation was also evident in the other source of immigration problems—the Chinese. This cooperation adds another element to the symbiotic relations of the twin-city complex integrating the U.S.-Mexico border. "Instrucciones para nombrar médico de la inspección sanitaria de los inmigrantes en Mexicali, B.C." and "El Inspector de Inmigración en Mexicali comunica la introducción de Chinos," AGN-IIH, 1912.110 and 1912.60.
38. "El Subinspector de Inmigración en Mexicali . . . informa sobre incidente en la deportación de la norte-americana Elena Warren, y lista de prostitutas radicadas en la localidad," November 25, 1912, AGN-IIH, 1912.117.
39. "El Subinspector de Inmigración en Mexicali . . . informa sobre incidente en la deportación de la norte-americana Elena Warren, y lista de prostitutas radicadas en la localidad" and "El Subinspector de Inmigración en Mexicali . . . a Secretario de Gobernación," November 25, 1912, AGN-IIH, 1912.117. Me permito respetuosamente suplicar a Ud. Jefe su atención en que el número de mujeres *blancas* supera al de *negras* (emphasis added).
40. "Administración de Aduanas en Mexicali informa acerca de las condiciones de imoralidad que prevalece en esa población," AGN-IIH, 1913.90 [6.41].
41. Ibid.
42. Ibid.
43. *Periódico Oficial*, April 10, 1914; "Sesión de Ayuntamiento de Ensenada, July 4, 1913," Sesión de Ayuntamiento de Ensenada, April 27, 1914, AHE. For a discussion of Huerta's blunders regarding the federal army, see Knight, *Mexican Revolution*, 2:47, 55–59, and 78–79.
44. I am grateful to Víctor M. Macías-González for having suggested the term *honor quest*.
45. Paul Vanderwood, *Juan Soldado: Rapist, Murderer, Martyr, Saint* (Durham, NC: Duke University Press, 2004), 46–48.
46. "Encarnación Sánchez y José Valencia. Piden Informe del Fusilamiento de los dos." AHE, Fondo Gobierno del Distrito del Norte, Sección Relaciones Exteriores, Serie n/a, 1903–1928, Exp. 3/1914; and "Mexican Officials Charged with Summary Execution of Americans New Year's Eve," *Chronicle*, January 2, 1914.
47. "Mexican Officials Charged with Summary Execution of Americans New Year's Eve," *Chronicle*, February 4, 1914.
48. "Inspector de Inmigración en Mexicali envía copia de la Circular que dirigió a los empleados de esa Oficina," February 21, 1914, AGN-IIH, 1914.10 [7.50], Caja 129, Exp. 59.
49. The report characterized Deputy Prefect Llaguno as a "capable and energetic man" but one who had committed "imprudent and incorrect executions." Immigration Inspector Pecina was guilty of committing "numerous abuses." See "El jefe político del Distito Norte de la Baja California propone de suprimir por innescesario los empleados Agentes de Inmigración," March 10, 1914, AGN-IIH, 1914.15 [8.5].

50. Ibid. Reforming the border gaming and prostitution sector was urgent and required honest men of solid "family values" (in the parlance of latter-day conservatives) who would not disgrace the patria.
51. John Kenneth Turner, *Barbarous Mexico* (Austin: University of Texas Press, 1969).
52. "Cantú Says No Export Duty On Cotton," *Chronicle*, January 5, 1915.
53. "Mexicali Scum Dumped into Calexico," *Chronicle*, February 16, 1915. Cantú's racial anxieties were acutely displayed regarding the presence of African Americans in the PLM-IWW invasion of Baja California Norte, 1911. See Adalberto Walther Meade, *Coronel Esteban Cantú Jiménez* (Mexicali: Instituto de las Américas, 1993), 77.
54. "Mexicali Scum Dumped into Calexico," *Chronicle*, February 16, 1915.
55. *Chronicle*, January 6, 1914. See also "Convict Labor May Solve California's Road Problems," *Westways-Touring Topics*, January 1914; "Convict Road Building Proved Economic Advantage," *Westways-Touring Topics*, July 1914; "Convict Labor Lowers Highway Cost," *Westways-Touring Topics*, December, 1914. I am grateful to Kerwin Klein for the tip on the Automobile Association. See Klein, "The Last Resort," 61; and Mark Reisler, *By the Sweat of the Brow: Mexican Immigrant Labor in the United States, 1900–1940* (Westport, CT: Greenwood Press, 1976), 11, 12, 36, and 41–42.
56. "Father O'Hara Has Wild Auto Ride," *Chronicle*, November 23, 1916.
57. *Vago* is defined as a person without a job, craft, or honest livelihood, not including the handicapped. It cites individuals who loiter or convalesce in public places, ranches, labor camps, and roads as well as cantinas, brothels, and other centers of profligacy; see *Periódico Oficial*, October 10, 1918, Del Gobierno del Distrito Norte, Sección II, Circular, #56, Of. 2791, AHE.
58. "Se entreguen los rateros siguientes: Cesareo Provencio, Kirby Short, Ricardo Wolf, Beit Hall, Alfonso Navarro, Guillermo Navarro, and Ramón Ontiveros," *Periódico Oficial*, October 10, 1918.
59. "To Clean Front Street of Mexicali," *Chronicle*, April 16, 1916; and "Casino en Mexicali: Concessión provisional otorgada a C. Withington," AFT, Fondo 11, Serie 010302, Exp. 2, "Concesiones," fojas 37–38, inventario 57.
60. "Rumor Reports Casino to Get Choicest Site," *Chronicle*, June 12, 1919.
61. Mexicali's municipal hygienist states that he had found three infected women who needed to be isolated and quarantined. See "El Ayuntamiento de Mexicali," *Periódico Oficial*, August 15, 1915.
62. "Reglamento de Sanidad para el Distrito Norte de la Baja California," Sección 7, Número 8, Ayuntamiento de Mexicali, B.C., 1915. Copy obtained from Ing. Adalberto Walter Meade and his generous staff at CIH, UABC, Mexicali; and Ayuntamiento de Mexicali, *Reglamento para las casas de tolerancia de la ciudad de Mexicali, Baja California, Decretado por el Ayuntamiento de dicha municipalidad y aprobado por la Jefatura Política del Distrito, por oficio de 13 de Septiembre de 1915* (Mexicali, n.p., c. 1915). I am grateful to Lic. Ignacio Guajardo (Mexicali, Baja California) for providing a copy.

63. "Mexicali Move Made Tonight," *Chronicle*, June 1, 1916.
64. "Casino en Mexicali: Concesión provisional otorgada a C. Withington, Segunda: Que tales casas para juegos y las que se construyan para departmentos de asignación deberán edificarse en los terrenos libres que existen sin finca alguna al otro lado del Rio de esta población, conforme a los locales que deberá designarles el Ingeniero de la ciudad . . . ," AFT, FAO 11, Serie 010302, Exp. 2; "Concesiones," fojas 37, 38, inventario 57.
65. "Catastro," 1917–1918, AHE. The streets that bordered the Owl—Reforma, Azueta, but especially Juárez—were principal thoroughfares for Chinatown, which had as its natural boundary the New River (Río Nuevo) cutting in a diagonal, north to southeast.
66. "Death Comes to Withington," *Los Angeles Times*, October 24, 1925.
67. Dr. Francisco Dueñas Montes tells us that Cantú imported the latest in building design and materials for the secondary school. Interview of Dr. Francisco Dueñas Montes conducted by Eric Schantz, May 12, 1997. Also, David Piñera Ramírez, "Testimonios de personas que vivieron la época," in *Panorama Histórico de Baja California*, 420–23; Modesto Rolland, *Informe sobre el Distrito Norte de la Baja California* (Mexico City: Secretaría de Educación Pública, 1993), 160; Harry Carr, "The Kingdom of Cantú: Why Lower California Is an Oasis of Perfect Peace in Bloody Mexico," *Sunset*, 3 (April 1917): 34; and "Border: Mexicali Is Tingling with Rumors of War," *Los Angeles Times*, November 19, 1916, I, 1:1.
68. The new school "command[ed] a general view of the main street in Mexicali," where red-light operations once dominated the commercial menu. "To Clean Front Street of Mexicali. Order Enclosure in New Plan," *Chronicle*, April 16, 1916.
69. "Mexicali Move Made Tonight," *Chronicle*, June 1, 1916.
70. "Niños Americanos Que Van a la Escuelas de México," *El Heraldo de México*, March 4, 1920. It said, "Los de Calexico pasan diariamente a recibir instrucción en Mexicali. Es quizas el único caso en que los niños de una nación reciben instrucción en las escuelas de otra." This statement is also supported by the oral history of Dr. Francisco Dueñas Montes. Interview by Eric Schantz, May 12, 1997, Mexicali; and Piñera Ramírez, "Testimonios de personas que vivieron la época," 421–23.
71. "Ayuntamiento de Mexicali, sesión extraordinaria, 28 de marzo, 1916," *Periódico Oficial*, May 11, 1916.
72. "Catastro," 1917–1918.
73. Jack B. Tenney, Oral History, Transcription. UCLA, URL Special Collections (1966), 140.
74. *Fichera* is colloquial, like "taxi dancer" or "percentage girl." For the latter term, see Harry Carr, *The West Is Still Wild* (Boston: Houghton Mifflin, 1932). They received a ticket or token called a *ficha* for each dance or drink they had with a patron and cashed these in at the end of the night.
75. "Mexican Monte Carlo Shut Up," *Los Angeles Times*, September 27, 1919.

76. "Mexican Monte Carlo Shut Up," *Los Angeles Times*, September 27, 1919.
77. "Carnival Saturday Night," *Chronicle*, May 13, 1922.
78. "Mexican Monte Carlo Shut Up," *Los Angeles Times*, September 27, 1919.
79. "Casino en Mexicali: Concesión provisional otorgada a C. Withington," AFT, FAO 11, Serie 010302, Exp. 2, "Concesiones," fojas 37, 38, inventario 57. The terms for prostitute used in the concesión contract were *hetera/hetaira* (see *Grijalbo: Gran Diccionario Enciclopédico Ilustrado* [Barcelona: 1998], 889) and *pupila* (see Ramón García-Pelayo y Gross, *Larousse Diccionario Usual* [Mexico City: Ediciones Larousse, 1985], 532).
80. "Catastro," 1917–1918.
81. "Mexican Monte Carlo Shut Up," *Los Angeles Times*, September 27, 1919.
82. "Owl Gambling House Is Destroyed by Fire Last Evening," *Chronicle*, February 10, 1920; and "Three Shot as Dash to Grab Coin Follows Gambling House," *Los Angeles Times*, February 10, 1920, I:1.
83. "Catastro," 1917–1918. The Owl's interior was described in the following urban census: "104 cuartos separados por pasillos. Un salón cantina y juego para *gente de color*, con salida para la calle José Azueta. Sobre el Lote numero 2, hay un Salón Restaurant y una peluquería, con frente a la avenida Guerrero."
84. "Plan de Propios y Arbitrios, Presupuesto de Egresos de Mexicali, BC, para el año 1917," AGN-IIH, 1916.42 [10.2], Artículo 87.
85. Reglamento de Sanidad para el Distrito Norte de la Baja California, Sección 7, Número 8, Ayuntamiento de Mexicali, BC, 1915, Artículos 14 and 25. Bliss, "Prostitution, Revolution, and Social Reform," 73, found that class hierarchy of prostitutes in Mexico City also corresponded to phenotype and ethnicity.
86. "Primera: Que el casino o salones que establezca para explotar los juegos serán atendidos por individuos de raza Blanca y con juegos que ésta misma acostumbra. Casino de Mexicali, Concesión provisional otorgada a C. Washington," and "Línea de Vapores entre San Diego, E.U., y Ensenada, México, Concesión provisional otorgada a George Beermaker," fojas 48–50, October 1, 1915. "Serán exclusivamente para la translación de mercancías cuyo comercio esté permitido legalmente en el territorio, pars las mercancias útiles y demás que necesite el Gobierno y para la conducción de pasajeros bajo el concepto de que le estará prohibido traer a cualquier punto del Distrito jornaleros extranjeros y en ningún sentido pasajeros que siendo extranjeros aunque se titularen capitalista, pertenezcan a la *raza amarilla, negra, o indostana*" (emphasis mine), AFT, FAO 11.
87. "Three Shot as Dash to Grab Coin Follows Gambling House," *Los Angeles Times*, February 10, 1920, I:1; "Owl Gambling House Closed," *Chronicle*, September 8, 1920; and "Mexican Monte Carlo Shut Up," *Chronicle*, September 27, 1920.
88. "Owl Gambling House Closed," *Chronicle*, September 8, 1920.
89. "Owl Women Ordered to Leave City," *Chronicle*, September 17, 1920.
90. "Mexicali 'Clean Up' Is Carried to Opium Dens. Drugs and Men Taken," *Chronicle*, September 22, 1920.

91. Juanita Deal to Presidencia Municipal, November 5, 1922, AHE, Gobierno del Distrito, Ayuntamiento 1916–1928.
92. It got worse the next year as gun battles waged in the streets of Mexicali punctuated the violent conflicts that ripped through local and national political bodies. For an excellent summary of the events, see Marco Antonio Samaniego López, "El Desarrollo económico durante el gobierno de Abelardo L. Rodríguez, 1924–1928," in *Mexicali. Una historia tomo II* (Mexicali: Universidad Autónoma de Baja California, 1991), 11 and 18–26. For "sins of commission," see Knight, *The Mexican Revolution*, 1:30. "Desconocimiento del Presidente Municipal, Otto Moller por parte del Ayuntamiento de Mexicali" and "El Gobernador del Distrito a Presidente Municipal," October 13, 1922, AHE, Fondo Gobierno del Distrito Norte, Sección Gobernación, Serie Asuntos Administrativos, 1917–1926, Exp. s/n, Sección: Ayuntamiento 1916–1928 and Exp. C.273.18, 1923.

CHAPTER 5

Theaters of Masculinity

Moviegoing and Male Roles in Mexico Before 1960

ANNE RUBENSTEIN

IN 1935 THE POPULAR MEN'S MAGAZINE *VEA* PUBLISHED THIS RACY, jokey anecdote:

> Walking in the darkness, a lady and a young woman were searching for a seat in a movie theater. At once a young male spectator called to the girl, "There's a space here, miss," pointing to the empty seat beside him. She thanked him and added, pleadingly, "Wouldn't you like to offer your seat to my mother?"
>
> "Oh miss!" said he, as he stood up, "I forgot that this space was occupied . . . but if you would like, your mother can sit here." The lady took the seat, and since both young people remained standing, he invited her to look farther back in the theater for a spot for them both.
>
> The first reel played. When the intermission came, the young people returned to the lady. Then the daughter, with every courtesy and now some familiarity, introduced her companion to her mother: "Look, mama, this is the attentive young man who gave you his place."

"What a pleasure!" said the lady complacently. "It's always so nice to meet attentive young men."[1]

What made this story funny to the men who wrote it, published it, and read it at the time? To begin with, there is a strained pun: the word *atento*, translated here as *attentive*, could also mean *calculating*. But the real humor of the situation arises from conflicting expectations of male behavior. There were two very different ways that men could act like men in movie theaters, and the young man in the story was trying to perform both male roles at once. First, he appeared to be enacting the respectable male role of protecting a mother and a family. Second, he was taking on the contrasting masculine role of acting as a sexual adventurer, relishing the opportunity to sit in the dark with an otherwise unaccompanied young woman to whom he has not even been properly introduced. This was funny because he was succeeding in simultaneously enacting both roles, when Mexican men in movie theaters usually could embody and perform their masculinity in only one of these two contrasting ways. And it was funny because the young man's performance required that the women around him play along, making their participation in these performances more obvious than it might otherwise have been.

This little story from *Vea* exemplifies the importance of movie theaters as a site for gendered performance, as much among members of the audience as on screen. Cinemas were theaters in more ways than one: men learned to use them as stages on which they could practice and perform their roles as men. (And women used them as stages for performances of femininity.) Movie houses were important sites for men to display the particular forms of masculinity that meant the most to them and the people around them. This article asks how and why that came to be true and examines what those forms of masculinity were.

We might assume that audiences were disembodied, that what mattered about moviegoers was the relationship between their imaginations and what they saw on the screen in front of them. But in fact moviegoers' bodies were at least as important, in historical terms, as their minds. Going to the movies was an intensely physical experience: it produced new sensations and experiences, and it suggested new forms of movement and behavior. Sometimes, what Mexicans saw on the screen was the least important aspect of moviegoing. The physical experience of sitting or standing in a movie theater, therefore, is where this inquiry will begin.

Discomfort, Danger, and the Physical Experience of Moviegoing

Movie theaters as distinct physical spaces evolved slowly, in Mexico as in the rest of the world, from origins in other public gathering spaces (usually theaters and auditoriums but also tent theaters, marketplaces, barns, warehouses, and churches). Movies first appeared as snippets of entertainment between live acts in variety shows and vaudeville. By 1920, some big-city venues had switched to film as their primary business, but it remained difficult to distinguish clearly between movie houses and other places of entertainment. In the early 1930s, some theater owners began to make the expensive renovations necessary for talking pictures. The resulting structures were the first true movie theaters in Mexico. But the physical conditions of moviegoing in the era of silent film created patterns of behavior and sets of expectations that carried over into the time of sound cinema, even after the rise of the movie palaces in the late 1940s. One way to understand these patterns of behavior is to read them as ways for moviegoers—especially male moviegoers—to claim pieces of the shared, public spaces of movie theaters as their own private domains.

To begin with, movie theaters were noisy. This was especially true in the era of silent film: because nobody had to hear a soundtrack in order to understand what was going on, many sounds competed with the musicians who accompanied the films in urban movie houses. Vendors moved up and down the aisles throughout the showings, hawking drinks, food, and sometimes cigarettes, as loudly as they could.[2] Despite efforts to silence them during the transition from silent film to the talkies, such vendors continued working inside the salones de cine for the subsequent half century: cartoonists made jokes about them, the 1938 fire code forbade their presence, and they were still there, at least occasionally, in 1987.[3]

Besides the noises made by musicians and vendors, audience members themselves frequently produced loud sounds. Many movies shown in Mexico after the arrival of sound cinema required subtitles because their English-language soundtracks had not been dubbed into Spanish. Subtitled English-language film has filled at least half of all movie screens in Mexico on any given evening from the 1930s to the present. Therefore, few people felt much need to listen to the movies even after there was something there to hear. Instead, literate people often added to the cacophony by reading subtitles aloud. This behavior was not limited to lower-class people or to the early days of cinema; even midcentury books of etiquette written for people aspiring to upper-class behavior warned against doing so. (And, too, they also warned against making too much noise by rattling programs or unwrapping candies.[4]) The safety inspectors who visited Mexico City movie theaters daily in the 1920s complained that male audience members whistled and hissed when shown an out-of-focus or scratched film, shouted comments (ranging from *piropos* to outright obscenities) at particularly interesting bits, and sometimes got into loud discussions with each other. Filling up movie houses with sound could be a way for men to stake a claim on these public spaces.

Movie theaters were not just noisy. Sometimes they stank. Theater operators, particularly those in poorer regions of the country, sometimes had to be threatened with fines and even jail before they would agree to install bathrooms.[5] Adding to the smells, people not only purchased food in the movie theaters but, as we shall see, often brought whole meals into the cinemas, making a trip to the movies a kind of Sunday picnic. The remains—tamale wrappers, corn cobs, orange peels—ended up underfoot. Moviegoers in the expensive sections of the theater feared being pelted with this garbage (and sometimes worse) from the cheap seats in the balconies above them. Whether or not this happened, or happened very often, the idea that it could happen certainly added to the perception of danger and discomfort connected to the experience of moviegoing.

Theater operators, government health and safety inspectors, and movie patrons struggled with each other particularly over control of women's bathrooms and related spaces, from which men were meant to be excluded. In 1928, the government of the Federal District attempted to ban children under the age of two from movie theaters, explaining somewhat hypocritically that this was "a question of sanitation and health, not morality." The regulation really intended to prevent women from breastfeeding in cinemas that lacked gender-segregated spaces and to exclude young mothers (and respectable women in general) from movie theaters.[6] Sometimes respectable women were excluded from movie theaters by other members of the audience. For instance, Tijuana sex workers in the 1950s adopted a local movie theater's women's room as a kind of clubhouse. They marked the space as theirs by leaving obscene drawings in lipstick on its walls.[7] A Mexican migrant man, who was working as a transvestite prostitute in Los Angeles in the late 1960s, reported similar behavior in an as-told-to memoir written in English:

> We was escared to go to the ladies room, but finally we just got to, so we go in and there were a lot of women there. Real Beverly Hills

> ladies, you know. Elegant. . . . And Speedy and me, we couldn't stop laugh. Believe me, we was screaming! Those ladies was look funny and evil at us.[8]

These two prostitutes succeeded, at least temporarily, in capturing the space for their own purposes by raising their loud, male voices in laughter.

Movie theaters were not only uncomfortable at times but also dangerous. They were sometimes overcrowded: journalists and safety inspectors began complaining that cinemas sold more tickets than they had seats around 1920, and they were making the same complaints in 1960. Safety inspectors also complained, in the days before regulations required that cast-iron seats be bolted to cinema floors, that rowdy young men in the audience were hurling wooden chairs down from the cheap seats in the balconies onto the heads of patrons who had paid more for their tickets. Sometimes the intense competition for space in the movie theaters was more than metaphorical.

Other physical dangers lurked in the movie houses. The technology of movie projection helped make movie theaters dangerous places in their early years. Fires started easily in the highly flammable celluloid of the early movies; such fires were frequent, sometimes deadly, and occasionally catastrophic. One such event took place in a working-class neighborhood of the port of Veracruz in the summer of 1924. El Teatro Esclava had been packed with spectators for an afternoon showing of *La ciudad de los espectros* when a cigarette butt dropped near the projector ignited a fire that killed thirty people, including some children, and injured seventy more.[9] There was a wave of movie theater fires, all taking place late at night and injuring nobody, between 1930 and 1932, which may indicate that theater owners who could not afford the expensive refitting and rebuilding needed to start showing sound pictures were burning down their buildings instead for the insurance. An accidental fire in a movie theater on a Morelos sugar plantation in 1937, which took place while a movie was showing on a weekend afternoon, was so terrible—killing more than forty people and spreading to nearby workers' housing to leave thirty-six families homeless—that it led to a public outcry and eventually the 1938 federal regulations on movie theater construction. Events like these gave moviegoing an aura of peril in the minds of many people, whether or not they went to the movies regularly.

The state of cinema technology helped to create violence, or the threat of violence. Reels of film were fragile and expensive, as well as flammable. Thus, in the 1920s, a single copy of a movie might be shown at several theaters in the same day, as cinema operators would send runners between the movie houses with each reel, a system that resulted in long delays and left the movies scratched, broken, and hard to watch. One inspector complained that when films wore out or were in poor repair, the first damage was always to the intertitles, "which at times cannot even be read . . . [the movies] are unintelligible and irritating to whoever has the bad luck to be present in the movie theater."[10] Delays, discomfort, and poor viewing conditions could produce "noisy public protest" (as another inspector described it), which included overturning chairs, throwing food at the screen, and fist fights.[11]

Well into the era of sound cinema, a columnist in a men's magazine was still complaining that problems with the physical conditions of movies, by the time they arrived at second-run cinemas, rendered them almost unwatchable:

> You might see a big new movie advertised loudly that is about to be premiered at the Regis Theater, and since it's out of the question to treat yourself to the luxury of going to the Regis, you tell yourself, "I'll go see it when it comes around to the Cine San Juan." But even though you might think so . . . well! You will go the San Juan, no doubt, but you won't see that picture there. You will see who knows what, and I'm going to explain this enigma. The Cine San Juan, like so many of the cheap little movie theaters, has the double charm of advertising one movie and showing another! And if that weren't bad enough, not even the producers of the movie that they show would be able to understand it. By the time these movies arrive at this type of movie house, they are so beat up and patched that they have scenes that end in the middle, and others that begin at the end. You have to use all your mental agility to follow the story . . . it's very tiring. I have spent entire nights in the Cine San Juan, receiving surprise after surprise. In the first place, they don't show any of the advertised movies. Then, I couldn't understand anything of the movies that they did show. And lastly, the equipment was so noisy that one couldn't hear even a word of dialogue, nor a single song.[12]

This journalist, in sum, was pointing out that waiting to see a movie at a cheaper cinema changed the physical experience of seeing the movie, especially with relation to sound. But these material differences added up to a difference in the social experience of going to the cinema: in the cheaper theaters, which were noisier and more crowded as well, moviegoers found it difficult to focus on the movie screen and easy to focus on the other people in the audience.

Moviegoers subjected themselves to other hazards as well. Sometimes violence erupted in movie theaters. Between 1918 and 1939 in Mexico City, and sometimes Guadalajara, Monterrey, and Puebla, too, frequent visits by municipal inspectors and the constant presence of a policeman in every theater ensured that everyone remained aware of the risks.[13] Sometimes such violence responded directly to the content of the movies, as in an infamous 1958 riot that pitted Elvis Presley fans against Elvis Presley detractors at the Mexico City premiere of his movie *King Creole*, but more often it resulted from contestation and conflicts among the audience members or between audiences and movie theater managers.[14] In one case, the lack of subtitles on an English-language talking film led to an incident in which "the public did not allow more than the first word in English to be heard" before "causing such an uproar that the exhibition of the film had to be cancelled" and the entrepreneur who had brought the equipment for showing sound film to Irapuato, Guanajuato, was obliged to leave town hurriedly.[15] The Mexico City theater inspectors' reports for 1917–1925 mention perhaps one such incident a week, though most seem to have involved such mild behavior as whistling rudely at the screen. These outbursts were sparked by uncomfortable or aggravating conditions in the cinemas, but they also belonged to a longer tradition of rowdiness among male theater patrons.

Movie theaters, particularly the less elite movie houses, were not places for people to sit passively, peacefully taking in a movie. They were places for audience members—especially men—actively to entertain themselves and each other, sometimes with violence and always with the thrill of the potential for danger. But physical discomfort and danger were not the only risks Mexicans ran in entering movie houses. Moviegoing also could harm audience members' reputations, or even their souls.

Gender and Moral Peril at the Movies

The first showings of movies happened as part of variety programs in live theater, and live performance alternated with movie viewing in some theaters well into the 1940s. Similarly, concerns over the moral dangers posed by moviegoing began with its connection to theatergoing. Theaters, in the Spanish-speaking world, had long since acquired a reputation as places where respectable gender norms could be challenged (and therefore had to be defended). The mere fact that actresses encouraged unrelated men to look at them was, perhaps, questionable. But the way that men and women might mingle in the audience presented much more of a moral risk.

These anxieties applied equally to theatergoing and moviegoing, and they extended almost unchanged over many decades and throughout the former Spanish empire. For instance, a popular mid-nineteenth-century guide to etiquette from Spain—the version cited here was printed in Paris in 1898 but purchased at a Guayaquil bookstore in the 1960s—offered careful, detailed instructions for male behavior in theaters, most still applicable to cinemas half a century later. Some of these rules made it easier for men to share a public space with a mixed-gender group of strangers: gentlemen were to avoid taking their seats late, which might force them to brush up against women they did not know; gentlemen were not to wear their hats in theaters where there were ladies among the spectators; gentlemen were not to rise from their seats, even during the intermissions, except in cases of "urgent necessity" to avoid "annoying one's neighbors"; gentlemen were not to smoke anywhere in the theater, to prevent the fumes from "penetrating into the places where the audience may be found, even when the spectators all are men"; and above all, gentlemen were to avoid making too much noise by moderating their applause and greeting poor performances with silence rather than shouts, hisses, or whistles. Other strictures on male behavior were less closely connected to movie house etiquette: these regulated flirtation, or even contact, with respectable women who might be in the private boxes (the only space open to honorable ladies in theaters). Gentlemen ought not to give ladies large, showy gifts of fruit or candy, and if they visited ladies in their private boxes, they must be sure not to take a seat belonging to another gentleman, nor to linger overlong.[16] In sum, the codes regulating elite behavior were designed to control and modulate potential conflicts between men, either over women or over public space. Underlying this was the assumption that theaters were places where men would be tempted to display themselves as men—making noise, emitting odors, bumping into each other, wearing eye-catching clothes—and that such displays could easily turn violent.

Similar worries over movie theaters as sites of immorality and potential male violence persisted throughout the Revolutionary and post-Revolutionary period in Mexico. Questions persisted as to who should join an audience. Certain types of theatrical performances were intended for male-only audiences, such as the daring revues presented by the Mexico City burlesque theater El Molino Verde in the early 1930s, in a continuation of a pattern of audience gender segregation for live performances. By emphasizing gender as the key to admission to the Molino Verde audience, one anonymous essayist wrote that divisions of "social status" could be overcome; the viewers could be "just men" together.[17] Similarly, movie theater operators seem to have tried segregating the audience by gender, at least occasionally, since they first went into business in Mexico. Or perhaps the audience segregated itself along gender lines: a 1918 photograph of the audience filling every seat in the Salón Rojo (then Mexico's premiere movie house) shows only women and girls in the first five rows of seats and only three men and one boy in the entire theater.[18] Similarly, in 1931, when Metro-Goldwyn-Mayer offered free screenings of the movie *Trader Horn* at the Cine Regis to Mexico City schoolchildren, the audience divided itself, with girls taking the entire right-hand main floor and the seven rows closest to the screen on the left side and boys occupying all the balconies and the remaining corner of the main floor.[19] As late as 1934, at least one movie house in Mexico City offered separate shows for "gentlemen" and "ladies."[20]

Some movie theater operators, aware that respectable women might hesitate to enter a cinema, offered women lower ticket prices than men, a practice that persisted well into the 1940s. But the price break was only for the most expensive seats on the respectable main floor; in the balconies, men, women, and children paid the same even though it was precisely in the balconies where women were least likely to sit. Differential ticket prices kept richer and poorer patrons apart, even when they attended the same cinemas: the main floor had the most expensive seats, the highest balcony had the cheapest seats, and the balconies in between also had intermediate prices. Although the Mexico City government regulated ticket prices at all movie theaters after 1919, it allowed prices to decrease sharply as patrons climbed higher up in the balconies. This policy encouraged a public understanding of the balconies as places where only boisterous young men could go.

Other government policies also helped establish movie houses as sites of moral danger. The powerful new Ministry of Public Education sponsored outdoor showings of educational films in the mid-1920s, at the same moment when Catholic conservatives were first articulating a critique of the state's new projects of educational, social, and cultural reform. Thus, moviegoing could be seen as part of government efforts to undermine religion, family, and "tradition." This linkage was solidified by the

Figure 5.1. Male audience in "El Molino Verde," Mexico City, from *El Molino Verde, Revista dirgida* [sic] *por Jiménez y Ortega* (Mexico City: Ediciones Montmarter, 1932), unpaginated.

Department of Public Health's campaign against venereal disease in 1928, which included free afternoon matinees of a film entitled *Pudor Falso* (*False Modesty*) at theaters all over the country. Since Salubridad Pública appears to have owned only one print of the film, it took six months to have one or two shows each in more than fifty theaters. Government workers hung banners in parks and across central plazas announcing the upcoming show, so anyone in town would know that this presumably racy movie was going to be shown soon, for free, as a "gift" of the state. This also allowed this government project to expand its impact well beyond the physical boundaries of the movie theater in each town and well outside the hours in which the movie was screened. Photographers traveled with the movie, taking photographs of the audiences (which were largely but not entirely male). The free screenings meant that the cinemas shown in these photographs were full to overflowing; but the topic of *Pudor Falso* was so shameful that audience members who happened to have turned toward the photographer at the moment she or he was taking a photograph of the audience often covered their faces with newspapers, programs, their hands, or their hats

Figure 5.2. Male audience members covering faces at "El Molino Verde," Mexico City, from *El Molino Verde, Revista dirgida* [sic] *por Jiménez y Ortega* (Mexico City: Ediciones Montmarter, 1932), unpaginated.

(as spectators at the Molino Verde burlesque theater also sometimes did). These moviegoers both wanted to see the erotic movie and wished not to leave a record of their presence there.

Government-made short films regularly formed part of the program at movie theaters across Mexico throughout this period. Some seemed morally innocuous—for example, the Department of Public Health took newsreel footage of official "donations" of running water to hundreds of small towns between 1935 and 1938, and much of this film ended up playing weekly before the features in big-city movie theaters—but other state-sponsored "educational" films, which included announcements about health, internal tourism, current events, and government services, seemed far more politically loaded.[21] Given the constant church-state tension of the era, anything that could be interpreted as pro-government would also be seen as irreligious. And the presence of the state-made newsreels, as with the visits from tax inspectors, health inspectors, and police, and the official signs that were supposed to be posted in every cinema listing state-approved ticket prices and other regulations, also connected moviegoing to political participation for at least some members of the audience.

Government relations with foreign and domestic film industries also helped connect the state, cinema, and immorality in Mexicans' imaginations. Formal and informal film censorship was the topic of gossip and speculation as well as occasional newspaper reports from the 1930s through the 1960s and beyond. And the government moved from taxing movie production and movie theaters heavily in the early 1920s, to supporting local movie production as a patriotic gesture—the cultural equivalent of import-substitution industrialization—in the Lázaro Cárdenas years. Newspapers covered this shift, and they also printed photographs of politicians attending the openings of new movie theaters, shaking hands with movie stars, and generally associating themselves with the cinema. Notoriously, too, certain high-level politicians conducted affairs with celebrities, including movie stars. And perhaps the most corrupt political family of the post-Revolutionary period, Los Alemán, also was well known to be involved in the movie business. So the images of politics (and especially political corruption), moral danger, and cinema became entangled.

The Catholic Church was the single loudest voice in establishing a moral critique of moviegoing. Catholic women's magazines consistently warned against being the kind of girl who would go to the movies instead of going to mass. Beginning in 1933, the Legion of Decency provided many urban dioceses with a weekly pamphlet, *Apreciaciones*, listing every movie showing locally and sorting them by degree and type of sins depicted, as well as rating them by appropriate audiences. Occasional campaigns against cinematic immorality from the 1940s to the present have involved thousands, sometimes tens of thousands, of Mexicans in actions ranging from listening to anticinema sermons in church to signing petitions to attending demonstrations.

One odd incident illustrates how Catholic critiques of cinema, "modern" ideas about gender, and the state dovetailed. On a Saturday night in February 1934, three teenage boys—high school classmates—went to see an American movie. The three boys sat politely through the first reel of *Tres Pequeños Vagabundos*, a melodrama originally titled *Wild Boys of the Road*, at the elegant Cine Montecarlo in central Mexico City. But during an intermission, while the reels were being changed, they elbowed aside the ushers and ran to the front of the crowded movie house. There they began making speeches, shouting their opposition to a government proposal to institute sex education in the public schools. The boys were, as they later explained, particularly concerned with protecting the honor of their female classmates by shielding them from seeing pictures or hearing explanations of reproduction. At first, the other moviegoers believed them to be making some sort of advertisement for upcoming movies, as the ushers often did during intermissions, and so the boys were ignored. Gradually—at least if the right-wing newspaper that recorded this event is to be believed—the spectators realized what was going on and began applauding enthusiastically. The account continues, "It is not known who informed the police, but suddenly they arrived and obliged the orators to leave their improvised podium."[22] A few days later, the boys were fined and sentenced to a brief jail sentence. They took advantage of the occasion to go on a hunger strike, during which they held a press conference to announce their exact political position and call for other students to join them in resisting the government's nefarious attempts to explain the mysteries of reproduction to Mexican girls.[23] After a few days of this, they were released from jail and quickly dropped from the public eye.

Elsewhere, I have used this story to illustrate political tensions in 1930s Mexico City between an expanding state and, in Alan Knight's term, a culturally "recalcitrant" citizenry.[24] Here, though, I repeat the story for two other reasons: it illustrates the links among moviegoing, the state, and immorality in the Mexican imaginary, and it marks the extreme end of a spectrum of comprehensible, if not entirely respectable, male behavior at the movies.

Theaters of Masculinity, Schools of Femininity

Movie houses became a logical site for rebellious assertions of masculine power through the period of 1920 to 1960, especially assertions of masculine power over feminine standards of behavior. Movie theaters were neither public nor private but had some of the qualities of both types of space: this made it possible for men to behave there in ways that would not have been acceptable in their homes, their workplaces, or on the street. One of ethnographer Oscar Lewis's informants vividly recalled occasions in the early 1940s when a local gang, "the terror of the neighborhood," visited the local cinema, where "they sat up on the balcony . . . and if the movie were a daring one, you could hear them saying dirty things." At the movies, sexual mores in particular might be transgressed; they offered young couples in urban areas an otherwise unobtainable degree of privacy. Oscar Lewis cited the recollection of a member of the "Sánchez" family (from about 1941, when

"Manuel" was thirteen years old): "I took her to the movies where we could kiss and embrace."[25] This would not have surprised cinema inspectors some two decades earlier, who insisted on good lighting not only to reduce the risk of catastrophe in case of fire but also as a gesture toward good manners and correct behavior, ruling that "dim illumination must be there even during the showing of the movies, so that the various rooms of the movie house will not be completely in darkness, thereby avoiding the immoralities that could occur in a similar place which lacked light completely."[26]

Masculine self-assertion and rebelliousness required some degree of participation from women—some women, at least, had to share an understanding with some men about what could happen in movie theaters, and they had to behave in ways that responded to male behavior with comprehension if not cooperation. In fact most people saw these male transgressions, even at their most sexualized and most aggressive, as so ordinary and acceptable that they were the topic of jokes; only foreign anthropologists took them seriously. Public concern on movie house immorality throughout this period usually expressed anxiety over female, rather than male, behavior. Moralists, politicians, and moviemakers (as well as ordinary people) viewed women's behavior at movie theaters as likely to slip beyond the bounds of the acceptable. The possibility for remaking the self that movies offered women, in particular, came in for a great deal of comment over the decades.

In the era of silent film, movies made abroad were thought to be especially appealing to modern young women as they provided international models for liberated behavior—beginning with liberation from restrictive clothing and heavy, long braids. Reviewers assumed that Mexican "*señoritas* would go to the cinema to witness the defense of or the attack on this new mode of feminine hairdo," the bob.[27] Similarly, when Mexico City periodicals in the 1920s printed reviews of movies made in Italy, Germany, France, England, and the United States, they frequently described the leading actresses—Pola Negri, Theda Bara, Constance Talmadge, Clara Bow, or Laura La Plante—as flappers; and reviewers seemed to believe that flappers were what female audiences demanded to see.[28] The association between new female fashions and the movies was reemphasized by the new architectural style of movie theaters built in the 1930s and especially the 1940s, as the new technology of sound produced new types of cinemas: grand staircases, wide atriums, and open balconies gave women wonderful spaces in which to pose themselves fashionably, surrounded by luxuries—especially the luxury of space—they were unlikely to find in other aspects of their lives in the booming city. These theaters did include grand ladies rooms with "lounges," replete with mirrors, countertops, and comfortable seating—one imagines them being pressed into service for diaper changing as well as breastfeeding.

But even in rural Morelos, where anthropologist Margaret Park Redfield spoke with an informant she called "Antonia," movie houses could be venues for displaying up-to-the-minute fashion (and associated loose morals). Antonia complained to Redfield that "my *marido* (husband) is going out with another woman. He says there is nothing wrong about it but he takes her . . . to the movies and he comes home and brags to me about her fine clothes."[29] (Note that this performance of masculine privilege required female actors too: both the wife at home and the morally questionable woman in the movie theater had roles to play in this little drama.) Women rarely attended movies without male accompaniment. Redfield found that respectable married women in Tepoztlán did not like joining local cinema audiences. Antonia went on to tell Redfield that "my daughter-in-law and I take the baby and went [*sic*] out to the movies one night as my son said we should go. But we were uncomfortable, two women alone with all those men."[30] Yet even in this small town, some women—including Antonia's husband's girlfriend—liked accompanying men to the movies.

But in Mexico City, around the same time, some respectable women visited movie houses frequently in the company of female relatives or friends. The family of Gloria Schoemann Vargas was, perhaps, a bit extreme in their passion for moviegoing in Mexico City in the 1920s: "Well, my grandmother was a fanatic about the movies, she went every day, and usually twice a day, she would leave one cinema at seven-thirty and go on to another," often bringing her two granddaughters along.[31] Schoemann Vargas and her family were unusually dedicated to cinema—the granddaughter who loved movies would grow up to become a very successful film editor—but their presence as women unescorted by men in the Mexico City movie houses of the day was not at all odd.

Young women used cinemas as backdrops to play out new feminine identities. The contents of the movies they saw and the dangerous pleasures of the moviegoing experience provided young Mexican women with a new model of the feminine self; some of them made these new ways of acting and appearing part of their own self-presentations. Juan Orol, who scripted, directed, produced, and acted in a long series of low-budget gangster movies and thrillers in the 1940s, described his impression of the feminine audience in Mexico:

> Those whom we might describe as *high life* [he used the English phrase] go to the movies to criticize them, they don't go just to watch a picture, the women go to see style, they go for the styles and if there are styles that they can use to make dresses for themselves, then they say that the film is very good; if there are no stylish clothes, if they can't borrow anything from the movie, they say that they don't like the movie and it isn't any good.[32]

This continued across the decades and across borders as well. A Tijuana-born migrant working in Los Angeles in the late 1960s complained about the film *The Wild One*: "I like that guy Marlon Brando . . . but that girl was a bust. I mean, she was nothing. She didn't give you no makeup, no fashion. That movie was just motorcycles, motorcycles, motorcycles, and they didn't give you no fashion at all."[33]

Cinemas offered similar options for self-fashioning to Mexican men as they did for Mexican women. Movie houses gave men a stage on which to enact manliness and a choice of male roles that they could perform. Enacting rebellious masculinity, like the young men who interrupted the screening of *Wild Boys of the Road*, was not the only possible way to demonstrate maleness at the cinema. For movie houses, paradoxically, also came to act as sites where exemplary gendered behavior, masculine and feminine virtue, could be defined and displayed. People loved going to the movies, despite all efforts from church and state to discourage them, and the opportunities it provided for gendered self-fashioning were an important reason why.

The Family Man at the Movies

In a brilliant 1938 essay, poet and critic Salvador Novo disagreed with those who complained about the immorality of movies and moviegoing. He called movie houses "modern temples" in which "the screen occupies the place of the altar, in symbolic and real ways," because there the audience could witness "an invisible god" arranging the destinies of the characters in the stories: "heaven for the just . . . hell for the sinners."[34] For him, the morality of the films—and he did not distinguish between foreign and Mexican-made movies—mattered more than the possibilities for immorality that movie theaters offered their clientele.

Over the years, the stars who meant the most to Mexican viewers—almost all male and Mexican, according to fan-magazine polls—tended to enact roles along a spectrum of exemplary masculinity, ranging from hard-drinking womanizers to tenderhearted, hardworking family men. The single most important star in Mexican cinema, Pedro Infante, managed to play both at once in his most popular movies, the *Nosotros los pobres* trilogy (*Nosotros los pobres*, 1947; *Ustedes los ricos*, 1948; and *Pepe el Toro*, 1952). In his role as Pepe el Toro, Infante was figured as a hardworking man (though he accidentally ended up in prison) who took good care of his young, orphaned sister and yet had a number of romantic partners. Other stars like Agustín Lara, Cantinflas, Jorge Negrete, Tin-Tan, and El Santo, though very different from each other, also tended to play roles in the movies and display public personae in which these somewhat opposed possibilities for exemplary masculinity were combined, with greater or lesser plausibility.

But even before Mexican cinema began to produce these stars, Mexican men used movie theaters as sites to perform many kinds of masculinity, not just for rehearsals of machismo. Chava Flores made a point of this in his memoir of his boyhood in Mexico City during the 1930s. The chapter in which he describes going to the movies begins with an exchange between Flores, his brother Enrique (nicknamed "Quico"), and his father:

> Papa asked us . . . You're going to the movies? Who with?
>
> By ourselves. Mama will let us, won't you, Mom?
>
> Mama assented, but Papa reproached us: "And your mother and your sister? Why not bring them?"
>
> . . . But I quickly recovered, and replied: "Because we can't. We're going to the top balcony and Mama and Trini [his sister] can't go there."
>
> "Then take them to the main floor," my father said, as if it were the simplest thing in the world.

But for a family of four to sit in the *luneta* section cost ten times the price of tickets for two boys to sit in the *gayola* (male-only balcony). The boy's father solved the problem by lending them a peso, saying that they could repay him "when you are big, when you have jobs."[35] In other words, preparing to go on a family trip to the movies was also preparation for adult male responsibilities. On the way to the movie theater, with Flores's father off at his job, the young boy's half-joking efforts at manly behavior continued:

> We went out happily and all wanted to take my mother's arm . . . When we arrived at the cinema, I felt my responsibilities. For those moments I was the head of the family and I went to buy the tickets . . . My mother looked at me seriously and later I saw her laugh, commenting to my sister . . . "clown!" The ticket window was a little high but my nose already could reach the counter.
>
> "Four orchestra seats, please," I told the ticket seller, proudly handing him one of my two pesos.
>
> I took the tickets and I ran to show them to my mother. Trini and Enrique wanted me to give them theirs, but my mother opposed this, adding to my importance.
>
> "Let him, let him carry them, you'll lose them."
>
> Trini wanted to buy popcorn, but Quico wisely responded . . . "First let Mom pick whatever she wants, then we'll see what's left over for us."[36]

Chava Flores vividly remembered this scene nearly fifty years later, even though he recalled almost nothing of the movie he saw once his family finally sat down in those expensive seats. For him, in other words, the lasting excitement of an afternoon at the movies came from the chance to enact—to embody—a responsible adult man. His father reinforced the lesson not only by helping Chava pay for the tickets, but also by showing up after the first movie had already played, with tortas for everyone—again, showing that a good man is a hardworking provider as well as a defender of feminine virtue. And Chava Flores did indeed learn this lesson well. He writes that when he finally did grow old enough to "earn my first pesos," he spent some of his first paycheck taking his mother, brother, and sister to that same movie theater, celebrating his arrival at adult responsibility in the precise place where he had so memorably played at maturity.[37]

In Chava Flores's story, he and his brother began their trip to the movies with the intention of sitting with the other men in the cheap seats, where they might partake in or (more likely) observe various forms of masculine agression, probably sexual agression. They were planning to play the male moviegoer's role of the boisterous young man. But their father convinced them to try out a different masculine role: to act as providers for and protectors of women, as good family men. To enact male respectability in this way required a bit more money than playing the part of the rowdy young man; choice of roles was informed by economic status and reflected social class (or social aspirations). But even more importantly, playing the part of the respectable family man at the movies required two sets of supporting actors. There had to be a respectable woman or women to be protected and provided for. And there had to be men playing the opposite male role, that of sexual agressor, so that the respectable man could defend the respectable women against someone. Neither of these supporting players had to be physically present in the movie house. They only had to exist in moviegoers' imaginations. But without these other actors, the part of the respectable family man at the movies—the role Chava Flores describes learning to play—would not make sense.

Space, Time, and Masculinity in Mexican Movie Theaters

Gendered behavior in movie theaters seems to have remained more or less stable across time from the 1920s through the 1960s. The only major change in moviegoing behavior was spatial. By the 1950s, most urban movie theaters had ceased to divide their audiences by ticket prices. Instead, distinctions among movie theaters became more obviously linked to their locations within cities, and this pattern was reinforced through differential prices among movie theaters rather than within them. Tickets at first-run movie palaces in wealthy areas cost more than tickets at second- or third-run movie houses in poorer areas. Movie theaters in wealthy areas probably were somewhat cleaner and perhaps more secure by the 1950s than they might have been in the 1920s and 1930s. This aside, though, very little had changed about the moviegoing experience in urban Mexico.

This is very surprising. This era saw enormous changes in motion-picture technology—the advent of sound, the rise of the movie palace, and at the end of this period the coming of television—as well as drastic shifts in demographic and economic patterns and political life. In this era, Mexico moved from a rural society to an urban one, while the majority of Mexicans learned to read. The feminism of the 1920s disappeared, while women got the vote in 1954. And the Mexican state, which had been improvising desperately in order to get control of the country in the 1920s, was by the 1950s a seemingly permanent, immovable monolith. Why, then, do we find such little change in what people did when they went to the movies and what the movies and moviegoing meant to them?

Here is one tentative explanation: moviegoing in the 1920s was a contingent response to the conditions of movie houses and cinema technology, to the vagaries of urban life, to the contents of the movies themselves, and to traditions of theatergoing. But it became a kind of laboratory for gendered modernity in which patterns were set that remained useful and understandable for two subsequent generations. The passage of time, change in understandings of gender roles and expectations, and processes of collective and individual memory would shift the meanings of those patterns. But they did not lose their utility or their importance until the arrival of television once again remade the private/public distinction—again, along gender lines—in urban Mexico.

NOTES

1. Boster, "Escenas Metropolitanas," *Vea* 1, no. 25 (April 19, 1935): 31.
2. "Como hacer clientela, 10 mandamientos," *Mundo Cinematográfico* 3, no. 14 (April 1931): 19.
3. One such cartoon can be found in "Los 'Latosos' de la Calle," *Vea* 1, no. 38 (July 19, 1935): 5; the fire code and related documents are in Archivo Histórico de Salubridad Pública, Sección Acuerdos Presidenciales, Libro 16. I witnessed such vendors at work in movie theaters in Oaxaca, Puebla, and Mexico City in 1987.
4. For instance, Irma Carlota Limantour, *Etiqueta, Urbanidad, y Distinción Social* (Mexico City: Libros y Revistas, S.A., 1941), 113. Thanks to Víctor M. Macías-González for the citation.
5. Archivo Histórico de Salubridad Pública, Sección Acuerdos Presidenciales, Libro 16, acuerdo de December 2, 1938.
6. La Sede Social de la Unión Cooperativa "Mujeres de la Raza" to Jefe del Departamento Administrativo, Gobernación, September 25, 1928. Centro de documentación de la Secretaria de Salud, Fondo Salubridad Pública (hereafter, Salubridad Pública), Serie Jurídico Consultivo, Caja 14, Exp. 26. See also Jefe de la Depto. Administrativo, Gobernación, to Jefe del Depto. de Salubridad Pública, September 25, 1928, and Secretario del Jefe del Depto. de Salubridad to Secretario General del Gobierno del Distrito Federal, October 6, 1928, Salubridad Pública, Serie Jurídico Consultivo, Caja 14, Exp. 26.
7. "Las 'Vivitas' en los Teatro," *Cine al Día* (Tijuana), no. 173 (July 10, 1955): 6.
8. Elaine Hollingsworth, *Zulma* (New York: Warner Paperback Library, 1974), 124.
9. "Mas de 30 niños muertos y como 70 heridos en Veracruz," *El Universal*, July 24, 1924, secc. 1, p. 1.
10. Hipólito Amor to the chief inspector, June 16, 1922, Exp. 250, Vol. 812, Diversiones Públicas, Gobierno del Distrito Federal, Archivo Histórico del Distrito Federal.
11. Hipólito Amor to the chief inspector, June 17, 1922, Exp. 230, Vol. 812, Diversiones Públicas, Gobierno del Distrito Federal, Archivo Histórico del Distrito Federal.
12. Ruherí, "Bagatelas," *Vea* 1, no. 46 (September 13, 1935): 10.
13. The records of the Oficina de Diversiones Públicos show that these safety inspectors did make very regular visits, often more than once every day, which was possible as each inspector was charged with visiting two, three, or at most four theaters, always in the same neighborhood. But inspectors frequently cited the theaters for the absence of either the police or the tax inspectors, occasionally both. See Vols. 812, 813, 853, and 854, Diversiones Públicas, Gobierno del Distrito Federal, Archivo Histórico del Distrito Federal.
14. Eric Zolov, *Refried Elvis* (Berkeley: University of California Press, 1998), 47–49.
15. "No quieren Películas Habladas en Inglés," *Mundo Cinematográfico* 1, no. 4 (June 1930).
16. Manuel Antonio Carreño, *Manual de urbanidad y buenas maneras*, 15th ed. (Paris: Librería de Garnier Hermanos, 1898), 146–51. Thanks to Juan Maiguashca for the

citation. See also Condesa de Tramar, *El Trato Social* (Mexico City: Librería de la Viuda de Ch. Bouret, 1906), 197–202. Thanks to Víctor M. Macías-González for this citation.

17. Anonymous, "Molino Verde, Espejo y Sombra" in *MOLINA VERDE, Revista Dirgida [sic] por JIMENEZ Y ORTEGA* (Mexico City: Ediciones Montmarter, 1932), 2.
18. Photo (from the fototeca of INAH) reprinted in Francisco H. Alfaro and Alejandro Ochoa, eds., *La República de los cines* (Mexico City: Editorial Clío, 1998), 17.
19. See photograph in "Sección Gráfica," *Mundo Cinematográfico* 3, no. 17 (July 1931): 19.
20. Advertisements for El Cine Alarcon in *Excelsior*, January 1–June 30, 1934.
21. These government-made short movies are now inaccessible to researchers due to the 1984 fire in the Cineteca Nacional. However, the process through which they were made, distributed, and projected left archival traces elsewhere. See, for example, Salubridad Pública, Serie Secretaría, Sección Presidenciales, Caja 12, Exp. 14, and also Salubridad Pública, Serie Acuerdos Presidenciales, Sección Presidenciales, Libro 10 (passim).
22. *Nuevo Regimen* 17 (February 19, 1934): 1.
23. *Nuevo Regimen* 19 (February 23, 1934): 1.
24. Anne Rubenstein, "Raised Voices at the Cine Montecarlo," *Journal of Family History* 23, no. 3 (1998): 312–23.
25. Oscar Lewis, *The Children of Sánchez: The Autobiography of a Mexican Family* (New York: Vintage, 1963), 31, 147. The continued use of downtown Mexico City cinemas as spots for illicit sexual behavior can be seen in Luis Zapata's novel of teenage street life in the 1970s, *El Vampiro de la Colonia Roma* (Mexico: Grijalbo, 1979).
26. Hipólito Amor to the chief inspector, June 12, 1922, Exp. 250, Vol. 812, Diversiones Públicas, Gobierno del Distrito Federal, Archivo Histórico del Distrito Federal.
27. Celuloide [Jaime Torres Bodet], review of *Pelona*, in *Revista de Revista*, November 29, 1925, cited in Felipe Garrido, ed., *Luz y Sombra: Los inicios del cine en la prensa de la ciudad de México* (Mexico City: Consejo Nacional para la Cultura y las Artes, 1997), 451.
28. See the reviews reprinted in Garrido, *Luz y Sombra*, 402–4, 410–12, 415, 418–20, 456.
29. "Antonia," (n.d.) (1933?): 21. Folder 3, Box 48, Redfield Papers, Special Collections, Regenstein Library, University of Chicago.
30. "Antonia," (n.d.) (1933?): 22. Folder 3, Box 48, Redfield Papers, Special Collections, Regenstein Library, University of Chicago.
31. Gloria Schoemann Vargas interviewed by Maria Alba Pastor, August 16, 1975. PHO/2/32, 3, Archivo de la palabra, Proyecto de cine mexicano, PHO, INAH.
32. Juan Orol interviewed by Eugenia Meyer, July 2, 1975. PHO/2/30, 25–26, Archivo de la palabra, Proyecto de cine mexicano, PHO, INAH.
33. Elaine Hollingsworth, *Zulma* (New York: Warner Paperback Library, 1974), 125.

34. Salvador Novo, "El Cine, templo moderno," *Síntesis* 15, no. 48 (December 1938): 437–39. Reprinted in Novo, *Crónicas y artículos periodísticos, viajes y ensayos II* (Mexico City: Fondo de Cultura Económica, 1999).
35. Chava Flores (Salvador Flores Riera), *Relatos de mi Barrio* (Mexico City: Editores Asociados, 1972), 101.
36. Flores, *Relatos de mi Barrio*, 104.
37. Ibid., 106.

PART 2

REPRESENTATIONS

CHAPTER 6

Toward a Modern Sacrificial Economy

Violence Against Women and Male Subjectivity in Turn-of-the-Century Mexico City

ROBERT BUFFINGTON

CONVENTIONAL WISDOM ASSURES US THAT "EVERY PICTURE TELLS a story," that "a picture is worth a thousand words."[1] These everyday maxims reinforce the widely held notion that images are more economical, more accessible, and more descriptive than written language. None of these reputed virtues, however, makes pictures any easier for historians to interpret. Take, for example, the political cartoon that appears on the March 23, 1905, cover of *La Guacamaya* (*The Squawking Parrot*), a satiric weekly newspaper that proudly proclaimed itself "the unconditional defender and friend of the working class." The image depicts two men squatting on a Mexico City street corner. They are smirking, pointing fingers, and commenting to each other on the "meatiness" of a passing woman's calves. Straw sombreros, scruffy moustaches, tousled hair, stooped posture, white cotton clothing, sandals, and bare feet mark them as typical *pelados*, a common if derogatory term for lower-class, mestizo (mixed race) urban men. Dainty umbrella, plumed hat, coiffed hair, bustled dress, frilly petticoats, striped stockings, and lace-up shoes signal the passing woman's bourgeois status—and, if distinctive fashion were not enough, her class privilege is reinforced by the

Tome III Año III México, Marzo 23 de 1905 Segunda época. Núm. 43

LA GUACAMAYA

DEL PUEBLO Y POR EL PUEBLO

PERIODICO HABLADOR Y DE BUEN HUMOR

Rebalsador y decidor de verdades, no papero ni farolero, azote de los burgueses, defensor incondicional y amigo de la clase obrera.

Ganado para el nuevo Rastro

El Mártes 21 del presente
Beneficio de nuestro estimado compañero de Redacción
FERNANDO DE P. TORROELLA
En el Teatro Lelo de Larrea.

—Oye mano pos no dicen que la carne está muy cara y que si Dios no nos oye nos lleva la chicharra.
—Pos es cierto Pitacio y eso que te digo dile.
Que el pobre dentro de poco ha de comer puro chile.
—Pero mira que chamorros, yo me agacho.
—Yo me acerco,
—Pero no seas tan madera. No vez que es carne de puerco

Figure 6.1. This *La Guacamaya* cover is titled “Cattle for the New Slaughterhouse.” The last two lines of the commentary read, “[first man] I’m going to get closer.” “[companion] But don’t be a blockhead. Can’t you see that it’s pig meat?” Source: *La Guacamaya*, March 23, 1905.

hatless, disheveled figure of a poor Indian-looking woman carrying a child in the distance. Mexico City's seasonal rains and inadequate drainage—for critics like the editors of *La Guacamaya* the drainage problem was a perennial symbol of municipal misadministration—have caused the bourgeois woman to hike up her skirts to avoid soiling her dress and petticoats, thus exposing her ankles and calves to the men. Their apparent glee at her evident discomfort suggests long-standing resentments about their marginalized social status coupled with a misogynistic disdain for bourgeois female frivolity—represented here as overindulgence in food and fashion.

The accompanying text complements and complicates the image.[2] The title, "Ganado para el nuevo Rastro [Cattle for the New Slaughterhouse]," references a newly constructed municipal meat market and serves to demean the woman by equating her with livestock and to hint at the latent violence in the encounter, especially as she lacks a male chaperone.[3] The dialogue that follows the image, rendered in *caló* (street slang) and full of *albures* (word plays), teases out the image's carnal and sexual implications. The first line, for example, begins with a comment about the high price of meat and ends with, "If God doesn't hear us we're finished" ("Nos lleva la chicharra"). The phrase *nos lleva la chicharra* translates literally as "We'll be summoned by the old harp" but also stands in for the obscene expression *nos lleva la chingada*, which means "We'll be taken by the fucked one" or, more colloquially, "We're fucked." Both common expressions signify being summoned or taken by death.[4] In addition, *chicharra* suggests the Mexican word for pork rinds (*chicharrón*) while *la chingada* represents the violated woman. The third line keeps the sexual connotations in play with the comment that "soon the poor will have nothing to eat but chile"—the hot pepper being a common Mexican euphemism for *penis* or *dick*. And finally, when one man threatens to move in for a closer look, his companion stops him with, "Don't be a blockhead [No seas tan madera]. Can't you see that it's pig meat?"

As this initial reading suggests, a careful eye and a good dictionary can provide useful clues to the cartoon's meaning. Nevertheless, this first level of analysis, crucial as it is, begs some important questions: Why are the two men's class resentments directed at a "helpless" woman rather than at bourgeois men? Why are their resentments expressed in terms of carnality, sex, and violence? Why are they being voiced in a public space? And what exactly is it that connects the bourgeois woman to the poor woman in the distance? To get at these more complex questions, we must look beyond the image itself to radical changes in the representation and performance of gendered identities taking place in turn-of-the-century Mexico City and consider the grim implications of those changes for women.

For the historian—largely dependent on mass media accounts like *la nota roja* (tabloids); bureaucratic sources like crime statistics, court records, and social workers' reports; criminological studies; or bourgeois prescriptive literature—the topic of violence against women seems especially intractable. The best histories for the modern period acknowledge the role of systemic violence in disciplining women and sustaining patriarchy but do not really explain how that patriarchal system is produced and reproduced other than by an unproblematic male desire to dominate women.[5] Even anthropologists working directly with abusive men or abused women can only hint at larger patterns of gendered violence.[6] Moreover, since the men involved in these studies are almost exclusively from the lower classes, even a careful reader might conclude that politically impotent, economically exploited, and socially marginalized men often have expressed and compensated for their understandable frustrations by beating women, sometimes to death, even though most scholars agree that violence against women regularly transcends class and racial boundaries.[7] This deceptively commonsensical explanation for male violence against women serves to perpetuate and reinforce negative stereotypes of working-class machismo. It also exculpates middle- and upper-class men as direct perpetrators of violence, supports the conventional view of the bourgeoisie as the "civilized" class, provides a convenient location (in socially marginal spaces) for most violence against women, and justifies the continued repression and exploitation of "uncivilized" working-class men.

In response, this article argues that widespread male violence against women in turn-of-the-century Mexico City resulted not from the inherent brutality of working-class men, but from a more generalized crisis of masculine subjectivity—of men's sense of themselves as men—that affected men and women of all classes.[8] By around 1900, the broad dissemination of "modern" notions of social organization in Mexico City had begun to alter the conditions of male subjectivity as regulatory norms (formal and informal rules of proper behavior) that prescribed heterosexual rather than homosocial intimacy and national citizenship rather than *patria chica* (local) loyalties and began to set new if often-contested standards for social acceptance and visibility.[9] These dramatic changes had a profoundly destabilizing effect on male subjectivity.[10] In this context, then, violence against women functioned symbolically and systemically to counter modernity's assault on traditional masculine subjectivities. This symbolic-systemic function produced a cultural logic of female sacrifice—a modern sacrificial economy—in which women figured as the designated scapegoats whose "sacrifice" would restore social order.[11]

While this essay intends to shed light on the larger historical problem of violence against women in modern societies, it is first and foremost a case study grounded in a particular time and place, focused on a particular social class and sex, and based on a particular source. The reasoning behind these choices is as follows: turn-of-the-century Mexico City provides an ideal site for historical investigations into the links between male subjectivity and sacrificial economies because it was in the throes of a full-blown modernity crisis with Oedipal overtones—Porfirio Díaz as tyrannical father, the Virgin of Guadalupe as the long-suffering mother—and because it was a central site for the development of the unstable "hybrid modernity" that still characterizes Mexican society.[12] Working-class men are the ideal subjects for this historical investigation because their marginal but still visible status in Mexican society exposes the fundamental instability of *all* modern male subjectivities (including those of bourgeois men) predicated on the mastery of self and female (or feminized) dependents. Moreover, their marginal visibility as political subjects meant increased state surveillance. For that reason, they appear more often in police reports, court records, and other official sources than middle- and upper-class men who were better able to shield their private lives from the prying eyes of policemen, bureaucrats, and historians.[13] The turn-of-the-century Mexico City satiric penny press supplies a crucial piece of this historical puzzle because it provided a forum or public space in and through which its working-class male clientele attempted to make sense of a cultural revolution that affected all aspects of their public and private lives—and most especially their sense of themselves as men.[14]

Penny Press as Proletarian Public Sphere

Any historical investigation into violence against women in turn-of-the-century Mexico City must begin with an attempt to recover the specific historical conditions of working-class male subjectivity. Those conditions had changed dramatically by 1900. The intricate web of causes, effects, and articulations behind these changes are too complex to do justice to here, but the essentials are something like this: by 1900, modernization efforts had begun to have a significant impact on relations of production and thus on class structures throughout Mexico and especially in the capital. For a variety of reasons ranging from land enclosures to incipient industrialization to expanding railroad networks (financed by foreign capital), Mexico City experienced a huge influx of migrants throughout this period, most of them from outlying rural areas and nearby states. This influx caused the city to more than double in size from 230,000 in 1877 to 471,000 by 1910.[15] As migrants flooded in, the middle and upper classes deserted the central districts for newer residential areas along the capital's showcase boulevard, the Paseo de la Reforma. At the same time, housing shortages drove up downtown rents and forced many poorer residents into less reputable neighborhoods like the notorious El Tepito and the working-class barrios that sprang up around the new penitentiary in San Lázaro. The class differentiation that resulted from these demographic and geographic shifts, although incomplete and permeable, encouraged the development of a working-class "consciousness" of sorts grounded in shared social spaces and shared cultural practices (like reading the satiric penny press).[16]

Conscious of itself or not, the Mexico City working class was hardly the industrial proletariat envisioned by Marxist theorists. Although the number of factory workers rose nearly 355 percent between 1895 and 1910 to around 10,500 people, they represented only 4 percent of the city's workforce, and nearly a third of that workforce was female. While many more did comparable labor in small- and medium-sized workshops, Mexico City workers employed in manufacturing actually declined as a percentage of the workforce from 37 percent in 1895 to 33 percent in 1910 (although the overall number of workers in manufacturing did grow substantially). In fact, the bulk of the capital's labor force was unskilled, with the majority working in sweatshops or service jobs. Moreover, by 1910, women represented 35 percent of the capital's waged workers. Over 35,000 of them were employed as domestic servants, more than three times the number of male and female factory workers. Workers' wages ranged from ten centavos a day for children to one peso for most routine factory work to two to five pesos for semiskilled mechanics. Women were invariably paid less than men.[17]

But the Mexico City proletariat did include a sizeable and influential contingent of skilled craftworkers, many of them former artisans. And literacy rates were remarkably high: 50 percent for the Federal District by 1910 despite the presence of large numbers of illiterate rural migrants. (The national literacy rate was closer to 20 percent.) To further complicate class matters, the literate and better-paid end of the proletarian spectrum often blended imperceptibly into Mexico City's financially precarious petite bourgeoisie. This was especially true in innovative industries like printing that had benefited tremendously from a spate of technological innovations that had significantly increased productivity and quality in the newspaper trade. Bolstered by the rise of mass dailies beginning in 1896 with *El Imparcial*, skilled printers remained among the best-paid craftworkers. Those with more traditional skills benefited less: petite bourgeois journalists struggled with notoriously low salaries, and artisans like master printmaker José Guadalupe Posada faced an exhausting daily scrabble just to make ends meet.[18] Class status for members of this group was fluid rather than fixed, circumstantial rather than predetermined. Even the status-obsessed reporter-protagonist in Porfirian novelist Emilio Rabasa's *El cuarto poder* (*The Fourth Estate*, 1888) admits that "we worked as scribes, not as writers; we weren't artists, but workers."[19] From this marginally respectable sector of Mexico City life—nominally *gente decente* (decent folk) but self-identified as working class (at least when it suited their purposes)—the satiric penny press drew its editors, writers, printers, illustrators, and much of its clientele. And it was principally their struggles with the changing conditions of male subjectivity that were recorded in its pages.

The Mexico City satiric penny press has a historical importance that belies its relatively brief appearance (roughly 1900–1915), uneven quality, and erratic publication record.[20] With mastheads that openly proclaimed working-class loyalties—*La Guacamaya* (*The Squawking Parrot*) called itself the "newspaper of gossip and good humor, agile and a teller of truths, not puffed up or snobby, scourge of the bourgeoisie and defender of the *Working Class*"; *El Diablito Rojo* (*The Little Red Devil*) said it was "of the people and for the people"; *El Diablito Bromista* (*The Little Joking Devil*) claimed to be the "organ of the working class, scourge of the bad bourgeoisie, and boogeyman of bad government"—the satiric penny press provided a forum or "public sphere" for working-class issues, contributed to the formation of working-class consciousness, and facilitated the imagining of a Mexican national community grounded on the honest, productive, and patriotic toil of Mexico's working classes.[21] In exchange, authorities allowed editors to criticize bourgeois political corruption, crony capitalism, and exploitation of the working class so long as editors did not personally attack President Porfirio Díaz or espouse overtly revolutionary ideas.

These qualities set the satiric penny press apart from the mass dailies like the government-subsidized *El Imparcial* and the pro-Catholic *El País* that dominated the Mexico City newspaper business during the late Porfiriato. Penny press stalwart *La Guacamaya* might claim as many as 29,000 copies sold for its hottest weekly editions but could not begin to approach *El Imparcial*'s daily sales, which had soared to well over 100,000 by 1910.[22] Nevertheless, anecdotal evidence suggests that the satiric penny press—purchased, borrowed, shared, stolen, or read aloud on the shop floor, in the *vecindad* (tenement) patio, or in the local *pulquería* or *cantina* (bar)—circulated widely among Mexico City proletarians and sometimes even among their provincial counterparts. An 1895 print from *El Periquito*, for example, carries the title "Biblioteca al aire libre [Open-Air Library]" and depicts a group of working-class men (including a gendarme) listening as the paper is read aloud and discussed.[23] The mass dailies used up-to-date news, sensational crimes, sports coverage, and homey advice columns to attract readers of all classes, but only the penny press actively promoted working-class concerns and openly encouraged reader submissions on everything from strike information to poetic sentiment. Moreover, unlike the government-subsidized *El Imparcial* (which also cost a penny), the satiric penny press relied entirely on daily sales to finance operations, a constraint that forced editors to pay special attention to the everyday concerns of their working-class clientele. For the same reason, they were less inclined to propagandize than papers like *La Internacional*, *La Voz del Obrero*, and *La Revolución Social*, which were sponsored by radical workers' organizations. The continued popularity of penny press stalwarts *La Guacamaya*, *El Diablito Rojo*, and *El Diablito Bromista* suggests that successful editors understood and represented working-class concerns quite well whatever their own class status (which was never more than petit bourgeois in any case) and despite their "unusual" literary skills.

The satiric penny press for workers had many obvious virtues: eye-catching graphics (Posada was a frequent contributor), acerbic political and social critique, and—in contrast to the didactic tone of many newspapers directed at the working classes—a sense of humor. It also had lots of poetry and page after page after compulsive page of mostly hackneyed verse, much of it submitted by loyal readers. To modern scholars, the juxtaposition of creative brilliance and oppressive banality is a bit unsettling, and most prefer to ignore the poems and focus on graphic images or political analyses. This sensible strategy has produced some thoughtful work on Posada's artistic innovations and on working-class political culture.[24] Still, it leaves important questions about other aspects of working-class life unanswered.

Figure 6.2. The two small prints on the left depict "the big press" and "the little press." The larger print on the right depicts an "open-air library." The caption reads, "The sons of the people struggle to read" (literally, "choke on reading"). Source: *El Periquito*, August 2, 1895.

Male Scripts and Modern Love

The connection between political activism—whether in the form of satirical cartoons, news stories, or editorials—and the penny press as a proletarian public sphere is fairly straightforward. Certainly, there is no reason to dispute María Elena Díaz's analysis of the political positions staked out by the principal papers or to question Posada's stature as a social satirist. That leaves the poetry. What was it about? Why did readers submit so much of it? What was its purpose?

Despite the pro-worker stance of most newspapers, penny press poets paid scant attention to politics. They wrote instead about women: good, bad, and, of course, indifferent. Unlike penny press editors who sometimes portrayed workers speaking in a quaint, tortuous vernacular, reader contributors favored a refined poetic style that lent seriousness to their efforts to engage the mysteries of the feminine.[25] An example, "Mi novia [My intended]," from *El Diablito Rojo*, illustrates the high romantic style:

Negros, muy negros sus ojos negros,
Suave, muy suave su tez rosada,
Y el tinte de oro de sus cabellos,
Medio rizados y en profusión,
Es lo más bello de mi adorada,
Es el idilio de mi pasión.

(Black, very black, your black eyes
Soft, very soft, your pink skin
And the golden hue of your hair
Lightly curled and in profusion
Is the most beautiful of my beloved
Is the idyll of my passion.)[26]

Poems in this style lauded the Virgin of Guadalupe, the faithful *novia* (girlfriend or betrothed), the loving mother; lamented the downfall of the golden-hearted whore, the too-trusting wife; and cursed mothers-in-law and women whose black eyes, soft skin, and golden hair disguised their "indifference to my sufferings." Some poems favored a more practical than romantic mode. Another from *El Diablito Rojo*, for example, provided a working definition of a good woman:

La joven que el bien conoce, cose;
la que odia la mancha, ó baba, lava;
la que a lo pulcro se engancha, plancha;
la que es al deber sumisa, guisa;
De aquí formando premisa,
Se deduce a mi entender
que toda buena mujer
cose, lava, plancha y guisa.

(She who knows good, sews;
she that hates stains, or drool, washes;
she that clings to neatness, irons;
she that submits to duty, cooks;
From the premise that emerges,
According to my understanding
all good women
sew, wash, iron, and cook.)[27]

Although, as these examples suggest, most poems were fairly predictable and decidedly misogynistic, the best demonstrate a subtle humor as in an *El Chile Piquin* story in verse about starstruck lovers—Alberto and the beautiful Clara—whose marriage (and sex life) are revived when Clara seduces the overworked Alberto into initiating sexual relations by pretending to be cold. After a few weeks of this ruse, an exhausted Alberto responds with, "Pues si tienes frío, chica / Pégale fuego a la cama [If you're so cold woman / Set fire to the bed]."[28]

Around the edges of these poetic contributions, editors provided jokes, anecdotes, and bits of advice. An editorial paragraph preceding the first poem cited earlier, for example, advised readers that "el corazón de la mujer puede muy bien compararse á un jardin, que si se le cultiva ofrece la continua sucesión de frutos y flores . . . más si se le deja inculto, sólo produce en abundancia malas yerbas [a woman's heart can be profitably compared to a garden that if cultivated offers an endless succession of fruits and flowers . . . but if left untended only produces an abundance of bad weeds]."[29] The flower metaphor was a favorite: filler from *El Duende* included the following aphorism: "La mujer virtuosa es una flor cuyos pétalos el hombre muchas veces marchita, arrojándola al vicio [The virtuous woman is a flower whose petals men often wither, throwing her into vice]."[30] To reinforce the point, the saying was accompanied by a graphic image depicting a seducer of women (*tenorio de barrio*) at work. Not all anecdotes were so smug and unambiguous. For example, a story appearing with the second *El Diablito Rojo* poem cited earlier told the humorous tale of a jealous philanderer who confesses to a *sacristán* hiding behind a talking statue of St. Anthony that he is having an affair with the sacristán's wife (at which point the sacristán pushes the statue and the philander flees in terror). The story ended with this moral:

Fue un milagro ese de ayer
El adulterio prever
quiere el santo . . . y autoriza
para que diaria paliza
dé el esposo a su mujer.

(A miracle happened just yesterday
In order to forestall adultery
the saint wishes . . . and authorizes
that a daily beating
be given by the husband to his wife.)[31]

Regardless of approach, these male discussions about gender relations provided a common ground for the exploration and interpretation of men's lived experience (which as the last poem suggests might include religiously sanctioned violence against women). At some archetypal level, these discussions may even have supplied scripts—confused, convoluted, contradictory scripts to be sure—for male life in the modern age.

A Spectrum of Female Virtue

Male scripts for modern living or not, penny press poems about women also offer useful insights into the psyches of working-class men (whether as authors or readers). Even a cursory glance at the poetry reveals a rather rigid spectrum of female virtue with the Virgin of Guadalupe representing the idealized woman at one end and La Valentina as the unrepentant prostitute at the other.[32] Each of these archetypes had its uses. For example, the author of an *El Chile Piquin* poem "A la Virgen del Tepeyac [To the Virgin of Tepeyac]" addresses Guadalupe as a trusted confidante to whom he can voice his innermost thoughts:

Oh virgen, de mi patria la más hermosa,
La más dulce y más tierna de las amigas,
Ya sabes mi ensueñita color de rosa;
Arrodillado espere que lo bendiga.

(Oh virgin of my homeland the loveliest,
The sweetest and gentlest of friends,
You already know my sweet rosy dream;
On my knees I ask that you bless it.)[33]

Another poet—writing this time for an Antonio Vanegas Arroyo broadside, "María la del cielo [Mary who art in heaven]"—appeals to her as the ideal mother-intercessor:

Concédeme ¡oh madre! la paz que yo anhelo
Mándame el consuelo, tened compasión
Que el rey de los reyes que junto a ti mora
Pídele Señora de esta alma el perdón.

Figure 6.3. Popular representations of the Virgin of Guadalupe by José Guadalupe Posada. In the top print, the Virgin appears in a maguey cactus. In the bottom print, a woman prays to the Virgin while her drunk husband rages.

(Grant me, oh mother, the peace that I desire
Send me consolation, have compassion
Of the king of kings who with you resides
Ask him, lady of my soul, pardon.)[34]

As the purest exemplar of Mexican womanhood, the Virgin of Guadalupe served penny press poets as a point of comparison to the women in their lives—a comparison encouraged perhaps by the extraordinary number of Mexican women named either María or Guadalupe. The author of "A la Virgen del Tepeyac," in another verse of the poem just cited, compares her to his novia, "Como tú morenita, como tú buena, / Tiene tus negros ojos, tu negro pelo . . . [Like you she's dark, like you good / She has your black eyes, your black hair . . .]." Others chose to compare daughters, cousins, and, of course, mothers. Most of these comparisons were flattering tokens of appreciation and love. Sometimes, however, poets kept the comparison deliberately vague as in "A Guadalupe [To Guadalupe]," submitted to *El Chile Piquin* by "Un carpintero, M. S. [A carpenter, M. S.]." In this poem, although the name and description match the Virgin, there is no mention of virtue, only a string of flattering physical characteristics—hair blacker than jet, wide eyes, well-formed nose, little mouth, red lips, white skin, tiny waist—and the final verse:

En fin, eres hechicera,
Hermosa, muy rebonita.
Sí mi Guadalupita
Te quiero yo de deveras.

(In conclusion, you're bewitching,
Lovely, oh so pretty.
Yes my sweet Guadalupe
I love you and that's for sure.)[35]

Regardless of approach, for penny press poets the Virgin of Guadalupe embodied the noblest female virtues—trust, compassion, virtue, beauty—and represented an ideal against which the women in their lives could, would, and even should be measured. The following editorial from *El Diablito Rojo* leaves no doubts as to the woman's proper role in a working-class household:

VALENTINA

NUEVO CORRIDO

Una pasión me domina,
es la que me ha hecho venir
Valentina, Valentina,
yo te quisiera decir:

Que por esos tus amores
la vida voy a perder;
si me han de matar mañana
que me maten de una vez.

Si porque tomo tequila,
cerveza o puro jerez,
si porque me ves borracho
mañana ya no me ves.

Valentina, Valentina
dicen que me han de matar;
queriéndome tú: mi vida
¿qué me importa lo demás?

Y sé que me andan cazando
de tu casa en el zaguán,
que tanto estoy ahí entrando
y que en él voy a quedar.

Valentina, Valentina
te suplico esta vez
que si me dejan tirado,
me vayas a recojer.

Si tú me quieres mi nena,
aunque no tengo temor
que me defiendan morena,
tus caricias y tu amor.

No hay quien se atreva conmigo,
pues saben que han de perder,
si me tantean tan seguido
que me hablen de una vez.

UnaJuana y otra Juana
dos Juanas tengo a la vez,
una me tiende la cama
y otra me da de comer.

Dicen que por tus amores
la vida voy a perder,
nada me hacen los traidores
tan sólo con tu querer.

Una pasión me domina
es la que me ha hecho venir,
Valentina, Valentina
yo te quiero hasta el morir.

Y si muero Valentina,
yé muerto te he de querer
y una flor en mi tumba
tú me tendrás que poner.

Esa flor, mi Valentina,
siempreviva ha de ser
que simbolice el cariño
y el amor de una mujer.

Que el amor cuando fué firme
aún muriendo debe arder
en el corazón que vive
como un inmenso poder.

Medio-paso de moda.

Triste está mi corazón
por verte de medio paso,
pues pareces un payaso
al salir de la función;
y siento desilusión
viéndote andar con trabajo,
que ya te vas boca-abajo
que te das un tropezón,
y mi pobre corazón
te mira como tasajo.

Yo te aconsejo Angelita
que la falda no sea angosta,
pues más pareces langosta
y no muchacha bonita;
ántes ibas tiernecita
por las calles caminando
y la cadera meneando
con donaire y con soltura,
y hoy pareces figura
de las que estan anunciando.

Si se trata de subir
o se trata de bajar,
las medias hay que enseñar
o la falda se ha de abrir;
por eso no has de lucir
el vestido tan pegado,
porque un cuerpo modelado
á cualquiera hace reír,
y tú debes concebir
que hasta parece pecado.

Si critico tu vestido
y digo que es un fracaso
es porque andando no das
ni siquiera el medio paso;
y si el género es escaso
o de mala condición,
no te pongas polizón
ni la cadera postiza,
que siempre causarás risa
en cualquiera reunión.

Acuérdate que en los toros
no te podías ni sentar,
porque la faldita angosta
se comenzaba a trepar;
y aunque eras puro jalar
la faldita de adelante,
no faltó ningún tunante
que te quisiera ayudar,
y tú ya estabas jadeante
de jalar y más jalar.

Para la escultura humana
no es forzoso el medio paso,
que belleza soberana
no de andar como payaso;
y si te pongo por caso
lo que dijo Campoamor,
es porque me dá dolor
verte como una escopeta,
o apretada cual maleta
y perdiendo hasta el pudor.

Imprenta de A. Vanegas Arroyo 2a. de Santa Teresa 40 México —1915.

Figure 6.4. An Antonio Vanegas Arroyo broadside of La Valentina. The first line of the famous song reads, "A passion dominates me / it is the thing that made me come." Source: Antonio Vanegas Arroyo, "La Valentina: Nuevo Corrido," 1915.

> In the household of the worker himself is the solution: it's the woman. With few exceptions, the companion of the worker is self-denying, virtuous, economical, and hardworking. She should cover up with intelligent manipulation, and even with her own work, the deficiencies of the father, of the husband, of the brother; she should balance the budget with economy: she should oppose the idiocies, dissipations, and unnecessary expenses of the spendthrift worker.[36]

Aside from the stress on household budgets, the virtuous, self-denying woman with the redemptive mission is a true Guadalupe of the worker's household—and much the moral superior of her lord and master.

Male devotion of a different sort characterized symbols of womanhood from the opposite end of the moral spectrum. La Valentina, the unrepentant whore with the heart of gold, who sent men singing valiantly to their deaths—"Si me han de matar mañana, que me maten de una vez [If they have to kill me tomorrow, let them kill me quickly]"—was a particular favorite despite and because of her impurity.[37] Other "indecent" women received similar attention. In a *La Guacamaya* poem, "A. Omar," praises the grace and beauty of the prostitute "Manola," adding that:

> No importa que tus miradas
> Ni tampoco tus sonrisas
> Ni tus ardientes caricias
> Estén por todas compradas.
>
> (It matters not that your glances
> Nor even your smiles
> Nor your ardent caresses
> Be all of them purchased.)[38]

Some men even expressed sympathy for the plight of disgraced women as well as admiration for their physical charms. In a don Cucufate poem aptly titled "La mujer caída [The Fallen Woman]," the poet admonishes the reader:

> ¡Nunca insultéis á la mujer caída!
> Nadie sabe qué paso la agobió,
> Ni cuantas pruebas soportó en la vida
> Hasta que al fin cayó.

(Never insult a fallen woman!
No one knows what step crushed her,
Nor how many tests she passed in life
Before she finally fell.)[39]

As these poems suggest, on the surface at least, the penny press spectrum of female virtue was far from subtle. That good women are associated with social reproduction (Guadalupe's ribbon signifies pregnancy) while bad women remain barren (in a social if not necessarily biological sense) is no great surprise. Nor is the typically Catholic virgin/whore binary. Nor is the trope of betrayal (originating of course with La Malinche/Eve) that serves as the boundary marker between good women and bad.[40] A short prose piece on "Perfiles femininos (Female profiles)" for *El Diablito Rojo* marked the difference: "The good woman is an angel, the bad woman is the devil: the first is a ray of light that illuminates the home: the second torments good and bad."[41] The focus, however, was more often on bad women. An *El Diablito Rojo* poet, borrowing a strophe from a popular poem for his humorous account of "Adán y Eva [Adam and Eve]" put it succinctly enough:

Una mujer fué la causa
De la perdición primera.
No hay perdición en el mundo
Que por mujeres no venga.

(A woman was the cause
Of the first perdition [fall from grace].
There's no perdition in the world
That does not come from women.)[42]

Even the intermediate mother figures are represented as crude archetypes. For instance, beloved mothers are spared the sarcastic wit of *El Diablito Rojo*'s annual *calavera* (skull) issue for Day of the Dead that included this effusive poem dedicated to "El Congreso de Madres [Mothers' Congress]":

Nardos y flores lozanas,
en aromático torneo,

perfuman el mausoleo
de las Madres Mexicanas;
y en las radiantes mañanas,
cuando el astro rey fulgura
se ve un ángel: la Ternura,
y en la callada quietud,
otro ángel: la Gratitud
nimba aquella sepultura.

(Tuberoses and other luxuriant flowers,
in aromatic competition
perfume the mausoleum of the Mothers of Mexico;
and in the radiant mornings,
when the star king shines
appears an angel: Tenderness,
and in the hushed quiet,
another angel: Gratitude
graces that tomb.)[43]

Less powerful than the Virgin, the mother's role was principally the consolation of male children (of all ages) as in the following verse from a poem, "A mi Madre [To My Mother]," written for *La Palanca* by a self-identified "worker":

Quisiera estar á tu lado
Recibiendo tu cariño
Como cuando yo era niño
Y no como hoy . . . desgraciado.

(I would love to be at your side
Receiving your affection
Like when I was a child
And not like now . . . forlorn.)[44]

Less frequent but no less laudatory are poems dedicated to beloved grandmothers and even an occasional wet nurse, "porque tus pechos me dieron de mamar cuando era niño [because your breasts suckled me when I was a child]."[45]

PLEITO DE LA SUEGRA CON SU YERNO.

YA LA VIEJA DE MI SUEGRA
NOMAS QUIERE REGAÑAR,
DEATIRO LA CORTA VERDE
NO LA DEJA MADURAR.

Suegra—Oye yerno del demonio,
Zambo, patas de Judío,
¡Ojalá que una venida
Te llevara en un gran rìo!
Con el silloncito mío
Moro te voy á poner,
Pues debes de suponer,
Que te quiero castigar:
Deatiro la cortas verde,
No la dejas madurar.

Yerno—Cállese vieja zorrilla,
Jorobada, patituerta;
No me venga á molestar
Ni se pare por mi puerta.
Porque á mí nada me cuesta
Darle una buena paliza,
Volverla cual longaniza,
Y después ponerla á asar:
Deatiro la corta verde,
No la deja madurar.

Suegra—¡Qué diablo de cacarizo
Gon su cara de pan crudo!
Ojalá se le metiera
En el cuerpo un diablo mudo
Solo mi pobre hija pudo
Querer á tan gran zoquete
Te he de llevar del copete
A tirarte al muladar:
Deatiro la cortas verde,
No la dejas madurar.

Yerno—Vieja de todos los diablos,
Retrato de Barrabás
De buena gana quisiera
Quemarla con aguarrás
No puedo aguantarla más,
Pues solo verla me choca;
Portal sin gente es su boca,
No para de rezongar:
Deatiro la corta verde,
No la deja madurar.

Suegra—Tienes hocico de perro
Buldó con tamañas getas
Colgando como cortinas
Y como un carbón de prietas
Tus piernas parecen zetas,
Tu cuerpo parece sapo,
Con figura de macaco
Se te puede retratar:
Deatiro la cortas verde,
No la dejas madurar.

Yerno—¡Ay! que vieja tan bonita
Con esas patas de polla
Y la barriga tan grande
Como el globo de cantoya!
Su ombligo parece olla
De esas de hacer nixtamal,
De su boca de comal
Nomás se oye murmurar:
Deatiro la corta verde,
No la deja madurar.

Figure 6.5. A Vanegas Arroyo broadside depicting a "mother-in-law's fight with her son-in-law." The caption reads, "And that old lady, my mother-in-law / Only thing she does is scold / Weeds should be cut green / Don't let them mature." Source: Antonio Vánegas Arroyo, "Pleito de la suegra con su yerno," 1911.

Mothers-in-law, on the other hand, were demons or worse. As one *El Diablito Rojo* poet lamented:

No me deja un punto en paz
y aguantarla más no puedo:
regañona, lenguaraz . . .
y luego es mujer capaz
de pegarle un susto al miedo.

(She never lets anything slide
and stand her I no longer can:
scolding, sharp-tongued . . .
and then she's a woman able
to put a fright in fear.)[46]

Another agreed that "pagué caro mi descuido de haber adorado á su hija [I paid a high price for the mistake of having adored her daughter]."[47] More horrifying still is the Vanegas Arroyo broadside, "Pleito de la suegra con su yerno [A mother-in-law's dispute with her son-in-law]," with its graphic depiction of interfamily violence (probably by Posada) and two pages of colorful invective.[48]

Regardless of considerable differences among poets—style, linguistic facility, word choice, talent—the symbolic content of these poems is remarkably static. In fact, at the structural level, the penny press spectrum of female virtue could serve equally well for the colonial era (and earlier), and this timeless quality doubtless served to naturalize and even sacralize it.[49] A closer reading, however, suggests that things were not quite as timeless as they seemed. In the traditional honor/shame complex, male honor and female shame (*vergüenza*) were first and foremost public qualities. Among the upper classes, loss of honor or shame could damage the reputations and thus the fortunes of entire extended families by undermining the social prestige essential to the family network's political and economic success. For the lower classes, community acceptance could mean the difference between rough times and starvation as dishonorable men and women were considered untrustworthy and unworthy of community aid. Betrayal in this context involved much more than personal feelings, and its consequences often reverberated throughout the patria chica. The fear of public humiliation hovers around the edges of penny press writings on gender relations, and turn-of-the-century court records indicate that it was still very much on people's minds.[50]

Betrayal and Intimacy

Nevertheless, the act that reoccurs with obsessive regularity in penny press poetry was of a different order altogether: a wrenching betrayal of personal intimacy and trust that sends the poet reeling toward madness, death, and the abyss. The nineteenth-century romantic tradition bears some responsibility, especially for the overwrought style. There is even an occasional touch of the Parnassian symbolism of Mexican modernist poets like Manuel Gutiérrez Nájera, Salvador Díaz Mirón, and Amado Nervo—all of whom tried their hand at journalism. But the layers of cloying sentimentality and classical allusion obscured a fundamental change in gender ideology—a "transformation of intimacy," sociologist Anthony Giddens calls it—with profound implications for male subjectivity.

In colonial society, men became recognizable subjects at least in a sociopolitical sense through their corporate identities and were just as likely to locate intimacy in homosocial as heterosexual settings. Personal relations

Figure 6.6. These popular collections of love letters published by Vanegas Arroyo and engraved by Posada depict the transformation of intimacy with its stress on romantic love.

between men and women (sons and mothers, husbands and wives, brothers and sisters) no doubt played an important role in forming and maintaining male subjects, but these relationships were not identified as the sine qua non of male subjectivity. In most societies with aspirations to modernity, however, male-female relationships based on heterosexual intimacy provide the privileged site for the formation and maintenance of both male and female subjects. A contributor to *El Chile Piquin*'s regular column "Piquines en vinagre [Hot chilis in vinegar]" explained it this way:

Dice Pepita Rabás,
Que *uno* y *uno* hacían dos.
Muy equivocada estás,
Le dijo su prima Amós.
Qué ha de estar equivocada?
No me cabe duda alguna.
Uno y *uno* hacen nada,
Querrás decir *uno* y *una*.

(Says Pepita Rabás,
That *one* and *one* makes two.
How wrong you are,
Her cousin Amos replied.
What do you mean wrong?
I have not a single doubt.
One and *one* makes nothing,
You mean to say *man* plus *woman*.)[51]

A *San Lunes* poet provided a typically romantic formulation of the same sentiment with the aptly titled "Intima [Intimate]":

Doquiera vayas, doquiera alientes,
Siempre á tu paso me has de encontrar.
Pues tú y yo somos como dos fuentes,
Que ciegas corren al mismo mar.

(Wherever you go, wherever you breathe,
You'll always find me right behind.

Because you and I are like two springs,
That run blindly into the same sea.)[52]

Traditional notions of honor and shame were generally understood by most everyone and apparently required little comment or explanation except perhaps in front of a judge or in community disputes where they were invoked for ritual effect. The powerful new linkages between heterosexual intimacy and male subjectivity were not so easily incorporated into everyday consciousness, hence the compulsive, anxious, derivative quality of most penny press verse.

Behind these constant reiterations of male anxieties about female betrayal lay the specter of violence against women. A poem from *El Diablito Rojo* addressed the issue head-on with the following "Consejos [Advice]" from a deceived man:

Y cuando [del amor] se trata
el que no es tonto, prefiere
al golpe con que se muere
el golpe con que se mata.

(And when it has to do with love
he that's not a fool, prefers
to the blow from which he dies
the blow with which he kills.)[53]

Most poets, however, focused instead on the psychic violence inflicted on them by their female tormentors as in this "Queja (Complaint)" from *La Guacamaya*:

Tú has aumentado esas penas,
Desdeñando mis amores.
Tú has marchitado las flores,
De mi primera illusión.
Tú me niegas inhumana,
La paz que anhela mi alma.
Tú me has robado la calma,
La quietud del corazón.

(You have increased these torments,
By disdaining my love.
You have withered the flowers,
Of my first illusion.
You deny me cruel one,
The peace that annihilates my soul.
You have stolen the calm,
The stillness of the heart.)[54]

That the women in their lives threatened these men even to the point of violence is clear, even though the direction of that violence is not. Still, there is something more going on in these poems than a straightforward female challenge to traditional male authority.

Abjection and the Male Subject

That something else, I would argue, is abjection: a psychological state or psychic condition produced by the gendered dialectic of desire and rejection (of desire) in which the subject (identified as male) is both irresistibly drawn to and inevitably repulsed by the abject (identified as female).[55] This dialectic occurs too often in penny press poetry to be merely coincidental. The just-cited "Queja" is only one example of hundreds of penny press poems about female betrayal. Most follow the same formula: innocent love → promise of fidelity → betrayal → abjection. "A una ingrata [To a disdainful woman]" from *El Diablito Rojo* provides a concise example of the genre:

A una mujer amé, tan solo en ella
cifraba mi ilusión
Y tranquilo, fiado en su cariño
felíz vivía yo.
Mas ¡ay! Mis esperanzas halagüeñas
eran humo nomás,
que el viento de la pérfida inconstancia
hubo de arrebatar.
Las horas de ventura que sencillo,
soñó mi corazón
trocáronse en amargo desconsuelo,
en pena y en dolor.

NUEVOS VERSOS
DEL APASIONADO.

BONITOS VERSOS DEL APASIONADO
QUE LO HIZO GUAJE UNA MUJER,
COMO LA SUPO QUERER . . . .
¡SEÑORES SE HA EMBORRACHADO!

¡Ay amigo qué dolor . . . . !
¿Qué le pasa querido amigo . . .?
¡Qué ya muy borracho estoy . . !
¿Y porqué querido amigo . . . .?

Por una mujer que quiero
La que es hoy mi perdición,
Me gastó mucho dinero;
Y me jugó una traición . . . .

Lo compadezco amigo . . . !
¿Búsquese un nuevo amor . . . .?
No puedo querido amigo;
Es muy grande mi dolor.

¡Pues qué le dijo ella amigo...!

Pues me dijo que me amaba
Con muy ardiente pasión;
Yo muchos besos le daba;
Y con ellos mi corazón.
Recuerdo que me decía
Gon amor, esa mujer,
Yo te quiero prenda mía;
Tu eres todo mi querer.

¿Y ahora que piensa amigo...!

Mucho aguardienta beber,
Por ella seguir tomando;
Mi gusto tiene que ser
El andarme emborrachando.
Tuve un sueño en que la ví,
Ella me decía; aquí estoy,
Al despertar la perdí;
Que desgraciado yo soy . . . .

Figure 6.7. This Vanegas Arroyo broadside depicts a man in despair over a heartless woman. The caption reads, "Pretty verses of a desperate man / made a fool by a woman / as you might expect . . . / Gentlemen, he had to get drunk." Source: José Guadalupe Posada Collection of Popular Mexican Prints (PICT 999-019-0076), Center for Southwest Research, University Libraries, University of New Mexico.

Loco, desesperado, delirante,
con ciego frenesí,
olvidando la vida y sus encantos
solo pensé en morir.
Y una noche, dejando la morada
donde habita la infiel,
fui al viaducto á arrojarme decidido
pero . . . no me arrojé.

(I once loved a woman, only in her
did I place my dreams
And tranquil, sure of her affection
I lived happily.
But, oh! My alluring hopes
were nothing more than smoke,
that the perfidious, inconstant wind
was bound to snatch away.
The hours of simple happiness,
I dreamed in my heart
changed to bitter disconsolation,
to suffering and pain.
Crazy, desperate, delirious,
with blind frenzy,
forgetting life and its enchantments
I only thought of death.
And one night, leaving the dwelling
where the unfaithful one lives,
I went to the canal, determined to throw myself in,
but . . . I did not do it.)[56]

In this poem, betrayal produces first despair and, by strophe four, insanity—a frenzied, disconsolate, delirious madness so intense that it nearly results in suicide. Given a Mexican popular imaginary that includes the ghost woman, La Llorona, condemned to search forever along the edges of rivers and lakes for her children drowned by her own hand, the decision to choose death by drowning as a response to female betrayal is no accident but an obvious symptom of abjection. The final line with its pregnant ellipsis is just as suggestive: just what did the poet do instead of drowning himself? If, as Martha Reineke argues, "any woman may be marked for murder when subjects who struggle to resecure their roles in the Symbolic invest her body with the effects of that abject struggle," then poems like these give the penny press hierarchy of female virtue a new, more ominous meaning.[57]

In this context, the issue of symbolic stability (rather than virtue) becomes paramount. The Virgin of Guadalupe and La Valentina represent stable female archetypes, while the ambivalent figures of the lover, novia (girlfriend), and wife (symbolized by Eve/La Malinche) inhabit the boundaries of the abject where symbols lose their stability and threaten the male subject with dissolution. The inherent symbolic instability of women is clearly delineated in this advice column, "Cómo debe ser la mujer [How a woman ought to be]," from *El Diablito Rojo*:

> Las mujeres deben ser como el sol, porque dan vida; pero no deben ser como el sol, porque tiene muchas manchas.
>
> Deben parecerse á la luna, porque es compañera inseparable de la tierra; pero no deben parecerse á la luna porque tiene muchas caras.
>
> Deben ser como los espejos, que reproducen con fidelidad las imágenes; pero no deben ser como los espejos porque no todas las verdades se pueden decir.
>
> Deben parecerse al vino, porque está lleno de espíritu; pero no deben parecerse al vino que trastorna el juicio de las gentes.
>
> (Women should be like the sun, because they give life; but they should not be like the sun, because it has many spots [stains].
>
> They should seem like the moon, because it is the inseparable companion of the earth; but they shouldn't seem like the moon because it has many faces.
>
> They should be like mirrors, that faithfully reproduce images; but they should not be like mirrors because not all truths can be told.
>
> They should seem like wine, because it is full of spirit; but they should not seem like wine, because it clouds people's judgment.)[58]

Most of the binary oppositions in this piece reflect long-standing male concerns about women's shame, trustworthiness, and desirability (especially to other men). The play with mirrors, however, is surprising and surprisingly revealing. While it is doubtful that penny press authors had read much psychoanalytic theory, this writer at least seems to have intuited (or perhaps gleaned from symbolist poetry) a psychic connection between mirrors and subjectivity. The woman's faithful reproduction of the male subject is fairly obvious; but just what were the "truths" that cannot be told? According to Reineke, the feminized abject also marks the principal site of physical violence as the desperate subject faced with dissolution engages in "killing substance to make it signify."[59] As in the previously cited "Consejos," confronted by the annihilating power of the abject, "el que no es tonto, prefiere / al golpe con que se muere / el golpe con que se mata [he that is not a fool, prefers / to the blow from which he dies / the blow with which he kills]."

Toward a Modern Sacrificial Economy

Signification, then, transforms the "random" act of violence into a sacrificial ritual in which the subject's otherwise inexcusable attack on the abjected woman restores psychological order in the subject and social order (as an "exemplary" punishment).[60] The onset of modernity in Mexico City dramatically altered the cultural logic of female sacrifice. In the corporate society of the patria chica, the community publicly acknowledged the threat to social order, ritualized the sacrifice (as in witch burnings), and then sacralized the victims in order to obscure the violence involved. The breakdown of community identity, although more an ongoing process than an accomplished fact even in a rapidly expanding Mexico City, made these "dominant fictions" more difficult to maintain.

Just as public displays of state power were "hidden" in modern societies as executions moved from public spaces to behind prison walls, so too was the sacrifice of women. Pushed symbolically and legally into the private sphere and the confines of heterosexual intimacy, female sacrifice could be dispersed throughout society, disguised as random acts, and disavowed as the work of uncivilized (usually) lower-class men while, at the same time, continuing to produce and reproduce the patriarchal social order. It is no coincidence, then, that Mexico's first serial killer, El Chalequero, would appear on the scene at just this time (with requisite images by Posada), where he would be joined in the pages of la nota roja and in the popular criminology of journalist-turned-police inspector Carlos Roumagnac by infamous wife killers like Arnulfo Villegas. These men—both from Mexico City's lower classes—represented the sensational "exemplary" perpetuators of violence against women.[61] More "routine" violence against women, however, was downplayed both in the press and by the judicial system. According to Pablo

Figure 6.8. Posada illustrations of murdered women. The print on the bottom right depicts the serial killer known as "El Chalequero." The horrified men in the upper prints and the priest and police on the lower left serve to differentiate "monsters" from "normal" men.

Piccato, "Courts interpreted most cases of domestic violence in the same way that they viewed same-sex violence about the urban poor: a feature of the less 'civilized' areas of urban life but nothing to be too concerned about."[62] This lack of concern is reflected in dismally low conviction rates for sex crimes: one in five men arrested for rape between 1897 and 1900 were convicted.[63]

Roumagnac explained the "obvious" difference between extreme and routine violence against women in terms of biological and social degeneration. Men like El Chalequero and Arnulfo Villegas, he insisted:

> Have no age, are not the product of a certain class; have been, are, and will be of all epochs and all types of men—I was going to write animals . . . and wherever we turn our eyes, we encounter, by the thousands, cases of these infractions that reveal to us the extremes that can be reached by the degeneration, exaggeration, or perversion of an instinct.[64]

While Roumagnac does concede that sexual predators (he was going to write "animals") come from all classes and races of men, he also deploys the scientific jargon of psychology—*degeneration*, *perversion*, *instinct*—to suggest that they are anomalous and atavistic (throwbacks to an earlier, more primitive stage of human evolution) rather than normal and civilized. This distancing strategy allows these predators to serve a disciplinary function but obscures the systemic aspects of violence against women and encourages women's subordination to men for the sake of protection. "Aberrant" acts thus support (add symbolic power to) less publicized forms of violence from "routine" wife beatings to piropos (verbal harassment) to psychological cruelty without implicating these "lesser" acts and their perpetuators in systemic violence against women. Moreover, despite Roumagnac's willingness to universalize and dehistoricize the perpetrators of extreme sex crimes, the specific historical circumstances surrounding the appearance of his work favored a classist interpretation. In Victorian England, public narratives about sexual predators like Jack the Ripper often featured upper-class men; in Porfirian Mexico the focus was almost exclusively on lower-class "monsters."[65]

Piccato makes a convincing case that violence against women occurred far more often in turn-of-the-century Mexico City than legal activity and criminological treatises would allow. And in answer to the rhetorical questions of why public opinion could contemplate such violence as a natural part of domestic life and how those men could avoid punishment, he responds:

> Patriarchal traditions are only part of the explanation. The answer also lies in the transformation of early-twentieth-century Mexico City, as urban communities adapted to the challenge of survival in an urban environment characterized by labor instability, migration, and an authoritarian regime. Marital instability and the need to control the family's labor were the factors which, in this context, made sense of private violence.[66]

These ideological and functional explanations for widespread violence against women are surely right. Certainly urbanization, changing relations of production, and political repression placed tremendous stress on the Mexico City working classes (and probably on the bourgeoisie as well) and prompted a patriarchal backlash that was both practical and defensive (for

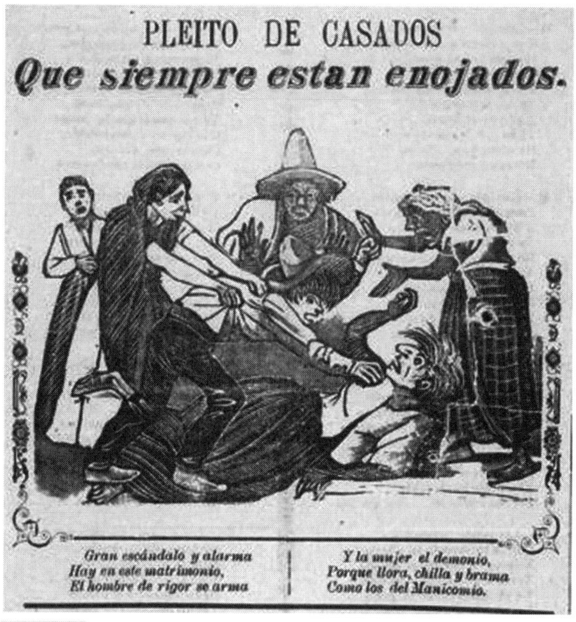

Figure 6.9. These images from Posada depict different styles of male violence against women. The top print of a working-class marital dispute, "Fight of a married couple who when they're not fighting are enraged," includes a knife-wielding man and community involvement. The couple in the four small bottom prints belong to the respectable middle classes; there's no weapon other than the man's fist, and there's no community involvement.

both classes). Nevertheless, Piccato's own evidence suggests an important psychological dimension as well. El Chalequero told Roumagnac that he had killed his victims because they had wounded "su amor propio del macho [his male self-esteem]," while Arnulfo Villegas proposed to his future victim with the astonishingly Oedipal, "The only thing I wish and hope to have found in you is someone to live with happily with God's blessing, someone I can proudly name as a substitute for my mother."[67] As the penny press poems cited earlier demonstrate, reactions like these were more ubiquitous than anomalous. And, since investment in heterosexual intimacy characterized male subjectivity, regardless of class status, these responses connect the systemic violence that they symbolically underwrite to middle- and upper-class men in ways that Piccato's more ideological and functionalist analysis cannot. Certainly the poetic sentiments expressed in the satiric penny press differ only in verbosity and artistic pretension from those of their "betters."[68] And, as Posada's images suggest, for working-class and bourgeois male subjects violence against women was often more a matter of style than substance.

The stress on psychic violence to men (rather than physical violence to women) in penny press poetry is perhaps the most egregious example of the cultural logic of the sacrificial economy at work. Violence against women may well have pervaded Mexico City life, but its systematic erasure from most texts—the ambiguous ellipsis in "but . . . I didn't do it" aside—served quite effectively to disguise its systemic nature. When poets, like the author of the previously quoted "Consejos," did acknowledge that fears of betrayal provoked male violence against women, it was nearly always as a joke—the tongue-in-cheek performance of male toughness for the benefit of other men. As noted in this chapter's introduction, the popular image from *La Guacamaya* of two squatting, working-class men throwing out piropos (suggestive comments) about a passing bourgeois woman's calves reveals a certain defensive resentment about their marginal social status and a covert threat of violence. The covert threat, however, takes on grim overtones when situated in historical context: Arnulfo Villegas was a self-employed butcher, and El Chalequero, known for expertly slitting the throats of his victims, had worked in his father's butcher shop as a teenager. "Ganado para el nuevo Rastro [Cattle for the New Slaughterhouse]" might use humor to make the potential violence more apparent to the reader, but the woman's worried expression suggests that she understands the seriousness of her situation (see Figure 6.1). Still, as Reineke points out, although "laughter is the primary symptom of rupture or breakdown in signification . . . in the eruption of laughter, as laughter passes to expression, laughter binds one over to order once again, preserving only for an instant that fragile movement of negativity that gives birth to subjectivity."[69] The joke might momentarily expose the act of violence that restores the subject to its place in the symbolic order, but its real purpose was "diversion"—the abrogation of responsibility for an act that the author did not in fact commit. Not exactly a conspiracy of silence but pernicious all the same. If there was some subversive, irrepressible "remainder" that might nag at a (male) reader's conscience, it was likely small consolation to the (female) victims of a new sacrificial economy.

NOTES

1. Special thanks to Elisa Speckman Guerra, Claudia Agostoni, Rachel Buff, Pablo Piccato, Ricardo Salvatore, Sandra Gayol, Natalia Lamberto, Eithne Luibhéid, and the Institute for the Study of Culture and Society Writing Group at Bowling Green State University for their help with this article.
2. The image appears in two issues of *La Guacamaya* with different verses on the subject of bourgeois women as "meat." "Ganado para el nuevo Rastro," *La Guacamaya*, March 23, 1905, and "Vigilia," *La Guacamaya*, December 28, 1905.
3. For more on Mexico City meat markets, see Jeffrey M. Pilcher, *The Sausage Rebellion: Public Health, Private Enterprise, and Meat in Mexico City, 1890–1917* (Albuquerque: University of New Mexico Press, 2006).
4. Francisco J. Santamaría, *Diccionario de mejicanismos*, 2nd ed. (Mexico City: Editorial Porrúa, 1974), 376; and Larry M. Grimes, *El tabú lingüístico en México: el lenguaje erótico de los mexicanos* (New York: Bilingual Press, 1978), 69.
5. See Pablo Piccato, *City of Suspects: Crime in Mexico City, 1900–1931* (Durham, NC: Duke University Press, 2001) and "'El Chalequero' or the Mexican Jack the Ripper: The Meanings of Sexual Violence in Turn-of-the-Century Mexico City," *Hispanic American Historical Review* 81 (2001): 623–51; Elisa Speckman Guerra, *Crimen y castigo: legislación penal, interpretaciones de la criminalidad y adminstración de justicia (Ciudad de México, 1872–1910)* (Mexico City: El Colegio de México/UNAM, 2002); Ana María Alonso, "Rationalizing Patriarchy: Gender, Domestic Violence, and Law in Mexico," *Identities* 2 (1995): 29–47; and Soledad González Montes, and Pilar Iracheta Cenegorta, "La violencia en la vida de las mujeres campesinas: el distrito de Tenango, 1880–1910" in *Presencia y transparencia: la mujer en la historia de México*, ed. Carmen Ramos Escandón et al., (Mexico City: El Colegio de México, 1987), 111–61.
6. For abusive men, see Oscar Lewis, *Five Families: Mexican Case Studies in the Culture of Poverty* (New York: Basic Books, 1959) and *The Children of Sánchez: Autobiography of a Mexican Family* (New York: Vintage Books, 1961); and Matthew C. Gutmann, *The Meanings of Macho: Being a Man in Mexico City* (Berkeley: University of California Press, 1996). For abused women, see Elena Poniatowska, *Hasta no verte Jesús mío* (Mexico City: Ediciones Era, 1969); Larissa Adler Lomnitz, *Networks and Marginality: Life in a Mexican Shanty Town* (New York: Academic Press, 1977); Sarah LeVine, *Dolor y Alegría: Women and Social Change in Urban Mexico* (Madison: University of Wisconsin Press, 1993); and Ruth Behar, *Translated Woman: Crossing the Border with Esperanza's Story* (Boston: Beacon Press, 1993).
7. Marjorie Becker, *Setting the Virgin on Fire: Lázaro Cárdenas, Michoacán Peasants, and the Redemption of the Mexican Revolution* (Berkeley: University of California Press, 1994). For a more carefully theorized version of a similar argument, see Steve J. Stern, *The Secret History of Gender: Women, Men, and Power in Late Colonial Mexico* (Chapel Hill: University of North Carolina Press, 1995). In

fairness to Stern, he is analyzing the cultural logic of a subaltern masculinity that predates the "transformation of intimacy."

8. This article also presumes that while male violence against women does indeed serve to maintain patriarchal domination, it more often occurs as a response to a perceived threat to male subjectivity rather than simply to restore male authority—although that is certainly one of its effects. On patriarchal ideologies and male subjectivities, see Kaja Silverman, *Male Subjectivity at the Margins* (New York: Routledge, 1992).
9. Homosocial intimacy and *patria chica* loyalties continue to characterize everyday social relations, however, and thus serve to heighten the prescriptive and administrative power of the regulatory norms that "restrain" them. The social construction of intimacy is theorized in Lauren Berlant and Michael Warner, "Sex in Public," in *Intimacy*, ed. Lauren Berlant (Chicago: University of Chicago Press, 2000).
10. According to sociologist Anthony Giddens, one of the principal social dislocations associated with modernity, "the waning of female complicity [in patriarchy]," has greatly exacerbated violence against women. He further insists that "a large amount of male sexual violence now stems from insecurity and inadequacy rather than from a seamless continuation of patriarchal dominance." *The Transformation of Intimacy: Sexuality, Love, and Eroticism in Modern Societies* (Stanford, CA: Stanford University Press, 1992), 122. Michael Kimmel reiterates these claims and provides statistical support in *The Gendered Society* (New York: Oxford University Press, 2000), 242–63.
11. On traditional sacrificial economies, see René Girard, *Violence and the Sacred*, trans. Patrick Gregory (Baltimore: Johns Hopkins University Press, 1977). My understanding of modern sacrificial economies is indebted to Martha J. Reineke, *Sacrificed Lives: Kristeva on Women and Violence* (Bloomington: Indiana University Press, 1997).
12. The best exposition of Mexican hybrid modernity is in Néstor García Canclini, *Hybrid Cultures: Strategies of Entering and Leaving Modernity*, trans. Christopher Chiappari and Silvia López (Minneapolis: University of Minnesota Press, 1995).
13. While most analysts, then and now, have accepted the premise that lower-class men are more likely to abuse women, there is no reliable evidence to support this foregone conclusion. We simply have more documents on the "private" lives of marginal men.
14. The links between subjectivity and cultural visibility are explored in Judith Butler, *Bodies That Matter: On the Discursive Limits of Sex* (New York: Routledge, 1993).
15. Secretaría de Economía, *Estadísticas sociales del porfiriato, 1877–1910* (Mexico City: Dirección General de Estadística, 1956), 9. During the same period, the Federal District grew from 327,500 to 720,750 (p. 7). In 1900 approximately half the population of the Federal District had been born somewhere else (p. 12). For Mexico City, the percentage of "outsiders" was even higher.

16. On these shifts in "social geography," see John Lear, *Workers, Neighbors, and Citizens: The Revolution in Mexico City* (Lincoln: University of Nebraska Press, 2001), 15–48. On the transgression of urban spaces, see Pablo Piccato, "Urbanistas, Ambulantes, and Mendigos: The Dispute for Urban Spaces in Mexico City, 1890–1930" in *Reconstructing Criminality in Latin America*, ed. Carlos Aguirre and Robert Buffington (Wilmington, DE: Scholarly Resources, 2000), 113–48; and Piccato, *City of Suspects*, chapter 2. On working-class consciousness and the satiric penny press, see María Elena Díaz, "The Satiric Penny Press for Workers in Mexico, 1900–1910: A Case Study in the Politicisation of Popular Culture," *Journal of Latin American Studies* 22 (1990): 497–525.
17. The statistics are from Lear, *Workers, Neighbors, and Citizens*, 49–85.
18. On the financial difficulties and poor working conditions of Porfirian journalists, see Florence Toussaint Alcaraz, *Escenario de la prensa en el Porfiriato* (Mexico City: Fundación Manuel Buendía, 1989), 57–60; and Henry Lepidus, "The History of Mexican Journalism," *The University of Missouri Bulletin* 29 (1928): 62–63.
19. Emilio Rabasa, *El Cuarto Poder* (Mexico City: Editorial Porrúa, 1970), 60.
20. Scholars as diverse as Jürgen Habermas, Raymond Williams, and Benedict Anderson have stressed the vital role played by newspapers in the development of modern societies. Habermas argues that the circulation of newspapers helped form a late-eighteenth-century bourgeois public sphere in which ideas about social organization and social justice could be freely debated (at least among the rising bourgeoisie); Williams notes their crucial contribution to bourgeois class-consciousness and revolutionary politics; and Anderson views them as essential to the construction of the "imagined community" that binds together the modern nation-state. Jürgen Habermas, *The Structural Transformation of the Public Sphere: An Inquiry into a Category of Bourgeois Society*, trans. Thomas Burger and Frederick Lawrence (Cambridge, MA: MIT Press, 1989); Raymond Williams, *The Long Revolution*, rev. ed. (New York: Harper and Row, 1961); and Benedict Anderson, *Imagined Communities: Reflections on the Origin and Spread of Nationalism*, rev. ed. (New York: Verso, 1991).
21. *La Guacamaya: periódico hablador y de buen humor, revalsador y decidor de verdades, no papero ni farolero, azote de los burgueses y defensor de la CLASE OBRERA*; *El Diablito Rojo: del pueblo y para el pueblo*; and *El Diablito Bromista: órgano de la clase obrera, azote del mal burgués y coco del mal gobierno*.
22. These figures probably exaggerate sales quite a bit—which is not to say that the papers were not widely distributed at least in Mexico City. For more on the thriving Mexico City newspaper business, see Phyllis Lynn Smith, "Contentious Voices Amid the Order: The Porfirian Press in Mexico City, 1876–1911," (PhD diss., University of Arizona, 1996); and Toussaint Alcaraz, *Escenario de la prensa en el Porfiriato*.
23. *El Periquito*, August 2, 1895. Reprinted in Jaime Soler and Lorenzo Avila, eds., *Posada y la prensa ilustrada: signos de modernización y resistencias* (Mexico City: Museo Nacional de Arte, 1996), 37.

24. There are several excellent works on Posada's prints, including Ron Tyler, ed., *Posada's Mexico* (Washington, D.C.: Library of Congress, 1979); Rafael Carillo A., *Posada y el grabado Mexicano* (Mexico City: Panorama Editorial, 1983); Soler and Avila, eds., *Posada y la prensa ilustrada*; and Patrick Frank, *Posada's Broadsheets: Mexican Popular Imagery, 1890–1910* (Albuquerque: University of New Mexico Press, 1998). Political analyses of the satiric penny press include Díaz, "The Satiric Penny Press for Workers in Mexico," and Lear, *Workers, Neighbors, and Citizens*, 91–106.
25. Editors' poems were often as refined in tone as those of their contributors but sometimes reflected a satirical bent that reader contributors generally avoided.
26. "Mi novia," *El Diablito Rojo*, September 17, 1900.
27. "Consecuencias," *El Diablito Rojo*, April 2, 1900.
28. "Que tengo frío," *El Chile Piquin*, January 19, 1905.
29. "El corazón de la mujer," *El Diablito Rojo*, September 17, 1900.
30. *El Duende*, November 15, 1904.
31. "La machincuepa de San Antón," *El Diablito Rojo*, April 2, 1900.
32. The Virgin of Guadalupe is the official Catholic patroness of Mexico (and all the Americas). In Mexican American gang culture, her image is often tattooed on men's bodies, although women are forbidden to do the same.
33. "A la Virgen del Tepeyac," *El Chile Piquin*, January 19, 1905. Tepeyac is the site where the Virgin of Guadalupe allegedly appeared to the poor Indian bearer Juan Diego in 1531; it is also the location of her shrine on the outskirts (at least in 1905) of Mexico City.
34. Imprenta de Antonio Vanegas Arroyo, "María la del cielo (danza)," 1911. Vanegas Arroyo ran the most important print shop in Mexico City but is best known for his patronage of Posada.
35. Un carpintero, M. S. "A Guadalupe," *El Chile Piquin*, February 19, 1905.
36. "Los dos grandes vicios de nuestros obreros: a quién debe encomendarse la moralización del proletario," *El Diablito Rojo*, June 1, 1908. Editors often printed romantic poems of their own composition but took a more didactic tone in editorials.
37. The song, a classic of the Mexican Revolution (1910–1920), was printed as a broadside along with an illustration of a curvaceous circus performer by Vanegas Arroyo. Imprenta de Antonio Vanegas Arroyo, "Valentina: nuevo corrido," 1915.
38. A. Omar, "A Manola," *La Guacamaya*, January 2, 1908. The author's pen name is derived from the Spanish word for love, *amor*.
39. "La mujer caída," *Don Cucufate*, September 3, 1906.
40. Eve and women as "the daughters of Eve" are mentioned often in the penny press; La Malinche—Cortés's translator, concubine, and alleged betrayer of Mexico—is not. Whether this omission is deliberate or not is open to debate. These days, however, those who "sell out," either economically or culturally, are openly condemned as *malinchistas*.

41. "Perfiles femeninos," *El Diablito Rojo*, April 25, 1910.
42. Emilio del Val., "Adan y Eva," *El Diablito Rojo*, September 3, 1900.
43. "El Congreso de Madres," *El Diablito Rojo*, November 2, 1908.
44. Gabino Néstor Cerrillo, Obrero, "A mi Madre," *La Palanca*, November 27, 1904.
45. For examples, see J. Manuel Huerta, hijo, "A mi Abuelita," and Pesares, "A mi nodriza," *El Diablito Rojo*, September 3, 1900.
46. Calixto Navarro, "Mi suegra," *El Diablito Rojo*, September 17, 1900.
47. "A mi suegra," *El Diablito Rojo*, October 8, 1900.
48. Imprenta de Antonio Vanegas Arroyo, "Pleito de la suegra con su yerno," 1911. This broadside is more ambiguous (and funnier) than most penny press poems because the mother-in-law gets to talk and fight back.
49. Archetypes like the Virgin of Guadalupe and La Malinche/Eve carry other meanings as well, many of them much more ambiguous than this structure would imply and some of them quite subversive of the regulatory norms it upholds. The point here is that penny press poets almost always deployed these symbols in "conventional" ways that upheld rather than subverted hegemonic notions of proper womanhood.
50. Piccato makes a strong case for popular honor in chapter 4 of *City of Suspects*.
51. *El Chile Piquín*, February 9, 1905. The play on the Spanish word for *one* (*uno*) and its feminine counterpart (*una*) makes this a typical *albur* (pun or wordplay).
52. "Intima," *San Lúnes*, November 4, 1907.
53. Ego, "Consejos," *El Diablito Rojo*, March 4, 1901.
54. "Quejas a . . . ," *La Guacamaya*, October 20, 1902.
55. For a psychoanalytic take on abjection, see Julia Kristeva, *Powers of Horror: An Essay on Abjection*, trans. Leon S. Roudiez (New York: Columbia University Press, 1982).
56. E. F., "A una ingrata," *El Diablito Rojo*, September 3, 1900.
57. Reineke, *Sacrificed Lives*, 27.
58. "Cómo debe ser la mujer," *El Diablito Rojo*, April 6, 1908.
59. Reineke, *Sacrificed Lives*, 30. The phrase is from Julia Kristeva, *Revolution in Poetic Language*, trans. Margaret Waller (New York: Columbia University Press, 1984), 75.
60. On traditional female sacrifice, see Girard, *Violence and the Sacred.*
61. Francisco Guerrero, a.k.a. "El Chalequero," assaulted and murdered several women in Mexico City during the 1880s. His modus operandi was to slit the throats of his victims, and the tabloids were quick to draw comparisons to London's notorious Jack the Ripper. Guerrero was apprehended in 1888 and sentenced to death. His death sentence was commuted, however, and he was released in 1904. In 1908, he was convicted of murdering another woman and sentenced to death again but died in prison two years later. Arnulfo Villegas murdered his fiancé when she attempted to break off their engagement in 1905. The grisly nature of the crime—he forced her to sit on his lap and then shot her in the head—attracted considerable interest from the tabloids. On the la nota roja treatment of these

and other sensational crimes, see Piccato, *City of Suspects*, chapter 5, and "'El Chalequero' or the Mexican Jack the Ripper"; Speckman Guerra, *Crimen y castigo*, 173–99; Frank, *Posada's Broadsheets*, chapter 1; and Alberto del Castillo, "Prensa, poder y criminalidad a finales del siglo XIX en la Ciudad de México," in *Hábitos, normas y escándalo. Prensa, criminalidad y drogas durante el porfiriato tardío*, ed. Ricardo Pérez Monfort (Mexico City: Centro de Investigaciones y Estudios Superiores en Antropología Social y la editorial Plaza y Valdés, 1997), 15–74.

62. Piccato, *City of Suspects*, 107.
63. Ibid., 126. Piccato's statistical table (p. 232) indicates that conviction rates were even worse for other sex crimes.
64. Carlos Roumagnac, *Crimenes sexuales y pasionales: estudio de psicología morbosa* (México: Librería de Ch. Bouret, 1906), 5–6.
65. In addition to a long-standing criminological discourse that depicted the lower classes as inherently criminal, Mexican elites were deeply concerned about Mexico City's international reputation as a dangerous city and consequently tried to downplay crime statistics by suggesting that violent crime was mostly confined to the lower classes. See Robert M. Buffington, *Criminal and Citizen in Modern Mexico* (Lincoln: University of Nebraska Press, 2000), 53. Since the Porfirian regime controlled the mainstream press, including much of la nota roja, references to upper- and middle-class violence could have been suppressed or at least discouraged. Just as important is the privacy that comes with class privilege.
66. Piccato, *City of Suspects*, 105–6.
67. Ibid., 113 and 118.
68. The connection between poetry about women and the changing conditions for bourgeois male subjectivity has yet to be tackled by historians. However, even a cursory glance at bourgeois newspapers and journals from the period reveals little substantive difference between upper- and lower-class concerns.
69. Reineke, *Sacrificed Lives*, 60.

CHAPTER 7

Nationalizing the Bohemian

The Mythogenesis of Agustín Lara

ANDREW G. WOOD

Soy un ingrediente nacional como el jepazote o el tequila.
(I am as Mexican as epazote or tequila.)[1]

—Agustín Lara

INTERNATIONALLY KNOWN MEXICAN MUSICIAN AGUSTÍN LARA MADE a triumphant visit to the beautiful river town of Tlacotalpan, just south of the Port of Veracruz, in the fall of 1967. Nearly everyone turned out for the occasion as the mayor presided over an extraordinary banquet honoring their guest. Praising Lara as one of their own, many offered warm remembrances of a "mischievous, frolicking, intelligent young boy who had gone off in search of fame and fortune." Even a wheelchair-bound, blind schoolteacher fondly remembered "his old student" as Lara and his admirers made their way about town after the meal. Indeed, it was a glorious day for Lara as he savored thoughts of "earlier times" amid the lavish praise heaped upon him by the townspeople of Tlacotalpan. Basking in the limelight of his adoring fans for what writer Javier Ramos Malzárraga dubbed his "last happy day on earth," Lara exuberantly exclaimed to the gathered multitude at one point: "*My* Veracruz is such a beautiful place" ("Que linda es *mi* Veracruz").[2]

As Carta Blanca Beer funded a television shoot that captured the composer's visit to Tlacotalpan, Mexicans across the country subsequently had the opportunity to join the celebration.

Yet despite all the pomp and circumstance celebrating Lara's connection to the area—including a freshly minted birth certificate drafted by Tlacotalpan municipal officials a few years earlier—the musician's Veracruz identity, along with his image as a romantic crooner, had in fact been constructed largely for publicity purposes. It turns out that Lara was no *tlacotalpeño* (a native of Tlacotalpan) or even a *jarocho* (someone born in the state of Veracruz). He was pure *chilango*—born and raised in Mexico City. So why all the hoopla surrounding his alleged hometown roots? As the following essay will discuss, Lara's mythic Veracruz origins played an important part in establishing his identity as a modern Mexican man just as a new cultural age was dawning throughout the Americas and western Europe.

The Veracruz Connection

Agustín Lara gained notoriety at a critical time in Mexican history when post-Revolutionary prosperity combined with advances in communications technology to spark the mass dissemination of illustrated magazines, phonograph records, radio, and film. Soon to become a major contributor to a dynamic new wave of cultural production headquartered in Mexico City, Lara crafted a celebrity identity that simultaneously appealed to feelings of national pride, post-Revolutionary optimism, and the simple desire on the part of many to have a good time.

Lara cemented his reputation by casting himself as a romantic bohemian originally from the tropical state of Veracruz. His was a melancholy, sentimental, occasionally nostalgic musical blend that drew upon the late-nineteenth-century modernist poetry of writers such as Amado Nervo and others. Lara gained a substantial following when he began appearing on radio broadcasts beginning in the early 1930s. This was soon followed by collaborations in cinema. Working with a talented group of singers and backing musicians, he composed a string of hugely successful songs that solidified his image throughout the Spanish-speaking world as a romantic crooner dedicated to his female muse. For his many fans, Lara's music was powerful sonic poetry.

Unlike other leading figures of his generation who tended to embody a muscular, "macho" male image, Lara presented himself as a musician-poet: an inheritor of European inspired romanticism, a connoisseur of wine, women, and song. He played the dandy—but with a Mexican twist, for Lara's romantic modernism included a complementary commitment to the traditional ideals of home and country. In Mexico's immediate post-Revolutionary age of often-dizzying social transformation, Lara cleverly crafted a public image that kept one foot in the past while at the same time riding the wave of technological and cultural change. His fundamental identity as an artist and a Mexican man rested on two mythic pillars: 1) his "total" dedication to his female muse and 2) his identification, however fabricated, as a jarocho. I begin with the question of his Veracruz "roots."

Agustín Lara was born Ángel Agustín Lara y Aguirre on October 30, 1897, in Mexico City.[3] Lara's thirty-eight-year-old father Joaquín Lara Aparicio came from a small town in the state of Puebla and worked in Mexico City as a doctor. His mother, María Aguirre del Pino, was six years younger than her husband and originally from a village in the state of Mexico. Together with Agustín's younger sister María Teresa, they lived a few blocks northeast of the Plaza de Santo Domingo in central Mexico City in a modest two-story residence on 16 Puente (or Callejón) del Cuervo—now República de Colombia.[4] When financial difficulties forced Agustín's father to search for work in Europe, Agustín went for a time to live with his aunt Refugio in the fashionable Mexico City suburb of Coyoacán. There he soon received his first piano lessons.

At the age of twelve Lara began working as a pianist in a Mexico City bordello, improvising tunes for the mix of businessmen, politicians, and assorted pleasure seekers who frequented the establishment. Agustín performed regularly until his father (having recently returned to Mexico) shipped the young Lara off to military school. These were the years of the Mexican Revolution (1910–1917), which resulted in more than one million deaths and much devastation before the conflict was over.

As the violence gradually subsided, Agustín resurfaced in the capital where he returned to the business of entertaining. Several opportunities soon presented themselves, and Lara began playing in a number of new clubs, cabarets, movie houses, and theaters—many located in the entertainment district along Santa María la Redonda Avenue. The young artist lived a bohemian lifestyle while acquiring the necessary survival skills to make it in the entertainment industry. Over the next decade, he would prove himself a skillful and prolific creator of popular song.

Lara began telling interviewers that he had been born in the tropical town of Tlacotalpan, Veracruz—just south of the Gulf of Mexico ports of

Veracruz and Alvarado on the banks of the Papolapan River. It is not exactly clear why he concocted this particular falsehood. Perhaps Tlacotalpan—having earned a reputation as a fashionable destination for elite and middle-class Mexicans around the turn of the century—afforded the *capitalino* artist a certain status he otherwise would not have enjoyed given that he had been playing the subterranean bordello circuit for some time.

Probably more important, however, is the currency one's regional identity had in post-Revolutionary Mexico. The late 1920s was a time when officials in Mexico City worked to reconstruct national identity through a mythic characterizing of specific regional "types." Among a wide array of these traditional "personalities" (including Puebla natives known as *poblanos*, and women from Tehuantepec known as *tehuanas*), people identified residents of the Veracruz region as *jarochos*. In this national mosaic, jarocho identity was well understood as a mixed heritage developed along the Gulf Coast through a combining of indigenous, European, and African peoples. Following this, jarochos were attributed a certain lowland "essence" made manifest in all areas of social and cultural expression: attitude, comportment, sexuality, food, drink, music, visual art, literature, and the like. Taken together, these assumed characteristics probably added a certain cachet to Lara's growing reputation as an artist because they provided him a geographic and cultural grounding in the "imagined community" eagerly promoted by post-Revolutionary nationalists.

One of the first published associations between Lara and Tlacotalpan can be found in a 1931 newspaper article titled "La Tierra de Agustín Lara."[5] In a purported testimony to his boyhood past, this short exposé included three photos of Tlacotalpan, including one of the house where Lara was supposedly born. A month later, while on tour in northern Mexico, Lara tempered his story somewhat by telling an interviewer that he was "originally from Tlacotalpan but had spent many of his early years in Mexico City."[6] Subsequent retellings of Lara's youth, however, did not shy away from full-blown myth making about his origins.

For example, a comic book series produced with Lara's cooperation titled *La vida de Agustín Lara* presented a sanitized history of the musician beginning with his invented experience in Tlacotalpan. These *historietas* painted a heroic portrait of the young artist making a way for himself in the Mexico City underworld. In the first of 135 issues, our protagonist offers his readers the following explanation regarding his alleged birth in Tlacotalpan:

> My father was working as a doctor in [the port of] Veracruz when one day a messenger came and told him that señor Malpica in Tlacotalpan needed his help because his wife was going to have a baby. My mother, who was also expecting, said she was going to go too. Then, almost by accident, my mother gave birth there in Tlacotalpan. When they hoisted me up to take a look, they said "how ugly." Still for me, Tlacotalpan was the most beautiful town you could ever imagine.

Associating the natural beauty of Tlacotalpan with his later development as a professional musician, Lara then speaks directly to his readers:

> My first memories are of swimming in the [Papaloapan] river when I was four. It was at that time that I first became aware of the musical rhythms being born in me. [Commenting to a childhood friend while swimming in the river] "Listen, do you hear that . . . ? There's music in the river!"

Establishing the town of Tlacotalpan as his creative source, Lara's tale also touched upon another essential element in his artistic image: his mother. Laying the basis for what would become a legendary commitment to his female muse, the musician shares his first impression of his beloved mother María:

> When I opened my eyes, I saw the face of my mother . . . and saw that she had the face of a queen; very tall, very straight with long and beautiful hair. With a mother so attractive, I knew that I could not be all that bad looking. In her love for me, maybe my mother knew something: that I would have sensitivity to the natural beauty all around. Indeed, some nights when everyone was asleep, I would open the window and listen to the sounds of the night . . . I realize now it was that little Veracruz river town that nurtured my musical talents.[7]

Forging a link between his mother and his adopted hometown, Lara then articulated the second of his core artistic identifications. Lara's reputation—supposedly rooted in maternal love—was as an artist completely dedicated to romantic ideals.

The Artist and His Muse

From the beginning, Lara sought to establish himself as a man who placed romance above all else. If thought to be the main protagonist in many of his songs, Agustín can often be seen searching for a female muse whether she be his own mother or aunt, a movie star, a cabaret dancer, or—like himself at one time or another—a "good" person struggling under difficult circumstances. Central to his image as a romantic artist was the idea that fans could see him as a visionary who could appreciate the inner beauty present in ordinary people. In this regard, Lara's work on the 1932 Antonio Moreno film adaptation of Federico Gamboa's turn-of-the-century novel *Santa* is an excellent example. As one of the first Mexican films to feature sound, *Santa* tells the archetypal story of a suffering Mexican woman who falls from grace after migrating to the city. Forced into prostitution in the shadowy underworld of Mexico City, *Santa* spoke to the many ways in which many Mexicans found themselves embroiled in a troublesome tangle of lost opportunity and moral ambivalence in the capital.[8]

Luckily for his career, Lara was asked to write music for the film. With Miguel Lerdo de Tejada acting as musical director, Lara's compositions included the title song "Santa," (played by Carlos Orellana), a fox-trot, a danzón (danced in the film by actress Lupita Tovar and a partner), as well as another piece to which the character Santa dances in her room. Lara also provided some vaguely Spanish-sounding music for the background of a party scene.[9] Above all, the musician's melancholy sound and poignant lyrics idolizing the fallen women resonated with audiences.

Lara's composition assumes the voice of blind bordello piano player Hipólito. In the film, Hipólito appears as one of the few remaining people who have not been corrupted by the big city. In Santa he senses a woman who, despite her working as a prostitute, is truly a saint. Lara's lyrics provide a love-struck Hipólito with a passionate ode to the young woman. Rendering his heartfelt confession, he essentially tells her "you light up my life":

En la eterna noche
de mi desconsuelo
tú has sido la estrella
que alumbró mi suelo
Y yo he adivinado
tu rara hermosura

y has iluminado
toda mi negrura

(In the eternal night
of my suffering
you have been the star
that lighted my way
And as I have discovered
your exquisite beauty
you have cast your light
into all my gloomy darkness)

Highly sentimental, the song idealizes the fallen woman whose descent into prostitution is caused by the city. As she sadly dies at the end of the film and is returned to her family village just outside Mexico City, the story of Santa served as a cautionary tale in popular culture with Lara's composition revealing the essential moral dilemma many felt at the time. Idolizing the fallen Santa in song, Lara smartly positioned himself as an important interpreter of social and cultural change by challenging audiences to reaffirm "traditional values" in the face of modern challenges to the moral order.

Lara's music invited his listeners to become enraptured. According to Carlos Monsiváis, Lara's songs conjured a kind of "logic of delirium [as listeners came to] fall in love with the idea of falling in love!"[10] Allegedly inspired by a mythic female muse, Lara wrote song after romantic song in the early 1930s. At the same time, he fashioned a corresponding public image of himself as a near-obsessed lover—someone the entertainment press could promote as a temporary escape from the drudgery of everyday life.

The dissemination of radio in Mexico added greatly to Lara's popularity. In 1930, impresario Emilio Azcárraga came up with the idea for a powerful station that would "unify the great Mexican family" while showcasing a wide range of new talent and turning them into stars. Shortly thereafter, Mexico City's XEW was born.[11] Owned by the Mexican Music Company (a subsidiary of RCA) and managed by Azcárraga, XEW became the Western Hemisphere's most powerful radio station and was soon known as the "voice of Latin America."

Lara's connection began in September 1930 when Azcárraga invited him to perform for the inaugural broadcast of XEW. A full-page ad in the Mexico City newspaper *El Universal* on September 18, 1930, announced the opening of the station and first evening program that included Lara and the young tenor Juan Arvízu among others:

> Today at eight o'clock the powerful radio station XEW will officially be on the air with its inaugural concert. XEW will begin a completely new and advanced era in the history of radio in Mexico as from a technical point of view there are few stations in the world that can equal it. Artistically, we can assure you that XEW will be of the highest quality—earning your respect and full attention. The station will be a revelation with its clarity, range and perfection. [Not only that] XEW's well-managed operations and constantly updated programming will no doubt make it your preferred station.[12]

In the years to come, XEW would broadcast a range of musical programming that often featured performances by artists playing popular song forms. Coupled with a growing accessibility of radio throughout Mexico, the station soon created a surge in Lara's popularity.[13]

In 1932, Emilio Azcárraga offered Lara his own one-hour show on XEW that they called "La Hora Íntima." Aired three times a week starting at 10:00 p.m., the program was initially sponsored by Tres Flores Brilliantine and later picked up by Bayer Aspirin of Mexico. Performing with singers such as Juan Arvizu, Luis R. Roldán, Chucho Martínez Gil, Pedro Vargas, Ana María Fernández, and Toña la Negra (for whom he would write his Veracruz-inspired *Tropical Suite*), Lara's music entered homes across Mexico. Making the most of the situation, Lara composed a number of new songs. Performing in theaters and on the radio several times a week, Lara's music caused a sensation as people sang his songs and journalists wrote about him in glowing terms.

As audiences yearned to hear his romantic melodies, Lara's partnership with Mexico's growing communications technology brought his body of work into the privacy of listeners' homes.[14] Commenting on Lara's powerful appeal during this time, Carlos Monsiváis writes:

> Lara's talent is enormous, but his fame really emerges from the fits and starts with which a modern sensitivity transforms traditional sensibility; for he dominates an epoch in which the electronic media (radio, records and film) complement, rather than contradict, the typically pre-modern extolling of love as fiery rapture and

> unfulfilled possession. This is why Lara's repertoire, the central pillar of the new culture industry, becomes part of the most cherished of national traditions.[15]

With Lara's entertainment formula well in place by the mid-1930s, promotional forces behind the scenes in combination with the artist's own drive to succeed turned "Agustín Lara" into a legendary figure (nicknamed *el flaco de oro* or "the golden beanpole") as he attained international celebrity status. Now at the top of his game, Lara represented an alternative Mexican male identity, one rooted in the past but thoroughly modern at the same time. In 1943 the artist achieved one of his greatest "conquests" when he courted the attractive film actress María Félix. It would be his shining moment as a leading romantic male as well as his ultimate undoing.

Félix had made a name for herself by playing the title role in the 1943 film *Doña Bárbara* directed by Fernando de Fuentes and based on the novel by Venezuelan Rómulo Gallegos. The actress played a tough-minded, untrusting, and fiercely independent woman—an artistic role she quickly developed in subsequent films and one that would soon contrast interestingly with Lara's romantic maleness. To help explain the character of doña Bárbara, we learn that she had been raped in her youth. The crime resulted in the birth of a daughter named Marisela (played by María Elena Marqués), who was subsequently abandoned. These tragic events turn doña Bárbara into the woman we initially meet as she presides over an extensive ranch essentially stolen from the family of a handsome young doctor named Santos Luzardo (played by Julián Soler). As the drama develops, doña Bárbara acts out a conflicted gender identity that rejects the attention of men so as to preserve her status as a powerful landowner. Acting out a seemingly "masculine" identity, she dons the local frontier-style clothing, smokes cigarettes, and rides a horse.

In spite of appearances, the underlying message of the film is one that encourages traditional family values and a strict adherence to standard heterosexual gender roles. Doña Bárbara is presented as an example of how not to be, and her story is a cautionary tale meant to warn of the "dangers" of blurring sexual identity. As we see María Félix portray a "manly" woman eventually in competition with her own (more feminine) daughter for the attention of Santos Luzardo, the message is clear: doña Bárbara is a devouring woman who is surely doomed.

After its release, *Doña Bárbara* garnered unprecedented box office receipts as well as significant praise for director Fernando de Fuentes and his female star. Enamored with her magnetic appearance and powerful persona, her unique celebrity status as an assertive woman began to grow as fans referred to Félix simply as La Doña. Her reputation as a strong, independent woman would soon be contrasted with that of the older, less attractive, yet exceedingly charming Agustín Lara when the two established a relationship in the early 1940s. It would not be long until the two began playing their "odd couple" role to the hilt for an adoring public and publicity-hungry entertainment press.

Lara met the thirty-year-old Félix through mutual friend Tito Navarro in the fall of 1943. The actress had begun work on a new film titled *La china poblana* at the same time *Doña Bárbara* premiered. After an initial courtship, the two began appearing together in restaurants, nightclubs, and other high-profile venues. Not surprisingly, they attracted the attention of the press who took tremendous pleasure in gossiping about the celebrity couple. At first, many accused Félix of seeking publicity. Yet the young actress stood firm in her commitment to the older Lara. She even confessed a fondness for debonair radio star Agustín Lara ever since she was a young girl. In her 1993 memoir she maintained that "Agustín was *muy sexy* [and had] the most exciting voice in the world."[16]

As winter descended on the Mexican capital, the celebrity odd couple could be seen attending theater openings, frequenting upscale restaurants, and visiting friends. Sunday afternoons were often spent at the bullfights. Courting the attractive young actress, Lara showered Félix with a number of gifts while introducing her to Mexico's cultural elite. For many, the pairing of the nation's most beloved bohemian with its favorite female star seemed a fabulous fairy tale.

Lara treated Félix with great care. He purchased a white grand piano for his new love on which he had inscribed, "On this piano will only be played my most beautiful melodies for the most beautiful woman in the world."[17] Indeed, as Agustín began writing songs inspired by his new muse, his music enjoyed new levels of popularity both in Mexico and throughout the Spanish-speaking world. At the same time, María attracted praise for her work in *Doña Bárbara*.[18]

Countless anecdotes about the two circulated throughout Mexico and the Spanish-speaking world. Singer Alejandro Algara recounted one late-night episode when he, Lara, and Félix had just left the Lírico Theater after a performance. Making their way across town, they came upon a prostitute while waiting at a stoplight. The woman approached the car and upon recognizing Lara, asked him for a cigarette: "Maestro, I'm very cold, could you spare me one of yours?" Obliging her, Algara tells that not only did the famous musician offer her one of his Pall Malls but also María's fur coat, saying, "Don't worry we'll buy another one for you tomorrow."[19] When asked, the attractive actress would repeatedly tell reporters of her happiness with the gentlemanly, albeit much less attractive, musician-poet.[20]

Lara and Félix eventually moved in together. Inviting journalist Robert Browning in for an interview during the winter of 1945, the two celebrities hosted the reporter with a round of highballs. Félix testified that she felt "very happy" and that Lara "was a true gentleman."[21] A follow-up interview later that year similarly portrayed the couple as sophisticated lovers listening to freshly pressed bolero recordings.

About the same time, however, Lara began to suffer from fits of suspicion and jealousy. Acting to shore up his insecurities, he marked the third anniversary of his meeting Félix with special zeal. Rumors circulated suggesting that the celebrities planned to wed.[22] The gossip was soon borne out as the two gathered in front of friends to join in civil union on Christmas Eve 1945. Capturing the moment, photographers pictured the couple surrounded by Mario "Cantinflas" Moreno, Dolores del Río, Pedro Vargas, Renato Leduc, Carlos Denegri, Libertad Lamarque, Jorge Negrete, Betty Davis, and several other stars. Félix and Lara then honeymooned in Acapulco. According to legend, it was there that Lara penned his famous waltz "María Bonita" in which he affectionately declares, "Amores habrás tenido, muchos amores . . . Pero ninguno tan bueno, ni tan honrado, como el que hiciste que en mí brotara" ("I've had many loves, but none so fine, so honorable as this").[23]

With the press framing their extensive coverage of the union as a fairy tale "beauty and the bohemian" romance made in heaven, the Lara/Félix story—as everyone suspected—eventually had to come to an end. Living with "the most beautiful woman in Mexican cinema," Lara's insecurities about the relationship began to show. Mocked by certain members of the press, reporters suggested that Agustín could occasionally allow his insecurities to get the better of him. As before, many wondered how someone "so ugly" could command the attention of such a beautiful younger woman. Clearly, Lara did not fit their traditional "macho" image of the "proper" suitor to such a ravishing beauty as Félix. Lara converted the situation into new material. With his long-standing reputation as a sensitive, romantic gentleman, several new compositions such as "Humo en los ojos" ("Smoke in the Eyes"), "Cuando vuelvas" ("When You Return"), "Revancha" ("Revenge"),

"Sombras" ("Shadows"), and "Pecadora" ("Sinner") effectively evoked the pathos of love.

Official word of the Lara/Félix breakup came on October 25, 1947.[24] In contrast to the publicity furor that had come before, newspaper reports revealed little as to why Félix and Lara had separated. María indicated that she had no interest in discussing the matter publicly.[25] Instead, she announced plans to leave for Los Angeles, California.[26] The next day a headline in *El Universal* declared that "the need for divorce for María Félix is not necessary." With this, the paper let the Mexican public in on their little secret: the celebrity couple had never been married in a religious ceremony but had chosen to marry only in front of a judge, in what Mexicans call a "civil ceremony."[27]

Lara and Félix did much to modernize the development of celebrity identity in Mexico. With the help of a national entertainment industry infrastructure made up of publicists, photographers, and promoters, their union during the mid-1940s invited Mexicans (and countless others throughout the Spanish-speaking world) to identify with the "modern love" the couple engendered and thus, in some small way, vicariously live the glamorous life through them. Together they expanded the way gender was defined in Mexico as Félix convincingly played the role of the tough, near-macho woman to Lara's sensitive, romantic male.

Yet Lara's "conquest" of the beautiful and younger Félix also put his reputation as a modern lover on the line. Many had always wondered how the unattractive, older Lara had won over the younger actress. Certainly the idea of his using Félix as his muse to compose (among other songs) the popular "María Bonita" no doubt added to his more-than-decade-long effort to build a reputation as a romantic artist. Still, as difficulties in their personal lives became a matter of public speculation, the older musician was often ridiculed in the press as an emasculated, jealous lover.[28] Following the breakup with Félix, Lara set out to restore his somewhat tarnished reputation.

Posterity and Pantheon

Having fully established himself as a public figure, Lara was the subject of *La vida de Agustín Lara*, director Alejandro Galindo's 1958 film depiction of Lara's life story that went on to preserve his image for posterity. To do this, Galindo chose not to have Lara play himself but instead cast the younger, more attractive actor Germán Robles in the part.

The film opens with a well-dressed woman and her younger female companion browsing in a Mexico City music store filled with brand-new pianos. In walks a dapper young musician apparently "just in from Veracruz" who sits down and begins playing a tune. Hearing this, the woman approaches him in a friendly manner and asks if he might be willing to teach her attractive associate. When the pianist agrees, she provides him with her address and a small advance payment.

In the next scene we see our man Lara arrive outside a fashionable home where a moving truck is delivering a new piano. Inside, there are several nicely dressed young women who all express their girlish excitement when Agustín begins to play. Soon, the woman who had propositioned Lara in the music store appears at the top of the stairs and orders the young women to "hurry up" and "get ready." Slightly confused, the young musician continues playing for a while before realizing along with the film audience that he has been hired to work in a bordello.

It is not long before one of the archetypical scenes from Lara's life is recounted. Playing night after night at the bordello, Agustín takes a fancy to a prostitute for whom he soon writes a song. Performing it for her one night, he sings "Rosa" but soon is crushed to see his new love swept up by one of the well-dressed johns and taken away. With everyone applauding his music, a disappointed Lara angrily takes a beer bottle and smashes it against a mirror as the scene ends.

A day or so later, he is again at the piano with the Rosa of his song again listening intently. When Agustín this time shows caution in dealing with her, she begins to grow anxious. Next, Lara is called into another room by a phone call. Following him, a possessive Rosa grows extremely agitated, breaks a liquor bottle, and violently slashes Lara's left cheek.

The scene dramatized the real-life incident in the late 1920s that gave Lara his trademark facial scar. As a formative event it served as the legendary means by which his physical appearance was officially made "ugly" while at the same time he was aspiring to create great beauty in his music. Lara from this moment develops an image of himself, according to Carlos Monsiváis, as "bohemian, dissipated, at the disposal of the Muse twenty-four hours a day, deeply in love, marked by ugliness and redeemed by genius."[29] Added to childhood feelings of inferiority, the bordello incident is critical in the development of the Lara legend for it forever combined his tormented appearance with his musical credential as a dues-paying professional. A large part of the subsequent "mystery" of Lara as an artistic man was that he takes his ugliness and turns it into something immensely beautiful.

Lara's alleged inner spark is dramatized in a scene from *La Vida de Agustín Lara* when, after performing on radio, he encounters a young woman who insists they must talk. Sitting down in a cabaret, Lara is very conscious of his still-healing scar and tells the attractive young woman that he has lived a worthless life in dance halls, drinking wine long into the night. Mesmerized by the piano man, she tells him that none of that matters, "she knows everything." Visibly shaken, Lara begins singing "Noche de ronda" ("Night Moves") to her as a way to convince the young woman that their love is not meant to be. Eventually, she realizes he is singing about a long-lost love whom he still cares for. Upset, she clutches her purse and abruptly leaves.

The next day, however, Lara appears in a police station where he encounters one of the Mexico City madams he knows. While smoothing out things with the authorities, she introduces Lara to an attractive high-class call girl called "Mariposa" ("Butterfly"). Seeing her, Lara is transfixed. Almost immediately the two are seen together on a date in the charming town of Xochimilco, happily cavorting and having fun. The apparently pure and passionate romance does not last, though, as one day one of Mariposa's clients jealously tracks her down. After finding them together kissing in her apartment, the jealous client pulls out a gun, forces Mariposa to dance to the Lara tune of "Aventurera" ("Adventuress"), and then shoots her when Lara tries to intervene with a broken bottle. As she lies on the floor, she calls to Lara to kiss her once again before she dies. Here again, Lara is characterized as an insightful, well-intentioned man who sees the inner value of the fallen woman.

In *La Vida de Agustín Lara*, even the depiction of Lara's real-life romance with María Félix takes a backseat to his romantic musings about the fictive character Mariposa. Despite courtship, marriage, a honeymoon in Acapulco, and a seemingly blissful life together on the set of one of María's films, the talented musician and his attractive film star wife eventually put their greatest stock in their careers and go their own way. This soon leaves Lara to return to the cemetery where Mariposa is buried to pay homage to his most honored muse. As the film ends, her memory for Lara soon becomes immortalized as he sees her in visions and reverently visits her grave while celestial music plays in the background and the camera pans upward to the heavens.

Conclusion

Agustín Lara died on November 6, 1970, at the age of seventy-three. His funeral was held the following day as thousands joined in a massive procession in Mexico City that circulated through many of the capital's central streets. Inside the Teatro Blanquita, where a memorial service was held, Lara's most renowned interpreter Toña la Negra sang a chilling rendition of "Noche de ronda" while many wept. That same day, a minute of silence paying tribute to the beloved artist was observed throughout the nation.

Knowing that Lara's passing signaled the loss of a living legend who had risen to prominence early in the post-Revolutionary period and subsequently helped shape Mexico's modern entertainment industry, Mexicans paid tribute to a man who in death would forever be considered a national treasure. Today, the image of Lara—in the company of several others who form the entertainment pantheon of Golden Age Mexican stars—can be found on postage stamps, collector's-edition glossy magazines, and commemorative classic films reissued on DVD and sold in department stores.

From early in his career, Lara had constructed an imagined yet powerful connection with the state of Veracruz. Known for its "four times heroic" defense against foreign invasion during the nineteenth and early twentieth centuries, the strong sense of Mexican nationalism associated with the area provided Lara another important credential needed to make it in the entertainment business. Moreover, the tropical sun, ocean breezes, beaches, music, rum, food, cigars, and romantic nightlife of Veracruz added important cultural capital to Lara's reputation as a romantic artist in post-Revolutionary Mexico. The connection between his adopted jarocho homeland and his muse is evident in his pseudo-autobiographical song "Veracruz" in which he sings:

Yo nací con la luna de plata
y nací con alma de pirata
he nacido rumbero y jarocho trovador de veras y me fui
lejos de Veracruz.

Veracruz, rinconcito donde hacen su
nido las olas del mar

Veracruz, pedacito de patria que sabe sufrir y cantar.
Veracruz, son tus noches diluvio de estrellas, palmera y mujer
Veracruz, vibra en mi ser algún día hasta tus playas lejanas tendré que volver.

(I was born under a silvery moon
And I was born with the soul of a pirate
I was born a jovial vagabond
A genuine troubadour and I went far away from Veracruz.

Veracruz, sweet little nook
Where the waves of the ocean meet to make their nest

Veracruz, sweet little piece of my country that knows of suffering and song.
Veracruz, your nights are a shower of stars, palm tree and woman
Veracruz, you vibrate within me, someday to your faraway beaches I'll have to return.)

Lara's apocryphal tale held a special appeal in post-Revolutionary Mexico. As changing economic and technological forces combined with a new wave of rural to urban migration, many found reassurance in the idea of a popular artist originally from a decent Mexican middle-class family in the provinces. Despite his history as a musician who had come of age playing in bordellos, Lara's invented boyhood testimonials and affected jarocho identity comforted audiences by revealing that he was a "good" Mexican man. No matter that the story was false, the idea that he had come from Tlacotalpan served as attractive public relations copy that—along with his impressive body of work—forever secured his position as a twentieth-century romantic in the hearts of listeners throughout the Spanish-speaking world.

NOTES

1. Lara quoted in Carlos Monsiváis, *Amor Perdido* (Mexico City: Biblioteca Era, 1982), 62.
2. Javier Ramos Malzárraga, "El último día feliz de Agustín Lara," in *Todo lo que quería saber sobre Agustín Lara*, ed. Guillermo Mendizábal and Eduardo Mejía (Mexico City: Grijalbo, 1993), 20–22, identifies the year as 1968. However, R. Delgado Lozano's short piece in *Life* magazine on the celebration titled "Muchas emociones para un solo día" was published as part of a cover story on Lara in January 1968 (*Life en español*, January 15, 1968, 59) and suggests it took place the previous fall.
3. While his birth certificate reads "Mexico City," some speculate he may have been brought to the capital from Tlatlauquitepec, Puebla, to Mexico City as an infant.
4. Gabriel Abaroa Martínez, *El Flaco de Oro* (Mexico City: Grupo Editorial Planeta, 1993), 18–25.
5. Unidentified Mexico City paper, January 14, 1931, Salvador Lara scrapbooks, vol. 3, Casita Blanca de Agustín Lara, Boca del Río, Mexico (hereafter CBAL).
6. S. R. Gallardo, "El creador de la canción actual está en San Luis." Unidentified newspaper clipping from San Luis Potosí, March 1931, CBAL.
7. Pedro Lete D'Erzell, ed., *Vida de Agustín Lara* (Mexico City: Editorial Arguments S.A., 1964, 1965). Aside from the occasional mention of 1964 as a publishing date, most other details regarding publication remain unknown. Issue no. 1 gives production credit to Antonio Gutiérrez, Jorge P. Valdés, Gustavo Vidal, Gabriel Madrid, and Guillermo Yépez, whereas issue no. 135 lists Rubén González, Jorge Avina, Gustavo Vidal, A. Acosta, and Gabriel Madrid.
8. Andrew G. Wood, "Blind Men and Fallen Women: Notes on Modernity and Golden Age Mexican Cinema," in *Post Identities* 3, no. 1 (Summer 2001): 11–24.
9. For a discussion of production history, see Emilio García Riera, *Historia documental del cine mexicano*, vol. 1, 1929–1937 (Guadalajara: Universidad de Guadalajara, 1992), 47–51.
10. Carlos Monsiváis, "Bolero: A History," in Carlos Monsiváis, *Mexican Postcards*, trans. John Kraniauskas (London: Verso Books, 1997), 181–83.
11. On the illustrious history of XEW, see Pável Granados, *XEW: 70 años en el aire* (Mexico City: Editorial Clio, 2000).
12. *El Universal*, September 18, 1930.
13. Advertisements for Westinghouse, Radios 80-RCA-Corporacion Radio Mexicana S.A., Brunswick ("el radio del futuro"), Atwater-Kent, and other brands can be seen in virtually all Mexico City newspapers at the time.
14. On the sexual power of recorded music in the home, see Wayne Koestenbaum, *The Queen's Throat: Opera, Homosexuality and the Mystery of Desire* (New York: Da Capo Press 1993), chapter 2.
15. Monsiváis, *Mexican Postcards*, 180.
16. María Félix, *Todas mis guerras* (Mexico City: Clío editions, 1993), 78.
17. Monsiváis, *Amor Perdido*, 83.

18. *Jueves de Excélsior*, February 11, 1943, featured a picture of Félix and commented on her as a "new star." "Agustín Lara murio en paz con el gran amor de su vida," unidentified clipping, November 8, 1970, Biblioteca Lerdo de Tejada.
19. Algara quoted in Benito Vázquez González, "María Félix: La mujer que más amo Agustín Lara," *Revista de Revistas*, November 19, 1990, 39.
20. Ángel Mora, "Grandes amores del cine mexicano," *Mexico Cinema*, April 1946.
21. "Yo soy una mujer con alma," *Mexico Cinema*, March 1945, 22–24; see also *Cinema Reporter*, May 12, 1945.
22. *Cinema Reporter*, August 31, 1945, covered this party where Sara Mateos, Gabriel Figueroa, Pedro Armendáriz, Rosa Castro, Efraín Huerta, Andrea Palma, and Ana María González attended while members of Lara's soon-to-be-formed "Sinfónica" played. "El Duende Filmo," [*sic*] reported in the Sunday, October 17, 1943, magazine section of *El Universal* that a young journalist unleashed "a torment" of gossip when he wrote that Lara and Félix had secretly wed. This rumor was subsequently denied by Roberto Soto and other friends (*El Universal*, October 22, 1943). Still, commentary would continue as seen in a cartoon printed in the paper two days later with a caption suggesting that "since Lara's songs had been used in film, what better than to marry the beautiful Félix" (*El Universal*, October 24, 1943).
23. Bing Crosby recorded a version that went on to sell thousands of copies. On Crosby, see Gary Giddens, *A Pocketful of Dreams: The Early Years, 1903–1940* (New York: Little, Brown, 2001). A Mexico City streetcar was for a time named María Bonita.
24. "Idilio roto: María y Agustín se separan," *El Universal*, October 25, 1947.
25. *El Universal*, October 24, 1947.
26. "Félix salió para L.A.," *El Universal*, October 26, 1947.
27. *El Universal*, October 27, 1947. Paco Pildora, "Revolviendo Papeles," *Notiver*, n.d. Lara would maintain that they had married and subsequently divorced.
28. On the relationship between Lara and Félix, see Andrew G. Wood, "The Public Romance of María Félix and Agustín Lara," in *The Human Tradition in Mexico*, ed. Jeffrey Pilcher (Wilmington, DE: Rowman & Littlefield/Scholarly Resources, 2003), 185–97.
29. Monsiváis, *Mexican Postcards*, 183.

CHAPTER 8

The Gay Caballero

Machismo, Homosexuality, and the Nation in Golden Age Film

JEFFREY M. PILCHER

ON MARCH 15, 1946, AT TEN O'CLOCK IN THE EVENING, THE LIGHTS flickered out all over Mexico City. Sitting in their darkened homes for fifteen minutes, until the power was restored, citizens had occasion to reflect on the political struggles that had inspired the blackout. Battles between rival unions had long been a source of inconvenience; street car closures impeded the daily commute to work, and butcher strikes made it impossible to buy meat. Yet unlike many labor conflicts, which were decided in backroom *arreglos* (deals) by shadowy leaders who were widely believed to be corrupt, this struggle involved the biggest stars of Mexican cinema. At stake was not the usual question of salary and benefits but the defense of the nation's masculinity. Rival versions of appropriate manly behavior, which had formerly played out onscreen, were suddenly crystallized in reality when union actors were locked out of a theater and replaced by a Spanish flamenco dancer, Miguel de Molina, who was denounced as a scab and, more importantly, a queer. Molina's performances, and the union struggles surrounding them, offered a dramatic political theater, staged for an audience of public opinion, with the outcome determined by the titular father of the nation, President Manuel Ávila Camacho.

Confronting the effeminate Spanish performer-dancer stood the Mexican cinematic ideal of masculinity, the *charro* (singing cowboy). Dressed in a broad sombrero and embroidered costume, he appeared in countless films, serenading his beloved with romantic ballads and belting back tequilas. While seemingly a figure of long-standing tradition, the mariachi is a comparatively recent phenomenon and did not become a national symbol until the late 1930s.[1] This essay surveys the construction of the modern myth of the Mexican macho within the cinema industry in the so-called "Golden Age" from the late 1930s through the 1950s. During this period, singer-actors Jorge Negrete and Pedro Infante defined the persona of the charro and made it a symbol of national identity through a series of enormously popular *comedias rancheras* (rural comedies).

An examination of their films and the fluid social context in which they were produced and viewed reveals a far from monolithic depiction of the macho, particularly when the screen is broadened to include the other leading actor of the period, comedian Mario "Cantinflas" Moreno. In its early days, the Mexican film industry engaged in considerable experimentation with gender roles as avant-garde directors sought to extend the recent social revolution to the domestic sphere. As a result, popular film characters often engaged in blatant gender transgressions. Yet this filmic homoeroticism produced a glaring paradox in the union struggle of 1946, when national champions Negrete and Moreno engaged in homophobic denunciations of the Spanish dancer Molina.

Projecting the Nation

After the Revolution, rival political factions sought to shape the memory of that decade-long civil war and claim for themselves the mantle of martyred leaders; cinema provided an important forum for debates about national identity. The valor of peasant soldiers, often of indigenous birth, also prompted a reappraisal of the place of Native Americans in the national life. Debates about race were closely tied to gender and the exemplary masculinity of such popular generals as Emiliano Zapata and Francisco "Pancho" Villa, whose images were diffused nationwide, beyond their *patrias chicas* (local power bases), in part through films, both documentaries and dramas, locally produced and imported from the United States. Moreover, the threat of renewed violence continued to haunt Mexican society. The power of cinema to shape popular attitudes therefore made studio moguls into powerful potential allies of the official party in its goal of forging social peace.[2]

Race assumed a prominent and divisive place in national debates of the post-Revolutionary era. The fight against Díaz and his European-centered vision of Mexico inspired a new nationalist, revolutionary ideology called *indigenismo*, although it was in fact dedicated to creating a mestizo nation. The two foremost advocates of indigenismo differed in their emphasis, with the archaeologist Manuel Gamio seeking to spread an appreciation for indigenous culture and education minister José Vasconcelos advocating a national identity based on the country's Hispanic heritage, but they nevertheless shared a common goal of assimilating Native Americans into Mexican national life.[3] The racial question was tied inextricably to gender stereotypes, complicating still further debates about national identity.

Gender appeared most prominently in the works of philosopher Samuel Ramos, particularly the influential title *Perfíl del hombre y la cultura en México* (*Profile of Man and Culture in Mexico*, 1934). Using the theories of psychologist Alfred Adler, Ramos diagnosed a national inferiority complex among Mexican men. The basis for this collective self-analysis was the figure of the *pelado*, a newly arrived migrant from the countryside who struggled to adapt to the vagaries of urban life. As an Indian seeking to assimilate to Hispanic civilization, the pelado represented the most basic expression of the mestizo national identity, yet he nevertheless posed a menace to Mexican society. Speaking in crude terms, using wordplay known as *albures*, he asserted his own masculinity and accused others of passive homosexuality. Ramos generalized this hypermasculine posturing to represent an inferiority complex among all Mexicans. Ironically, this debate over the nation's masculinity was often framed in albures; for example, the editors of the influential journal *Contemporáneos*, to which Ramos frequently contributed, were viciously gay baited.[4]

Cinema became a focus of such national debates, as Joanne Hershfield has shown through an insightful discussion of opposing racial images in the Golden Age. An idyllic version of the indigenous race inspired by Gamio's vision came to life in the films of Emilio "El Indio" Fernández, such as *María Candelaria* (1943), even though the title role was played by Dolores del Río, a striking beauty without any recognizably Native American features. Conservative Hispanismo, the rival nationalist movement embraced by Vasconcelos and based on Iberian cultural traditions, reached popular audiences through the *comedia ranchera*, in which Jorge Negrete and Pedro

Infante portrayed independent rancheros from the western state of Jalisco, the purported home of the purest Spanish descendants, supposedly untainted by race mixture. The mestizaje celebrated by official ideology appeared in the pelado character of Mario "Cantinflas" Moreno, who used quick wits and fast wordplay to outwit Hispanic elites, just as the revolutionaries triumphed over the Porfirian elite.[5]

Cinema also projected gendered images, already embedded in popular culture, onto the emerging national identity, thereby helping to create the myth of the Mexican macho. As Américo Paredes has shown through an important study of *corridos* (folk songs), for hundreds of years the word *macho* was used only in a negative sense to refer to the empty bravado of a cowardly buffoon. Only about 1940, with the election as president of Manuel Ávila Camacho, did the rhyming word *macho* become a favorable term for a valiant man. By that time, authentic corridos were no longer written about Revolutionary heroes such as Pancho Villa and Emiliano Zapata. Instead, these ballads had become tools of the entertainment industry, used in the motion pictures of Jorge Negrete and Pedro Infante, and depicted an exaggerated masculinity designed to fit on the big screen. Paredes thus made two important points: the male ideals of courage and virility were common to many societies, but the parody of masculinity that appeared on film in the 1940s owed more to the psychoanalytical imagination of intellectuals such as Samuel Ramos than to actual popular culture.[6]

Moreover, cinematic constructions of gender roles rarely fit in neat categories.[7] Portrayals of men were complicated by filmmakers' divergent goals of shaping national identity while maximizing box office revenue. Conservative studio moguls, many with financial ties to the ruling party, sought to ameliorate the threat of Revolutionary violence by transferring the masculine image of Pancho Villa to the singing cowboy Jorge Negrete, just as racial conflict was tamed by conflating the dangerous pelado with the humorous Cantinflas. To accomplish this cinematic alchemy of transmogrifying popular culture into national symbols required considerable experimentation, particularly in the case of gender roles, and even then, such images remained open to contestation.

"The Great Operatic Macho"[8]

Of the "many Mexicos" portrayed in Golden Age cinema, the comedia ranchera offered perhaps the least accurate and most widely embraced vision of the nation. The genre was so appealing precisely because it turned its back on the social transformations of the day, looking instead to a mythic past, and in doing so it constructed a nostalgic image of *lo mexicano*. At a time of agrarian revolution, the ranchero comedy depicted an idyllic rural world inhabited by benevolent landlords and respectful peasants. Ignoring the accelerating pace of industrialization and urbanization, the films celebrated a folkloric pageant of rustic handicrafts and costumes, mariachi music and dancing, boisterous barrooms and rodeos. Yet the very modernity of the audience subverted this mythologizing project, and the resulting imperfections in this fabricated national identity bedeviled, in particular, efforts at depicting the macho.

Allá en el Rancho Grande (*There on the Big Ranch*, 1936) launched the comedia ranchera as an international phenomenon, entrancing audiences throughout the Americas with its distillation of a folkloric Mexican national essence. Local viewers, however, found it vaguely dissatisfying, and it premiered for twelve days, better than the average film's run of a week, but only marginally.[9] Like much early cinema, it drew heavily on the popular *carpa* (tent) theater, alternating between musical numbers and comic episodes. The story derived from a Porfirian drama, *En la hacienda* (*On the Hacienda*), in which a young Indian woman was raped by the landlord and her beloved killed for seeking revenge. Rebel leaders had encouraged the play as propaganda, but director Fernando de Fuentes made crucial changes in the plot in keeping with his political opposition to the Revolution.[10] The hero was no longer a downtrodden indigenous peon seeking revenge against an oppressive landowner; rather, Hollywood veteran Tito Guízar took the role of a ranch foreman and childhood friend of the hacienda owner, played by René Cardona. Through a twist of fate, the two became rivals for the hand of Guízar's beloved, Esther Fernández, but Cardona refrained from using his power as hacienda owner to force her to marry him. Guízar, thinking that his old friend had betrayed him, sought vengeance in a tavern, but once the truth became known, they burst into folkloric song.

This reconciliation between ranch owner and hand thereby preserved onscreen a conservative social hierarchy in which wealthy landowners looked out for their peons with paternalistic care. It seemed particularly reassuring to the middle classes at a time when agrarian radicals in the countryside were invading haciendas to claim land that had been promised to them by Revolutionary reformers. In the movie version, moreover, the drama remained secondary to the local color provided by musicians such as the

Trío Tariácuri, a "Jarabe tapatío" danced by "Indio" Fernández, and comic jousting between the profligate Carlos "Chaflán" López and the shrewish Emma Roldán, both renowned carpa performers. This folkloric content of *Allá en el Rancho Grande* established Mexican cinema in the international marketplace and inspired a host of imitators. Local audiences, however, remained unimpressed by Guízar, whose Hollywood reputation as a Latin lover did not translate back to Mexico.[11]

The triumph of the comedia ranchera in Mexico had to await the arrival of an actor, Jorge Negrete, who could provide a suitable interpretation of the true macho. Negrete had a weak chin but a powerful baritone voice that he had trained operatically to such a broad range that he was often mistaken for a tenor. A graduate of the military academy, he had played war heroes and bullfighters and refused at first to be cast as a simple mariachi singer. Nevertheless, *¡Ay, Jalisco, no te rajes!* (*Hey, Jalisco, Don't Back Down*, 1941) established a formula for the singing charro that carried him through the rest of his career. The Rodríguez brothers—Joselito, Roberto, and Ismael—directed many of these films in an over-the-top style that became characteristic of the charro's machismo. In this film, the action took place during the Revolution, but the only reference to that social movement came from the chief villain, who had usurped the title of *general*, and the setting was the famously conservative Los Altos region of Jalisco. Negrete introduced the character of El Ametralladora (the Machine Gunner), so named because of the rapid fire from his revolvers, which he used to avenge his father, who was murdered in the opening scene. Cinema historian Emilio García Riera attributed the success of the film to "the arrogant, brave temper of the mustachioed hero [Negrete], a temper of reinforced machismo that differentiated him from the more pretty boy [*afeitado*] and less pugilistic Tito Guízar of *Allá en el Rancho Grande*; in that film by Fernando de Fuentes there were neither shots nor punches, and without doubt the macho violence five years later, with *¡Ay, Jalisco, no te rajes!*, gave new life to the ranchero genre."[12]

Negrete's character was dedicated to gaining mastery over men and women alike, thus giving cinematic life to the macho stereotype created by contemporary intellectuals. The opening sequences set a misogynistic tone for the film in which, after the death of his father, the hero was raised by a bartender who began his education with a poker lesson and a warning that a woman "was the most venomous animal on earth." In exacting revenge on the men who killed his father, Negrete worked through a catalog of standard masculine activities. He shot his first victim during a cockfight, another over a game of cards, and a third who had fallen to his knees, begging—a clear violation of the macho code. Finally, the ringleader was gunned down during a *jaripeo*, the folkloric rodeo that provided the inevitable conclusion to any ranchero film. In Negrete's hands, even the romantic serenade of Gloria Marín degenerated into a fist fight. The female lead was thus reduced to little more than a plot device; the love triangle with the foppish son of the ringleader provided simply another venue for the macho hero to defeat his rivals.

Despite the gratuitous violence, at least by contemporary standards, *¡Ay, Jalisco, no te rajes!* remained a comedy, interrogating as much as affirming the macho ideal. The film emphasized Negrete's machismo by contrasting it with the behavior of those around him, but at the same time, this approach could also unsettle the star's masculinity. For example, the challenger for Gloria Marín's affections was a citified dandy in a fedora and scarf, which highlighted the rural foppery of Negrete's embroidered charro costume. This ambivalent contrast also emerged in the frankly homoerotic environment created by Negrete and his comic sidekicks, Chaflán and Ángel Garasa. The former gave his trademark performance of drunken and ineffectual macho posturing, shooting with his eyes closed and chasing clumsily after women. The Spanish actor Garasa adopted a darker role as Malasuerte (Bad Luck), an accomplice in the murder of Negrete's father, who repented and offered to point out the killers for a bounty. Garasa had no sooner appeared before he was shot by an unknown gunman, and although he survived the wound, it left him weakened and passive, a feminine stance that continued throughout the movie. This gender crossing began in a scene as the trio set out to track down the killers; Chaflán tenderly arranged a pillow on the wagon for the injured Garasa, laid a blanket over his legs, and then sat down beside him to drive the horses, like a frontier couple setting out on the overland trail in a Hollywood western. An appearance by Lucha Reyes, a popular ranchero singer who was notorious for lesbian love affairs, reinforced this assignment of gender roles. Just before the first shootout, the formidable woman performed the title song as a challenge: Negrete sat impassively; Chaflán made a lustful grab that she easily parried; and Garasa she slapped dismissively in the chest. Later, in a drunken barroom scene, a classic setting for gendered ambiguity, Negrete performed a William Tell act by having Chaflán and Garasa hold a lime between their teeth, pressing together in a mock kiss. When Negrete fired, the comic pair passed out in a lovers' embrace. In the final gunfight, Garasa was shot in atonement for his culpability in the original crime, and a crying Chaflán begged him, "Don't leave me alone."

¡Ay, Jalisco, no te rajes! crystallized the monolithic modern stereotype of the Mexican macho, but nevertheless conveyed a more complex picture of masculinity. First, even while presenting Negrete as a new, positive image of the macho, it preserved older, derogatory meanings of the word *macho* in the calculated bravado of Chaflán and Garasa. Moreover, the film implicitly recognized an unspoken range of gender roles, including not only the heterosexual male but also the feminized man of popular albures, who was revealed as untrustworthy, continuing the misogynist theme in a transvestite guise, as well as the bisexual man who took the dominant role with both male and female partners. Even the sexuality of Negrete was muted by his tepid interest in Marín; the only character in the entire film who seemed genuinely to enjoy the company of women was the ever-affable Chaflán.

In any event, the cinema industry quickly retreated from the heights of machismo. In subsequent films, Negrete came increasingly to spoof the macho hero of *Ay, Jalisco*. For example, in *Me he de comer esa tuna* (*I'll Have to Eat that Prickly Pear*, 1944), the masculine rivalry between Negrete and Antonio Badú amounted to little more than sophomoric pranks and punches. Moreover, the rugged star was soon challenged for top billing by another singing charro, Pedro Infante. Although born into a lower-middle-class family in Sinaloa, long reputed to be the most violent state in Mexico, Infante brought a boyish charm to the role that was quite distinct from the aloof Negrete. Infante not only showed a genuine affection for his female costars, he was also far more willing to interrogate the rigid definitions of masculinity portrayed by Negrete.

This alternative version of the macho was clearly seen in one of Infante's most popular vehicles, *Los tres García* (*The Three Garcías*, 1946) and its sequel *Vuelven los García* (*Return of the Garcías*, 1946). The three García cousins each represented a different, dysfunctional version of Mexican machismo. Víctor Manuel Mendoza portrayed an elegant *catrín* (fop); Pedro Infante appeared as a boisterous but dissipated flirt; and Abel Salazar played a touchy and impecunious rancher. The three Garcías fought for the affections of a beautiful, blonde cousin, Marga López, who had been born in the United States and ultimately chose the least effectual of the machos, Salazar. Throughout the films, the Garcías cling precariously to their macho ideal, which was in constant danger of being overshadowed by strong female figures, especially their cigar-chomping, cane-wielding grandmother played by the beloved but craggy-featured actress, Sara García. In *Vuelven los García*, the catrín played by Mendoza fell in love with a masculine, gun-slinging daughter of the rival

López clan. At another point, Infante and Mendoza wrestled about in an overenthusiastic embrace until the grandmother pulled them apart with the warning, "Hombre, the people are going to think something else."[13]

The world of the ranchero comedy was not simply a nostalgic evocation of times past but specifically packaged to encourage consumption within a growing national market. The recording industry worked closely with film-makers to publicize artists and tunes that were simultaneously sold on vinyl to wealthy households and broadcast to the masses by radio stations like the giant XEW. Cinematic depictions of folkloric handicrafts and small-town festivals meanwhile encouraged the burgeoning domestic tourism business. The singing charro thus functioned in part as a salesman peddling a very modern national identity geared to industrial production.

Yet at the same time, the operatic macho of Golden Age cinema performed an ambivalent masculinity. On the one hand, he exaggerated his valor to the point of indifference to death, a sentiment expressed in corridos such as the title song of an Infante vehicle, *Si me han de matar mañana* (1946), which proclaimed, "If you're going to kill me tomorrow, better to get it over with today." Yet at the same time, the cinematic macho was placed under the control of powerful female figures such as Sara García or exposed as a latent homosexual. Although earlier examples are easy to find, Jorge Ayala Blanco dated the definitive loss of charro innocence to the film *Dos tipos de cuidado* (*Two Rowdy Guys*, 1952), when Jorge Negrete and Pedro Infante finally appeared together, serenading one another and announcing, "When a woman betrays us, we forgive her and that's it, because she's just a woman, but when the treachery comes from our best friend, *ah Chihuahua* [darn!] how it hurts."[14] The blurring of the macho with the *mandilón* (female-dominated man) and the *maricón* (passive homosexual) was not simply a comic strategy for drawing nervous laughs from middle-class audiences but also a reflection of the cinema industry's hegemonic goal of sublimating Revolutionary violence—still a very real threat in Mexico during the 1940s. The cinema clearly assigned this dysfunctional masculinity to the lower classes by constructing the charro as a plebeian figure, despite story lines lifted from Spanish drama and the aristocratic arrogance that Negrete brought to the part. This can be seen in the charro's affinity for tequila, which remained a drink of the construction worker (*albañil*) until it became fashionable toward the end of the twentieth century. Thus, the studios constructed an image of working-class manhood rendered impotent by fears of inadequate masculinity, yet such an image had to be carefully balanced, as was demonstrated by the case of Cantinflas.

Carlota's Mustache

The most serious threat to the hegemony of the comedia ranchera at the Mexican box office in the early 1940s came from the urban comedy of Mario "Cantinflas" Moreno. His character likewise arose from the carpa theater, where a standard performance featured the comic encounter between a pelado and a catrín, a peculiarly Mexican version of the universal theme of the country bumpkin and the city slicker. Ethnic conflict appeared in the contrast between the slim Moreno, with his relatively dark skin and the ridiculous wisps of a mustache, poised like dimples over the corners of his mouth, and the lighter complexion of his stage partner, Manuel Medel. If song provided the charro's aesthetic, Cantinflas's pelado became known for his nonsense speech, based on the peculiar dialect of working-class neighborhoods in Mexico City, where people used slang and circumlocution to confuse outsiders. The pelado's humor, both in the barrio and onstage, featured contests of one-upmanship using albures. By recording these verbal jousts on celluloid, Cantinflas's first films provided invaluable, hilarious historical documents of plebeian popular culture. However, to gain widespread acceptance among middle-class audiences, Cantinflas had to tame the more threatening aspects of his character, particularly the strong homosexual allusions.

Avant-garde director Arcady Boytler was the first to transfer Moreno and Medel's stage persona to the screen. The film *Aguila o sol* (*Heads or Tails*, 1937) records a classic stage encounter between the pelado and the catrín in which sexual albures appeared prominently. At one point in the extended verbal joust, Medel berated his partner for his crude and combative manner, saying, "What gets me is the way you talk to the cop . . . When he says, 'Come with me,' what do you answer?" Cantinflas replies, "You're not my type." The homoerotic innuendoes continued after they took their bows on stage and retired to a local bar. There they huddled together over shots of tequila, arms around each other's shoulders, leaning perilously close until their lips practically met. Cantinflas gently pushed Medel's face back and mumbled an apology, only to move in again for another feigned kiss. The joke continued in the next scene as they staggered back up to their hotel room. Medel took the lead in helping prepare his partner for bed by taking his pants off. The action quickly degenerated into a mock rape scene, with Medel insisting that it was uncouth and unhealthy to sleep in pants and Cantinflas plaintively repeating, "Don't force me." By the end of the film, Cantinflas had returned to his girlfriend, restoring heterosexual norms, but the final gag involved a pair of coconuts knocking the comic team into an unconscious embrace.

Cantinflas and Medel transgressed gender roles even further in their next screen appearance, *El signo de la muerte* (*The Sign of Death*, 1939), a pre-Hispanic version of the Hollywood horror genre directed by Chano Urueta and featuring a neo-Aztec cult reviving the practice of human sacrifice to drive out the Spaniards and restore the rule of Quetzalcoatl. The film actually showed one of the sacrifices on camera, a scene made all the more shocking when the priest tore off the maiden's dress before plunging the obsidian dagger into her naked breast. Equally startling was the appearance of Cantinflas in drag, although only on two brief occasions, the first when he dressed as a woman to investigate the maiden's disappearance and the second when a drunken Medel imagined himself to be the Emperor Maximilian and saw Cantinflas as his consort Carlota.

The outrageous nature of the film derived in part from the avant-garde artists behind the scenes, particularly the screenwriter and artistic director, Salvador Novo. A leading figure of the Contemporáneos group and a devastating political columnist, Novo behaved in an outrageously effeminate manner in a country of macho politicians. Ridiculed by albures such as "Nalgador Sobo" (Buttocks Fondler), he responded by plucking his eyebrows, while at the same time facing down opponents with the wit of a Hispanic Oscar Wilde.[15]

But no simple reference to Novo's behavior will explain the appearance of Cantinflas dressed in drag, let alone the transgressions of previous movies. Cantinflas and Medel derived humor by pushing the boundaries of gender roles, forcing the audience to laugh at the breakdown of family norms that became increasingly apparent in modern urban life. Naturally, producers had to take care to provide anchors for the audience to prevent them from becoming uncomfortable. One method was to heighten the sexuality of other scenes; for example, exposing the damsel's breasts before she was sacrificed in order to offset the troubling appearance of Cantinflas in a dress.[16] Another cinematic convention for reassuring audiences about gender-crossing scenes involved the consumption of alcohol, which allowed the macho to drop his guard and express his emotions. Filmmakers also took care, on the one hand, to emphasize the difference between temporary transvestites and genuine homosexuals and, on the other, to restore heterosexual gender roles by the conclusion. The cantina scene in *Aguila o sol* contained a brief appearance by a stereotypically effeminate male, allowing Cantinflas to distance himself from social transgression with a punned warning to Medel: "Watch out around here or you'll be *pegado.*" Literally *poked*, the albur implied passive homosexuality but at another level meant *imitated* in their affectionate embrace.

Yet these multiple provisos notwithstanding, the gender reversals reflected a carnivalesque element of the early Cantinflas, who used cross-dressing as a strategy for turning the world upside down. And here he seemed to have had the last laugh, for in the resolution of each film, ambiguities remained about heterosexual norms. *Aguila o sol* ended with Cantinflas and Medel in a lovers' embrace, albeit an unconscious one. The triumph of Cantinflas stealing Medel's girl in *El signo de la muerte* was equally ambiguous. The object of their mutual affection was a farcical Margaret Dumont character to Cantinflas's Groucho Marx. Instead of signaling his victory with a kiss, she started speaking his nonsense language, demonstrating that Cantinflas was more interested in the chase than in the consummation. The humor of Cantinflas thus lay precisely in the ambiguity of his character, in his ability to exist simultaneously within and outside gendered norms.

While these early movies have since become classics, for commercial success at the time, Cantinflas had to retreat from these gender transgressions. Abandoning such avant-garde filmmakers as Arcady Boytler and Salvador Novo, as well as his partner Medel, he signed instead with the self-styled "King of the Box Office," Grovas-Oro Films, and then formed his own production company, Posa Films. In the breakthrough movies *Ahí está el detalle* (*That's the Point*, 1940), *Ni sangre, ni arena* (*Neither Blood nor Sand*, 1941), and *El gendarme desconocido* (*The Unknown Policeman*, 1941), Moreno replaced the homoerotic scenes with a new plot line—still somewhat unsettling to traditional gender roles—in which he became the object of romantic desire. His films of the 1940s usually featured two female leads, one plebeian, the other wealthy, fighting for his attention. Cantinflas invariably chose the common girl, reaffirming his ties to Mexican popular culture. A touch of effeminacy lingered within Cantinflas's character, but it served a different purpose, questioning the masculinity of others through albures rather than the complete subversion of gender norms depicted in *El signo de la muerte*. It was this less ambivalent Cantinflas that joined with the charro Negrete in a union struggle to determine the future of the Mexican cinema industry.

Cinematic Machos Versus Union Bosses

The valiant charro and the clever pelado were transformed from abstract symbols of national identity into real-life political agents when the motion picture industry became embroiled in a national union struggle in the mid-1940s. As leaders of the screen actors' guild, Jorge Negrete and Mario Moreno attempted to break away from a corrupt national union, and in the resulting battle for public opinion, their celebrity status offered a potent weapon against colorless bureaucrats in the labor hierarchy. Nevertheless, elements of their cinematic personae, like the charro's tendency to shoot from the hip and the pelado's nonsense language, proved ill-suited to effective political action. Ultimately, the struggle came down to a contest between rival forms of masculinity when the union bosses sought to undermine the actors by hiring the Spanish dancer, Miguel de Molina. A refugee from the authoritarian regimes of both Francisco Franco in Spain and Juan Perón in Argentina, Molina had impeccable artistic credentials. Nevertheless, his reputation for homosexuality prompted Negrete and Moreno to abandon the gender transgressions of earlier years and perform idealized versions of masculinity.

The use of an effeminate scab seems all the more ironic given the union leaders' careful cultivation of their own masculine image, but macho posturing had actually led to the showdown of 1946. Labor organizing in Revolutionary Mexico had followed the model of syndicalism, in which workers formed industry-wide unions in an attempt to gain control over the means of production. The screen actors thus formed part of a broad Syndicate of Cinema Industry Workers (STIC), which was dominated by projectionists and other technicians and headed by Salvador Carrillo. In February 1945, the internationally renowned cinematographer Gabriel Figueroa, who headed the artistic branch of STIC, including screen actors, publicly denounced corruption within the union. When Fidel Velázquez, national president of the Confederation of Mexican Workers (CTM), called Figueroa in for a conference with Carrillo, the burly STIC boss became enraged and punched the slim cameraman in the face, putting him in the hospital. The filmmakers, led by Negrete and Moreno, then proceeded to form an independent union, the Syndicate of Cinema Production Workers (STPC). The STIC leader attempted a lame public apology, which he promptly sabotaged by explaining that the blow had been an "instinctive reaction against an injury that no man could tolerate."[17]

Aware that the clumsy Carrillo had little hope in a public relations battle with cinema idols, Fidel Velázquez brought in the Spanish dancer Molina to help stop the breakaway union. One can only speculate on the union leader's logic: perhaps he thought that to defeat the effeminate artistes of the movie industry, he would need a queer of his own. Regardless, the CTM boss had a clear imperative of preventing a secession movement in this high-profile industry, which might encourage other independent unions and undermine the official party's labor confederation. The need to crush the dissidents became all the more pressing when President Manuel Ávila Camacho, perhaps mindful of the favorable publicity to be gained from siding with the actors, issued a decree on September 3, 1945, awarding recognition to the STPC. The national union played its final trump in January 1946 when STIC projectionists declared a boycott of films made by the STPC. The first motion picture to be affected by the strike was Jorge Negrete's latest effort, ironically entitled *No basta ser charro* (*It's Not Enough to Be a Charro*, 1945). Molina also formed part of this attempt to undermine public support for the Mexican actors by playing at the Esperanza Iris Theater, where CTM workers had locked out the STPC actors and their stage allies. The dancer from Seville had a checkered past, but he was an internationally known artist, having toured Paris and London before the war, and his company of eighty dancers and musicians promised a gala spectacle of Spanish folklore.[18]

During the preparations before his Mexican premiere, Molina refused to consider the political ramifications of his performance. Moreno, who had met the dancer a year earlier on a tour of Argentina, tried to explain personally that Velázquez was using him as a scab against Mexican actors who had been locked out of the Iris Theater. The STPC even offered to compensate him for the costs of changing the venue, but the dancer ignored their pleas. Finally, a day before the show opened, the actors gave up on him and appealed to the public. A full-page newspaper ad denounced Molina as a "farcical dancer shamefully expelled from the Argentine Republic who now seeks to trample the sacred rights of authentic Mexican workers, cowardly betraying and mocking them by performing his hybrid art on a stage picketed by artists who have not made common cause with nefarious leaders."[19]

The opening performance by Molina at the Esperanza Iris Theater on March 8, 1946, therefore became a powder keg of potential union violence. Fidel Velázquez, delighted to have an international artist dancing for the Mexican national union, was determined to allow nothing to disrupt the premiere. STIC replaced the usual doormen with union enforcers and distributed free tickets to CTM butchers, long considered the most sinister of all tradesmen because of their association with blood and death. Velázquez calculated that knowing that they were present in the audience would discourage any attempts by the STPC to disrupt the performance. Meanwhile, the actors' union enlisted allies among breakaway segments of the CTM, who gathered nearby to break up the performance. President Ávila Camacho asked both sides to maintain the peace and just to be sure, ordered the district governor, Javier Rojo Gómez, to fill the streets outside the theater with police.[20]

These circumstances called not for the machine-gunning macho played by Negrete but rather the more calculated bravado of Cantinflas, ever ready to turn and run in the face of superior force. Numerous conflicting versions make it impossible to reconstruct exactly what happened in the Esperanza Iris Theater, but the basic outline of the night's events remained relatively consistent throughout the accounts. Molina was performing his second act when Moreno presented a ticket to the STIC doormen. They could not have failed to recognize the celebrity but expected to confront whole brigades of STPC thugs. The audacity of coming alone, or—in some accounts—with one companion, got Moreno past the front gate. Once inside the darkened theater, he made his way down the central aisle to the orchestra seats and shouted, "Traitor!" twice. He then tried to make a speech denouncing the show, but spectators booed and attempted to throw him out of the theater. Before STIC thugs could grab the actor, however, the police intervened and escorted him safely back to STPC headquarters while Molina resumed his performance.[21]

The diverse interpretations given to these events, and the subsequent public relations struggle between the STPC and STIC, further demonstrate the crucial role of masculine performance in this union conflict. Supporters of STIC, such as the theater critic for *Excélsior*, portrayed the event as an artistic duel in which the Spanish dancer had triumphed over the Mexican comedian. Molina came across to readers as a genial artist in a magnificent spectacle, the finest theatrical presentation of the times and a brilliant social event. This contrasted sharply with Cantinflas, who tried to win the audience over, only to be shouted down. "For the first time in his magnificent career, the public did not respond. Morally beaten, pale, and looking sad, Cantinflas abandoned the Iris."[22] Moreno rightly questioned such theatrical metaphors for what he considered to be a political struggle. Far from a disappointment, he described that night as one of the greatest triumphs of his life because it was real. "Now [there is] no more playacting [teatro]," he told reporters after returning from the Iris. "Today [there are] only deeds."[23] But regardless of the real physical danger, his deeds were a form of theater, intended to gain the approval of the Mexican public and their political leaders.

As a result, the question of just who attended the Iris Theater on March 8 assumed real significance. The STPC had launched a massive public relations campaign against Molina, so those who showed up had essentially repudiated the actors and their struggle against the STIC. The rude reception given to Moreno—telling him to shut up and get out—had compounded the insult. The comedian denied that the people in the audience constituted "the public" and insisted that they were merely STIC thugs and other CTM workers sent by Fidel Velázquez to fill the seats, a captive audience like those common to political rallies staged by the Mexican ruling party. But that seems implausible given that negative publicity draws crowds more surely than positive advertising. The critic for *Excélsior* described the usual mixed theater crowd, ranging across Mexican society, from wealthy Bohemians to the working class. He noted large numbers of pistol-toting STIC thugs but also many Spanish refugees nostalgic for the folklore of their homeland, currently under the dictatorship of Francisco Franco. The STPC's public statements before the performance had specifically called upon Spaniards to repudiate the scab dancer, and Moreno described the crowd as "undesirable individuals," not legitimate refugees.[24]

But even if Molina had triumphed before a crowd of Spanish refugees, as the newspaper reported, Moreno remained a heavy favorite in the theater of Mexican public opinion. To convince the public, and more importantly the president, of the justice of their cause, the screen actors played upon fears of foreign intervention and social dissolution. In a special assembly held on Monday, March 11, the STPC called for an executive order expelling Molina from the country under Article 33 of the Constitution of 1917, which gave the president the power to deport foreigners who threatened Mexican society. Supporters of the actors pointed to Molina's immorality, which meant effeminacy, in an attempt to convict the Spanish dancer before the court of Mexican public opinion. *El Universal* reported that Moreno had yelled not *traitor* but *maricón* and that the audience had taken up the chant. Another strong supporter of STPC, or rather critic of the CTM, the conservative *La Nación*, added that the Spanish dancer was known throughout Argentina by the feminine form "La Miguela." Moreno himself apparently never publicly used albures questioning Molina's masculinity, although Negrete could scarcely mention the man without some reference to his lack of manhood. Salvador Novo avoided the polemic by taking a nationalistic stance, denouncing Molina for his failure to appreciate Mexican culture but refusing to endorse the filmmakers' attacks.[25]

With public opinion turning against him, Molina attempted unsuccessfully to explain himself. When questioned about the events of March 8, he claimed that onstage he could not see what had happened and that if he had known, he would have invited Moreno up to explain his position. He gave an equally lame response to the charges of immorality by stating that he had not been physically thrown out of Argentina, just asked to leave. Finally, he published a forlorn letter in *Excélsior* insisting that he had no political agenda and wanted only to gratify Mexicans with the joys of Spanish art. But the Mexican people, already annoyed by the boycott, rallied behind the national film industry. When the actors threatened to relocate to Hollywood, announcing, "He goes or we go," the cry went up for Molina's expulsion. The president reportedly received numerous petitions requesting Article 33 treatment for the Spanish dancer. Nevertheless, crowds continued filling the Iris Theater to see the notorious act.[26]

The actors finally shut down their rival, Molina, and won the union dispute, through the assistance of an independent electricians' union. During the labor struggles of the previous year, Moreno had worked assiduously to recruit allies, and on March 13, workers of the powerful Mexico City Electricians' Syndicate (SME) pulled the plug at the Esperanza Iris Theater. The audience took the cancellation stoically, and most accepted rain checks for the next day's show, but that was likewise shut down. On March 15, the electricians increased pressure on the government by shutting off power to all of Mexico City for fifteen minutes, with promises of nightly blackouts until an agreement was reached. Once again, President Ávila Camacho intervened on behalf of the actors by ordering the CTM to accept the settlement he had decreed the previous September.[27]

Conclusion: The Shadow of the Macho

The internecine struggle between cinema industry unions reveals the ambiguity of the macho ideal within the broader Mexican society at midcentury. On the one hand, the masculine performance of STIC leader Carrillo, punching out the cinematographer Figueroa, prompted widespread outrage. On the other hand, the overt homosexuality of Miguel de Molina proved equally threatening to audiences. Actors Negrete and Moreno used their public personae to wage the battle, but in the moment of truth, it was the posturing pelado rather than the true macho who confronted the CTM thugs. Thus, the public rejected the extremes of male behavior, both the macho and the maricón, portrayed by Golden Age cinema.

The Mexican film industry, ever attuned to shifts in audience ratings, responded rapidly by altering its depictions of the national identity from rural charros to urban comedies and melodrama. For Jorge Negrete, who was incapable of reinventing himself, the change heralded the decline of his stardom. Increasingly, he dedicated his efforts to the management of the screen actors' guild before his untimely death in 1954. Pedro Infante revitalized his career by abandoning the charro role for an urban setting in films such as the comedy classic *Nosotros los pobres* (*We the Poor*, 1948), thus challenging Cantinflas on his home territory. Mario Moreno, meanwhile, reinvented his own style of filmmaking by fitting his distinctive persona into a different setting with each movie, portraying a fireman, a politician, and even a charro in the devastating parody *El siete machos* (*Seven Machos*, 1950)—a name taken from a popular brand of cologne. Apart from such star vehicles, the cinema industry focused on the cabaret underworld in a series of melodramas about women trapped in prostitution. By the late 1940s, the moment of rural nostalgia had passed and Mexican audiences became increasingly interested in the modern, urban society in which ever greater numbers of them lived.

The undeniable popularity of his movies notwithstanding, Jorge Negrete provided not so much a model of masculine behavior for any particular class of Mexican men but rather a mythic image of a past that never was. In Hollywood at the same time, John Wayne was attempting to define his own mythic vision of a masculine, Anglo-Saxon frontiersman as the national identity. In retrospect, he appears hunkered down inside the walls of an Alamo before a rising tide of civil rights and women's liberation. Certainly among working-class men in contemporary Mexico City, the macho represents a negative stereotype of dysfunctional masculine behavior.[28] While the crowds may have enjoyed watching the charro strut onscreen, the challenge in real life, as in the union struggle at the Esperanza Iris Theater, was to forge a modern masculine identity that would resolve the contradictions of a patriarchal society.

NOTES

1. See, for example, Enrique Serna, "El charro cantor," in *Mitos mexicanos*, ed. Enrique Florescano (Mexico City: Aguilar, 1995), 189–93.
2. Ilene V. O'Malley, *The Myth of the Mexican Revolution: Hero Cults and the Institutionalization of the Mexican State, 1920–1940* (New York: Greenwood Press, 1986); and Thomas Benjamin, *La Revolución: Mexico's Great Revolution as Memory, Myth, and History* (Austin: University of Texas Press, 2000).
3. Alan Knight, "Racism, Revolution and *Indigenismo*: Mexico, 1910–1940," in *The Idea of Race in Latin America, 1870–1940*, ed. Richard Graham (Austin: University of Texas Press, 1990); and David A. Brading, "Manuel Gamio and Official Indigenismo in Mexico," *Bulletin of Latin American Research* 7, no. 1 (1988): 75–89.
4. Samuel Ramos, *Profile of Man and Culture in Mexico*, trans. Peter G. Earle (Austin: University of Texas Press, 1962).
5. Hershfield identified another category of Afro-Mexican films recognizing the prominence of the mulatto population, particularly in coastal states such as Veracruz and Michoacán, where slavery had been widespread in the colonial period. See "Race and Ethnicity in the Classical Cinema," in *Mexico's Cinema: A Century of Film and Filmmakers*, ed. Joanne Hershfield and David R. Maciel (Wilmington, DE: Scholarly Resources, 1999), 81–100.
6. Américo Paredes, "The United States, Mexico, and *Machismo*," in *Folklore and Culture on the Texas-Mexican Border*, ed. Richard Bauman (Austin: Center for Mexican American Studies / University of Texas, 1993), 215–34.
7. Julia Tuñón, for example, has shown how women appeared on screen in far more nuanced roles than the stereotypical archetypes of the virgin and the whore. See her *Mujeres de luz y sombra en el cine mexicano: La construcción de una imagen, 1939–1952* (Mexico City: El Colegio de México, 1998).
8. The phrase is from Carlos Monsiváis, *Escenas de pudor y livianidad* (Mexico City: Editorial Grijalbo, 1988), 107.
9. But see Mary-Lee Mulholland, "Mariachis Machos and Charros Gays: Masculinities in Guadalajara," in this volume.
10. In *¡Vámonos con Pancho Villa!* (*Let's Go with Pancho Villa*, 1935), for example, Fuentes depicted the Revolutionary leader as a bloodthirsty and opportunistic bandit. For stage versions, see Armando de María y Campos, *El teatro de género chico en la revolución mexicana* (Mexico City: Biblioteca del Instituto Nacional de Estudios Históricos de la Revolución Mexicana, 1996), 46.
11. Aurelio de los Reyes, *Medio siglo de cine mexicano (1896–1947)* (Mexico City: Editorial Trillas, 1987), 142–52; and Emilio García Riera, "The Impact of *Rancho Grande*," in *Mexican Cinema*, ed. Paulo Antonio Paranaguá, trans. Ana M. López (London: British Film Institute, 1995), 128–32.
12. Emilio García Riera, *Historia documental del cine mexicano* (Guadalajara: Universidad de Guadalajara, 1993), 2:204.

13. Quoted in ibid., 4:92. See also Jorge Ayala Blanco, *La aventura del cine mexicano* (Mexico City: Editorial Posada, 1985), 76–82.
14. Ayala Blanco, *La aventura del cine mexicano*, 86.
15. Carlos Monsiváis, *Amor perdido* (Mexico City: Biblioteca Era, 1978), 265–96. See also Víctor Macías González and Anne Rubenstein, "Introduction: Masculinity and History in Modern Mexico," in this volume.
16. Just as *Some Like It Hot* (1959) balanced the drag scenes of Tony Curtis and Jack Lemmon with visions of Marilyn Monroe. Chris Straayar has defined an entire genre of such films in "Redressing the 'Natural': The Temporary Transvestite Film," *Wide Angle* 14 (January 1992): 36–55.
17. *El Universal Gráfico*, February 27, 1945; and Elena Poniatowska, *La mirada que limpia: Gabriel Figueroa*, vol. 3 of *Todo México* (Mexico City: Editorial Diana, 1996), 58–62.
18. For a fuller discussion of this union struggle, see Jeffrey M. Pilcher, *Cantinflas and the Chaos of Mexican Modernity* (Wilmington, DE: Scholarly Resources, 2001), chapter 4.
19. *El Universal Gráfico*, March 7, 1946.
20. *El Universal Gráfico*, February 2, March 8, 1946; *La Prensa*, March 9, 1946; and *La Nación*, March 16, 1946.
21. The city's major newspapers ranged from the pro-STIC *Excélsior* to *El Universal*, which favored the STPC, with *La Prensa* staying relatively neutral.
22. *Excélsior*, March 10, 1946.
23. *El Universal Gráfico*, March 9, 1946.
24. Transcript of STPC Assembly, March 11, 1946, 432/64, Manuel Ávila Camacho, Archivo General de la Nación (hereafter AGN), 13–14.
25. *El Universal*, March 9, 1946; *La Nación*, March 16, 1946; Salvador Novo, *La vida en México durante el periodo presidencial de Manuel Avila Camacho* (Mexico City: Consejo Nacional para la Cultura y los Artes, 1994), 499. In his autobiography, the Spanish dancer recalled Moreno as being conciliatory and blamed Negrete for all the trouble. See Miguel de Molina, *Botín de guerra* (Barcelona: Planeta, 1998).
26. *Excelsiór*, March 10, 11, 1946; *La Prensa*, March 13, 1946.
27. *El Nacional*, March 15, 1946; *El Universal Gráfico*, March 12, 1946.
28. Matthew Gutmann, *The Meanings of Macho: Being a Man in Mexico City* (Berkeley: University of California Press, 1996).

CHAPTER 9

Mariachis Machos and Charros Gays

Masculinities in Guadalajara

MARY-LEE MULHOLLAND

> A baby boy born in Guadalajara gets a finger up the ass. Why? To see what he'll be . . . If he kicks, he'll be a soccer player. If he screams, a mariachi. And if he laughs, he'll be a homo [*maricón*[1]].
>
> —*Amores Perros* (2000)

ON APRIL 13, 2002, OVER 40,000 CITIZENS OF GUADALAJARA, JALISCO (known locally as *tapatíos*), were treated to a historical concert: the one and only time that local father and son *canción ranchera* singers Vicente and Alejandro Fernández would sing together in a complete concert. Calling it the *Lazos Invencibles* (Invincible Bonds) tour, father and son performed dressed in *trajes de charro* (cowboy outfits) and backed by mariachis. They sang for over four hours, exchanging references to family frequently with particular emphasis on the bond between father and son. This bond was demonstrated by several embraces between Vicente and Alejandro and sealed with a kiss on the lips. The following week, the picture of the kiss was on the cover of many local and national newspapers and magazines, including one tabloid that held the caption, "*¡El Potrillo y Chente se besan amorosamente en la trompita! ¡Pero no son CHARROS GAYS! Le hizo cosquillitas*

Figure 9.1. Press coverage of Vicente and Alejandro Fernández kissing.

con el bigote de Zapata" meaning "El Potrillo ["The Colt," nickname for Alejandro Fernández] and Chente [nickname for Vicente Fernández] kiss lovingly on the lips! But they are not GAY CHARROS [cowboys]! Tickling him with his Zapata moustache."[2]

Mariachi is a musical ensemble consisting of eight to twelve performers dressed in traditional cowboy outfits, called *trajes de charro*, that play a range of string instruments, including several violins, guitar, *guitarrón* (a large bass guitar), *vihuela* (a small, five-string guitar with a rounded back), occasionally a harp, and one or two trumpets. The music played by mariachis includes different genres of songs such as *rancheras*, *sones*, *jarabes*, *huapangos*, *corridos*, and *boleros* that narrate nostalgic, humorous, and emotional stories of love, heartache, death, drinking, and place. Mariachis are most commonly comprised of men and are heavily associated with drinking, melodramatic sentimentality, fiestas, and cowboys and are virtually interchangeable with the stereotype of the Mexican macho. Ranchera music (canción ranchera) is a genre of Mexican music wherein individual performers dressed in trajes de charro sing accompanied by mariachi. Trajes de charro are stylized cowboy outfits consisting of matching pants and a short jacket adorned with silver buckles or embroidery, cowboy boots, thick bow ties, and sombreros.

Guadalajara, Mexico's second largest city, is a rich site to examine sexuality and masculinity in particular. Capital of the western state of Jalisco, Guadalajara is known for its conservativism and Catholicism. It is the birthplace of three well-known Mexican "traditions" and important national symbols: tequila, *charrería* (horsemanship, similar to rodeo), and mariachi. As a result, Guadalajara, and the state of Jalisco as a whole, is reputed to be home to the authentic Mexican macho: the tequila-drinking, singing charro. Paradoxically, Guadalajara is known as being Mexico's "gayest" city, often referred to as the San Francisco of Mexico.[3] At first glance it appears that Guadalajara is a site of competing narratives of male sexualities, of machos and maricones. However, I will argue that in fact the two are not competitive opposing discourses, one oppressive and the other oppressed, but rather they are entangled performances of the ambiguity and messiness of Mexican masculinities.

Specifically, I will examine how public perceptions of Vicente and Alejandro Fernández's sexuality work as performative sites, in which perceptions and anxieties regarding male sexuality in Guadalajara are produced and interrupted. I will illustrate how this concert, and the provocative kiss, worked as a flash point of male sexual ambiguity in Guadalajara, a city where the meanings and boundaries of masculine sexual landscapes are a daily contestation. That is, the kiss revealed the tension in Guadalajara between the privileging of an idealized Mexican macho against the increasing visible Mexican maricón.[4] In this tension, the seemingly contradictory performance between the macho and the maricón become intertwined with the gay merging into the macho and the macho into the gay.

Jalisco and the Macho Trinity: Mariachi, Charros, and Tequila

Y me gusta escuchar los mariachis,
Oír cómo suenan esos guitarrones
Y echarme un tequila con los valentones
Tus hombres son machos y son cumplidores,
valientes, ariscos y sostenedores,
no admiten rivales en cosa de amores
Su orgullo es su traje de charro, traer su pistola, pasear en el pinto
¡Ay, Jalisco no te rajes![5]

And I like to listen to the mariachis,
Listening to the sound of the guitarrones
And taking a swig of tequila with braggarts
Your men are macho and dependable,
brave, surly, and supportive,
who do not allow rivals in matters of love
Their pride is their traje de charro, carrying their pistol, taking their pinto for a ride
Ay, Jalisco don't give in [chicken out]!

Popularized by singer-actor Jorge Negrete (see essay by Jeffrey Pilcher in this volume), "Ay, Jalisco no te rajes" is a ranchera song that boasts the virtues of Jalisco, including its beautiful women, macho men, mariachi, and charros.[6] Performed in one of Mexico's earliest and most popular *charro cantor* (singing cowboy) or comedia ranchera films, *Allá en el Rancho Grande* (1936), the song and the movie combined three important symbols—tequila, mariachi, and charros—in the nostalgic imagining of Mexican nationalism and masculinity.[7]

In the 1930s, the Mexican state promoted nationalism through a renaissance of all things indigenous and the valorization of *patrias chicas*, or the notion that Mexico was comprised of several regional cultures.[8] With the intent to "unify all things Mexican," images of the rural and Revolutionary past, including charros, mariachi, ranchera music, and tequila, became important in the myth making of an imagined Mexico.[9] The state supported cultural industries such as painting (particularly the muralist movement), nationalistic music, folkloric ballet, and folklore studies. Furthermore, emerging cultural industries such as film, radio, and popular music became extremely powerful and active in the promotion and articulation of Mexicanness, or *lo mexicano*. This era produced several important cultural institutions including the charro cantor genre of film. Combining the music of mariachi and the cowboy tradition of charros, these films produced an image of the idealized Mexican man: a rural, mestizo cowboy who possessed a loyal, brave, and stubborn character. That is to say, a macho.[10]

These images are often associated with Jalisco, so that Guadalajara is often described in tourism literature as "the most Mexican city," and the secretary of tourism in Guadalajara has claimed in their latest tourism campaign that "Jalisco es Mexico [Jalisco is Mexico]." As part of this campaign, the municipal government and the local chamber of commerce promoted tequila, charros, and mariachi in tourism literature, festivals, heritage sites, and academic research. Sponsored through this tourism campaign, the historical study *El Origen del mariachi Coculense, una cultura entre mariachis, charros y tequila* (*The Origin of the Mariachi of Cocula: A Culture of Mariachi, Charros and Tequila*) by Efraín de la Cruz González details the origins of these three traditions, especially mariachi, in Jalisco. Then secretary of culture Pablo Gerber Stump introduced the book by stating that

> certainly Mexico and Jalisco are recognized around the world for the mariachi, tequila and charrería traditions that are very much our own. [This] book underlines the legitimate and irrefutable attention these elements receive as unequalled symbols of our authentic Mexican identity.[11]

Other state-sponsored promotions of these traditions include the Museo de la Ciudad in Guadalajara, which has sections on the charro, tequila, and mariachi; two mariachi museums in the towns of Cocula and Tecalitlán; and a tequila museum in the town of Tequila. Perhaps two of the most visible tourism projects are the Tequila Express and the annual Encuentro Internacional del Mariachi y la Charrería sponsored by the Guadalajara Chamber of Commerce and the state of Jalisco's secretary of culture. The former is a tourist package (approximately US$65) that takes tourists (Mexican and non-Mexican) by train to the tequila museum and a tequila factory. On the train tourists are entertained with live mariachi, Mexican food, and, of course, tequila samples. The latter is an annual international festival that includes a national-level charrería competition as well as a multitude of events exhibiting local, national, and international mariachis. At the ninth Encuentro Internacional del Mariachi y la Charrería (2002) a song commissioned by the secretary of culture entitled "Jalisco es Mexico" was performed at each of the gala events by "Mexico's most famous mariachi," Mariachi Vargas de Tecalitlán.

These traditions are not limited to state sponsored-tourism and heritage projects but are also part of the everyday lives of tapatíos. Tourists and tapatíos alike enjoy the music of mariachi in many bars and plazas in Guadalajara, there are several *lienzos charros* (arenas for charrería) throughout the city, and tequila, of course, is consumed at a variety of spaces and occasions. Furthermore, these three traditions are often combined together in the performance of *jalisciense* identity. Mariachis wear trajes de charro and perform at charrerías that are sponsored by a local tequila company, songs sung by mariachis are often about charros and tequila, and tours of the nearby town of Tequila and its tequila factories are accompanied by mariachi. While there are other important symbolic and cultural forces that work toward the construction of masculine identities in Guadalajara (such as religion), it is the official and everyday performance and consumption of tequila, charrería, and mariachi as cultural traditions that is of interest here.

Not only are these three cultural traditions purported to be authentically jalisciense and representative of lo mexicano, but they are also overtly understood as masculine and as part of the sexual landscape. The image of the rough, hardworking, hard-drinking singing cowboy is explicitly invoked in the promotion of these three traditions and symbols. Furthermore, the spaces and actors involved in their performances are masculine. Not only is charrería a sport restricted to men and mariachi a profession dominated by men, but the places and spaces where tequila, mariachi, and charro come together are highly masculine spaces, always controlled by men if not restricted to them.

Tequila is Mexico's legendary alcoholic drink and possibly its most famous cultural export. The majority of Mexico's tequila production is in the state of Jalisco with the majority of that production taking place in and around the town of Tequila (one hour west of Guadalajara). Tours of tequila distilleries (such as Sauza and José Cuervo) as well as the Tequila Express have made this both a successful industry and a successful tourist attraction. Furthermore, tequila is extremely popular with jaliscienses, often served at weddings and fiestas, and is a popular choice at bars, discos, and cantinas. Despite the consumption of tequila at a variety of events and places in Mexico, tequila, and drinking in general, is still considered very much part of the masculine domain. For example, cantinas and plazas are male spaces that few "decent" women frequent, and the ability to "handle" liquor is a positive male attribute. As one friend reminded me, *tequila* is a masculine noun (*el tequila*) after all. This link between tequila and masculinity or, perhaps more aptly, between tequila and machismo is situated in the mythic and historical representation of tequila as the drink of the men who fought in the Revolution. In the preface to a cultural history of tequila, Carlos Monsiváis comments that in "the mythical world of the cartridge belt and thick mustachios, of flashing eyes, the wide sombrero, and shouts of 'Viva Mexico, sons of . . . !' it is tequila that is revered by the fearless and avoided by the gutless."[12] In the representation of revolutionaries, machos, and mariachis in popular culture, the image of the macho in a cantina challenging, embracing, and consuming tequila is not only a verification of his manliness but also his Mexicanness.

The image of the charro in Mexican popular culture, particularly film, and its role in the construction of Mexican national identity has been extensively examined in anthropology, history, and cultural studies.[13] In her analysis of the history and symbolism of the charro, anthropologist Olga Nájera-Ramírez argues that the charro is a "master symbol of Mexican culture" that illustrates how gender, nation, and class are involved in the evolution and creation of lo mexicano.[14] Popularized during the Golden Age of cinema, the image of the charro is embedded in a nostalgic yearning in Mexican nationalism for a Revolutionary and rural past. In particular, Nájera-Ramírez argues that the image of the charro is "a cultural construction of maleness" that "represented the Mexican male as a brave, hardworking man who stood up for his rights, defended his family and country."[15] In Guadalajara, there are several lienzo charros, statues of charros, exhibitions in museums on the charrería, and it is part of the annual Encuentro Internacional del Mariachi y la Charrería (International Mariachi and Charrería Competition). The performance of the sport and the individual charros are important aspects in the construction of cultural and sexual identity in Guadalajara.

Similar to rodeo, charrería is a popular sport throughout Mexico, often described as Mexico's national sport.[16] However, it is particularly popular in the western states such as Jalisco, Guanajuato, Zacatecas, and Aguascalientes. Starting as informal competitions between cowboys, the charrería developed into a formalized sport and profession whose membership, dress, and behavior is governed by associations such as the Federación de Charros and La Asociación de Charros de Jalisco. Generally held on Sunday afternoons (except when there are special competitions), the charrería is a competition between two teams of charros (all men) in nine separate events that demonstrate riding and roping skills. The name *charro* is not one that can be used by any ranchera singer, mariachi, or cowboy, but rather it is a title that must be earned, used only by men who are members of charro associations. Although men dominate the sport, women do participate in the charrería in two ways. First, women participate as wives, sisters, and daughters of charros who occupy supportive roles and often have parallel associations. Second, women participate as *escaramuzas*, the women members of synchronized riding teams that perform a detailed riding pattern at the events. While the latter is an important and popular part of the charrería, it is not a judged event and is incorporated more as a performance than as a sport.[17]

Nájera-Ramírez argues that the involvement of women in wife-supportive roles or as objects of beauty reinforces patriarchal norms of femininity in Mexican culture. In addition to this, I would argue that lienzo charros are overtly masculine spaces in that they are a space controlled by men wherein the performance of masculinity is highly regulated and patrolled. In particular, regulations are quite strict regarding the dress of the charro (traje de charro) and membership with the associations. First of all, those wearing a traje de charro (whether it be mariachi, ranchera singers, or charros) must respect the costume and its history by following a code of behavior and conduct that includes no fighting, no drunkenness, maintaining a clean-shaven appearance (mustaches allowed) with short hair, and always wearing the entire costume (no removal of the bow tie or use of tennis shoes). Second, membership with charro associations and participation is completely restricted to men. In this highly regulated performance of history and tradition, the charro performs a nostalgic longing for Mexican masculinity wherein the charro is part of a brotherhood, respecting a set code of behavior defined by family values, loyalty, and bravery.

From religious festivals in villages, weddings, and birthdays to state-sponsored spectacles, mariachi is a vital and salient part of the identity of tapatíos. Not only performed in public spaces and tourist locations, mariachi is also heard in churches, homes, schools, bars, and, of course, in serenades. When I arrived in Guadalajara and explained that I intended to research mariachi, the response was always one of excitement and pride. Musicians, friends, and taxi drivers often tested my knowledge of the history of mariachi. I was questioned on my favorite artists and songs and recommended potential lines of research to pursue. Although it is somewhat costly (a mariachi for an hour can cost anywhere from US$200 to US$300), hiring a mariachi for serenades, patron saint fiestas, weddings, birthdays, graduations, or special events at work is quite common. In Guadalajara there are several places to hear mariachi, including the Plaza de los Mariachis, where there are several mariachis for hire by the song or by the hour, and several bars and restaurants that have live mariachi.

Although representations of mariachis in Mexican popular and official discourse are never stable, they are most frequently portrayed as male, macho, heterosexual, and mestizo. Many mariachis are constituted entirely by men, singing songs about drinking, love, or heartbreak and performing in overtly male spaces such as the Plaza de los Mariachis, lienzo charros, *palenques* (cockfighting arenas), and cantinas. There are, of course, many exceptions to this stereotype of mariachi such as all-female mariachis, traditional or indigenous mariachis, and the performance of mariachi in gender-neutral spaces such as restaurant-bars, family events, and churches.[18] The participation of women in mariachi and ranchera is nothing new. Women have a long and significant history with the mariachi as singers and musicians. For example, Lucha Reyes is one of Mexico's earliest and most famous ranchera singers, and Jalisco is home to several all-female mariachis, such as Mariachi Femenil de Tecaltitlán and Mariachi Femenil Las Perlitas Tapatías. Despite the strong presence of women in mariachi and ranchera, their participation is, at times, viewed as exceptional, leaving the image of mariachi as a masculine genre and vocation to persist. While female ranchera singers, such as Lucha Reyes, had a great deal of success, few female mariachi ensembles have achieved significant popularity, and none of the major mariachis include female musicians regardless of the growing presence of female musicians in the field. Partly due to the association of mariachi with fiestas, drinking, and overtly male spaces, the inclusion of women musicians into "mixed" mariachis is not very common.[19]

Working mariachis often keep late nights playing at restaurant-bars, fiestas, serenades, and the plaza, where drinking is common. For example, the Plaza de los Mariachis in Guadalajara is not recommended for women or, for that matter, tourists because of its reputation as a place of pickpockets, drug dealers, and prostitutes. Considered safe during the late afternoon or early evening, it is possible to enjoy the music and ambience of the plaza in safety (in fact, many argue that its reputed danger is inflated), although it is generally nearly empty with little activity. In comparison, at nighttime, particularly after midnight, the plaza is buzzing with activity. Mostly local men fill the tables of the plaza at night drinking beer or bottles of tequila or rum while mariachis wander from table to table playing songs requested and paid for by the customers (each song costs between US$8 and US$10). Meanwhile, other mariachis stand on street corners and meridians nearby, hoping to be hired for a party or a serenade, and, less visibly, drug dealers and prostitutes hope for customers of their own. Similarly, many neighborhood cantinas in Guadalajara are also almost exclusively male spaces where men go to drink and listen to ranchera music on the jukebox. Partying, late nights, drinking, drugs, and rough men are all part of the environment of many working mariachis.

The masculinity of these spaces, particularly of cantinas and the plaza, are regulated through implicit codes of propriety (or lack of propriety) for men and for women. Due to the reputation of these spaces as sites of heavy drinking, late nights, and potentially drugs and prostitutes, they are considered less than ideal working or social environments for "decent" women. As one female mariachi informed me, many parents are concerned about their daughters working in mariachis, particularly in the plaza, because "mariachi and tequila always go together, and sometimes playing at fiestas it is possible that people will fail to show proper respect." This plays into the stereotype of the macho Mexican man unable to resist the impulse to be excessive in his consumption of alcohol and his sexual desire for a woman. It is natural to assume, then, that a man who has been drinking will be more vulnerable to his natural weaknesses, and thus women who place themselves in circumstances where men are drinking in excess are willing to expose themselves to attention lacking in "proper respect."

Despite the perception of an overtly male (and dangerous) working environment for mariachis, there are several female mariachis working in Jalisco. Moreover, most musicians and friends I spoke with were supportive of women in mariachi, often commenting that it is a "very beautiful thing." However, few would, given the choice, hire an all-female mariachi over a male mariachi. When pushed on this point, many people responded that while female mariachis are "beautiful," they are unable to capture the same *feeling* that is so important to the experience of mariachi and ranchera. This feeling, not surprisingly, is linked to the highly charged drinking atmosphere often associated with mariachi, mariachi's perceived history, and the themes of many of the songs. A folklorist, media personality, and self-proclaimed mariachiphile in Guadalajara claims that women are not capable of playing mariachi with the same sentiment or force as men and that it should remain a "cosa de los hombres [man thing]." Speaking during the ninth annual Encuentro del Mariachi y la Charrería, Cornelio García stated that, "Female mariachis are something very modern. Yes, there were some groups of women in the forties and fifties. But, look, in order to pull the cords of a guitarrón one needs the composure, muscles and temperament of, well, a macho."[20] Later, I spoke to him about his statements made during the festival regarding the place of women in mariachi, and he explained that it is not just that he believes only men can play, but only Mexican men and, preferably, Mexican men from Jalisco:

> If I have to choose from a feminine group playing *sones* [a type of song commonly played by mariachis], and I have to choose, I would always choose the men. Because the origin of the sones comes from the countryside, from the land-work, as people that sweated all day long being exploited by the *hacendado*, working fifteen–twenty hours a day under the sun picking the maize, plowing the land, working hard. So this music belongs to the peasant, to the man that worked the land. And the feeling and the rage he had expresses itself through the strings of the guitarrón being pulled with guts.

He went on to say:

> They [women and foreigners] can play with feeling, but it is going to be a European feeling or a feminine feeling that is not the same as the macho jalisciense from a ranch, from the countryside. It is similar but not the same.

The opinion that only men can capture the essential feeling of mariachi is not uncommon, particularly when mariachi is associated with drinking, the land (that presumably the men worked), and matters of the heart (caused by the actions of women). In other words, hiring a female mariachi for a municipal celebration is fine, but when your lover has left you, you are lonely, and you want to go to the local plaza or cantina to console yourself with a tequila and a mariachi, a standard male mariachi is best. The sentiment associated with mariachi is best exemplified by one of the most requested and popular songs, "Ella [She]," written by one of Mexico's most prolific and revered singer-songwriters José Alfredo Jiménez:

> Me cansé de rogarle, me cansé de decirle
> que yo sin ella, ¡de pena muero!
> Ya no quizo escucharme, si sus labios se abrieron
> fue pa' decirme, "¡ya no te quiero!"
> Yo sentí que mi vida se perdía en un abismo
> profundo y negro como mi suerte
> quize hallar el olvido al estilo Jalisco
> pero aquellos mariachis
> y aquel tequila, ¡me hicieron llorar!

> (I'm tired of begging and I'm tired of telling her
> that without her I'll die of pain!
> She didn't want to listen to me anymore, if her lips opened
> it was to tell me, "I don't love you anymore!"
> I felt that my life was lost in a deep, black abyss, like my luck
> I wanted to forget, in the style of Jalisco
> but those mariachis
> and the tequila made me cry!)

The expression of angst performed with "guts" is essential to the popularity and success of mariachi and ranchera singers. Many ranchera singers, including Pedro Infante, José Alfredo Jiménez, and now Vicente Fernández, are famous for their expressive performance of the music, and the authenticity of this performance is based on their humble beginnings (*del pueblo*). This authenticity of expression not only stems from the performers' humble origins, but also their image as womanizers, hard drinkers, and machos.

The promotion and production of tequila, mariachi, and charros as true jalisciense traditions and Mexican national treasures work together with Guadalajara's religious and social conservatism to produce a strong masculine landscape of the city and of the state characterized by the hard-living, hard-drinking, honorable, macho mariachis.

El ambiente tapatío: "In Guadalajara, Men Are Either Mariachis or Maricones"

Known both for its macho sexual landscape and its religious and social conservativism, Guadalajara[21] enjoys a contradictory reputation as the "gayest" city in Mexico. There is a sense that *el ambiente* (the gay world) in Guadalajara is larger and more visible then in other Mexican cities. [22] In his study of sexuality in Guadalajara, Héctor Carrillo remarks on the dual reputation of Guadalajara as both gay and macho:

> Guadalajara has been a site of intense ideological clashes about sex and sexuality . . . On the one hand, the city is considered to be one of the most conservative and traditional in Mexico . . . Yet, on the other hand, Guadalajara has for long also been regarded as being the most homosexual city in Mexico . . . and many jokes about the city jointly invoke *machismo* and *homosexualidad*.[23]

The reputation of Guadalajara as gay is the result of a combination of several factors including the social and political activism of the community, the robust gay nightlife in Guadalajara and Puerto Vallarta (Jalisco's main beach resort), the popularity of Guadalajara and Puerto Vallarta as destinations in Mexican and foreign gay tourism, and the perpetuation of this reputation in jokes (such as the one at the beginning of this chapter), rumors, and media representations of the city.[24]

The political and social activity of el ambiente in Guadalajara became most active during the late 1980s and early 1990s in conjunction with the HIV and AIDS awareness movement in Mexico. During this time, Guadalajara was witness to the birth of several gay organizations, a surge in gay night spots, and the beginnings of an annual march and conference celebrating Guadalajara's sexual diversity. The year 2002 marked the XII Semana Cultural de la Diversidad Sexual (Sexual Diversity Cultural Week) and the VI Marcha por la Diversidad (March for Diversity) in Guadalajara.[25] The Semana Cultural de La Diversidad Sexual includes several different activities: cultural events, academic discussion, sporting competitions, and the march for diversity. The different activities, particularly the march, receive a fair amount of press coverage, counterdemonstrations, and a range of attention from the municipality, from opposition to support or complete ambivalence. The XI Semana Cultural de la Diversidad Sexual (2001) was important for el ambiente in Guadalajara because it marked the birth of the Movimiento Unificado por la Diversidad Sexual Jalisco (Jalisco Unified Movement for Sexual Diversity), which unified all organizations in the region in the common fight for human rights and sexual diversity.[26]

While some might argue that the degree of organization and activity in el ambiente somehow demonstrates a tolerance and liberal attitude toward sexuality in Guadalajara, thus making it the San Francisco of Mexico, quite the contrary is true. In fact, government, Church, and citizen associations in Guadalajara are active in the negation of el ambiente. The International Gay and Lesbian Human Rights Commission (IGLHRC) has stated that Guadalajara is a priority for them because despite the community's well-developed organizations, it also confronts a situation "particularly complicated" due to the opposition of certain sectors of the Catholic Church.[27] Furthermore, police harassment of the gay community, particularly the extortion and abuse of transvestite prostitutes, is common.[28] Likewise, conservative citizens' associations, such as the Unión Nacional de Padres de Familia, are influential in lobbying the different levels of the state and private business to deny any support, such as permissions for marches, to el ambiente.

The tension between el ambiente and the conservative segments of Guadalajaran society came to a head in 1991 when Guadalajara was selected to host the XIII International Association of Lesbians and Homosexuals Conference (ILGA). The city was selected by the ILGA because of its desire to host a conference in the third world for the first time, Guadalajara's reputation as having a large and active gay community, and the initial positive response organizers received in their discussions with city and private-sector officials. However, this amicability was short lived. Due to pressure from the Church, conservative citizens' associations, and a growing level of hostility of Guadalajarans toward the notion of a gay conference in their city, pressure to cancel the conference was enormous. Many tapatíos objected to the portrayal of Guadalajara as a "gay" city and were concerned with the preservation of Guadalajara's reputation as a conservative religious city and birthplace to Mexican tradition. The resistance to the conference included the appearance of antigay graffiti. Worse, the hotels and restaurants refused to provide service to conference attendees, and the city refused to provide security for the conference. As a result, the conference was moved to Acapulco.[29]

In addition to the visibility of Guadalajara's gay community in terms of political activism, the popularity of Guadalajara and Puerto Vallarta in gay tourism has also had an influential role in the production of Guadalajara's "gayness." In his study on queer tourism in Mexico, Lionel Cantú (2002) writes that Guadalajara and the coastal town of Puerto Vallarta have become arguably the most popular destinations in gay tourism in Mexico for both Mexican and non-Mexican tourists.[30] This popularity is a result of the presence of well-developed *zonas de tolerancia* (tolerant zones) in the cities that include gay-friendly bars, discos, hotels, and restaurants and the reputation that men in this region are gay and handsome. Specifically, Cantú examines the representation of male Mexican sexuality in tourist literature and argues that the attraction of these locations in queer tourism is the sexual intrigue of meeting "real" men and, therefore, the possibility of the macho gay. "In the Western queer imaginary Mexico and its men are somehow locked in a spatiotemporal warp of macho desire. Mexico seems to represent a place fixed in time where 'real' men can be found."[31] Here macho male sexuality collides with the gay male sexuality of Guadalajara, making a homosexual macho sexual landscape possible. To illustrate, he includes the covers of three queer tourism guides, one of which presents a shirtless man wearing pants from a traje de charro.[32]

Guadalajara and Puerto Vallarta reportedly have Mexico's best and most active gay nightlife. In a recent survey, it was reported that Jalisco boasts 20 percent of Mexico's gay bars with at least twenty-five each in Guadalajara and Puerto Vallarta. While Monterrey has a few more with twenty-eight, and Mexico City with forty-two, Jalisco dominates the Mexican gay nightlife with fifty in total. (The mayor of Guadalajara remarked that Guadalajara can no longer be considered the gayest city in Mexico since Monterrey and Mexico City have more gay bars than Guadalajara.[33]) Many of these bars in Guadalajara have been in business for over twenty years and are important institutions in the production of el ambiente in the city.

Finally, beyond the active and visible el ambiente in Guadalajara and its popularity in gay tourism, the reputation of the "gayness" of Guadalajara is perpetuated in jokes and rumors that circulate about the city in popular culture and in day-to-day discussions. For example, the joke told in the film *Amores Perros* cited at the beginning of this chapter is well-known and has several different forms, all ending with a similar punch line stating that Guadalajara is made up of three types of men: soccer players, mariachis, and homosexuals. I heard this joke in several different contexts while talking to musicians, fans, and friends, including one mariachi visiting Guadalajara from northern Mexico who answered his own question when asking me why I chose to do my research in Guadalajara: "There are only two things in Guadalajara: mariachis and maricones." Once, while visiting a friend's hometown in western Jalisco, I heard a group of young men discussing the origins of a mutual associate. One responded that the person in question was from Guadalajara; however, while saying this, he mimicked a tone of voice, effeminate gestures, and a bouncing walk meant to be read as gay.

El Charro de Huentitán and El Potrillo: The Fernández Family in Guadalajara

As well as being home to mariachi, tequila, and charros, Guadalajara is also the hometown of Mexico's most famous and popular ranchera singer today, Vicente Fernández. Also known as "El Charro de Huentitán," "Número Uno," or, more simply, "Chente," Vicente Fernández has released over one hundred albums and fifty films over a thirty-five-year career.[34] Starting as a singer at restaurants, bars, and the Plaza de los Mariachis in Guadalajara,

Vicente Fernández has performed at charrerías, palenques (cockfighting arenas), plazas de toros (including La Plaza México bullring in Mexico City), Carnegie Hall, Madison Square Garden, and countless other venues throughout the Americas during his prolific career. At times he has been compared to ranchera singers from Mexico's Golden Age. Although his acting career has been less impressive, Vicente Fernández has been instrumental in the immense success that ranchera music has enjoyed recently. Not surprisingly, he was recently honored at the 2002 Latin Grammys with the Person of the Year Award to acknowledge his long and influential career in Latin music.[35] His son, cleverly nicknamed "El Potrillo" ("The Colt"), Alejandro Fernández has also had an immensely successful career singing ranchera and ballads and is one of the best-selling Spanish-language performers in the world and Mexico's hottest sex symbol.[36]

The Fernández family is able to generate a great deal of pride and support in their hometown, due largely to their performance of traditional and conservative notions of Mexican identity and Mexican masculinity. Vicente and Alejandro Fernández embody and perform traditional notions of masculinity and lo mexicano in their private lives and in their music. Whether it is their performances dressed in trajes de charro backed by mariachi, the sponsorship of and participation in charrería, or their paradoxical reputations as both family men and womanizers, Vicente and Alejandro Fernández are overtly dedicated to the protection and reproduction of Mexican traditions, including the macho. However, their performance of Mexicanness and machismo is constantly interrupted and challenged by criticisms of their contamination of tradition and rumors questioning their masculinity due to their insincerity, questionable manliness, and homosexuality.

Born and raised in the small town of Huentitán outside of Guadalajara, Vicente Fernández moved to Guadalajara as a young man determined to make a living as a singer in local bars, restaurants, and in the Plaza de los Mariachis. With the end of the Golden Age of ranchera film and music marked by the 1966 death of Javier Solís (regarded as the last of the ranchera singers from this era), a void was created in Mexican popular and vernacular music. Vicente Fernández was approached in the late 1960s by record companies who had heard of the singing charro in Guadalajara known for his powerful voice, expressive performances, and authentic "del pueblo" ("of the countryside," "of the people") background. Eventually signed with Mexico's most powerful entertainment company, Televisa, Vicente Fernández would become a living legend in the genre embodying the image that charros cantors before him had possessed: down to earth, proud of his rural origins, dedicated to family, a ladies' man, and a man's man.[37]

Taking great pride in his humble rural origins, Vicente Fernández is extremely active in rural life, choosing to reside on his famous Los Tres Potrillos (The Three Colts) ranch. Located just outside of Guadalajara, the ranch includes a competitive charro team, a lienzo charro, a charro school, a western clothing store, a conference center, a breeding program of miniature horses and cocks (for fighting), and a guitar-shaped pool. Earning his title as "El Charro de Huentitán," Vicente Fernández is active in Mexico's "national sport" of charrería, sponsoring his ranch's charro team, attending events, and identifying with the traditions and values promoted by charro associations. Tourists used to be granted access to this ranch, but since the kidnapping of Vicente Fernández's oldest son in 1998, security at the ranch has been strengthened. The son, Vicente Fernández Jr. (currently trying to establish himself as a ranchera singer as well), was held for four months before his eventual release on payment rumored to be US$8 million. During the ordeal, the kidnappers cut off three of his fingers.[38]

In conjunction with his reputation as being "del pueblo" and a charro, Vicente Fernández also has a reputation as a dedicated family man and a womanizer. While at first these two may seem paradoxical, they reconcile in the image of the macho. First, Fernández often memorializes his parents in concert and interviews, speaking on how their lives were true and honest ones and their deaths the saddest times of his life. Second, he is extremely affectionate toward his wife, commenting on her loyalty, forgiveness, and toughness. During the famous "Lazos Invencibles" concert in Guadalajara Vicente Fernández announced that

> I want to thank one woman whom during thirty-nine, almost forty years, has given me love, respect, and her trust when I had nothing, sometimes only beans, sometimes nothing. She has given me my four children: Vicente, Gerardo, Alejandro, and Alejandra. She is here, and I want you to give her a round of applause. Back then, when Vicente was born [he begins to cry], she gave me the strength to move forward . . .[39]

Interestingly, when Vicente Fernández speaks of his children he never includes his son from one of his extramarital affairs, which were rumored to be quite common earlier in his career. Now, when speaking in interviews or in concerts, Fernández says that he prefers a quiet home life spent at the ranch with his wife, children, and grandchildren to the craziness that characterized the earlier part of his career.[40] When asked if he considers himself a good husband, Vicente Fernández replied, "Everyone knows that I have not been a saint. Alejandro, who is criticized a lot, is my apprentice."[41]

The performance of Mexican tradition and masculinity by Vicente Fernández is particularly overt during his expressive and energetic concerts. Like many popular music artists in Mexico, Vicente Fernández performs the majority of his concerts at palenques during city or town fairs and festivals. The concerts generally begin at midnight after the cockfighting tournament, when the arena is quickly transformed into a stage for the musical performances. While many young ranchera singers include pyrotechnics, confetti, special lighting, and flashy dancing mariachis that perform on a carpet covering the blood-stained floor, Vicente Fernández enters into the palenque accompanied only by his all-male (slightly aging) mariachi band. Without any attempt to transform the space into something cleaner or flashier, Vicente Fernández is clearly comfortable in this forum. The space, like him, is Mexican, gritty, and unapologetically masculine. Not surprisingly, he is an avid fan of cockfighting and raising cocks and has even written a song about them.[42]

The informality, or perhaps more accurately the simplicity, of a Vicente Fernández concert is augmented by the rapport he establishes with the audience by chatting, kissing women in the audience, shaking hands with the men, and sharing in a drink and a cigarette. During his interactions with the fans, he often talks about his humble roots, his gratitude to God and his fans, and his love of his parents, wife, and children. Consistently during these "chats" with the fans, Vicente Fernández is famous for becoming overcome with emotion and crying. He is also famous for, despite his dedication to family life and in particular his wife, kissing women fans at his concerts and kissing them quite passionately. The public nature of these kisses gives him the opportunity to express a sexual prowess and appetite while at the same time the controlled context of the kiss, a public concert, does not necessarily tarnish his image as a family man. Furthermore, he promises in every concert to sing for as long as the people applaud, making his concerts extremely long and seen as a way of expressing his gratitude and, perhaps, a demonstration of his virility. In addition, the length of his concerts situates him in the public as a regular man with an admirable work ethic untainted by his money. That is, despite his financial and popular success, Vicente Fernández has remained a hardworking man "del pueblo" and has not transformed into a pampered upper-class star. Occasionally, he engages in shoving matches and arguments with drunk and disorderly fans. At one concert I went to he became frustrated with a drunken fan who kept grabbing at him. Finally he lost his temper, threw down his drink, and shoved the fan, yelling, "Ya y ya, cabrón [Enough already, asshole]!"

Unable to claim the same humble origins as his father, Alejandro Fernández has been able to perpetuate an image of a macho, artist, and nationalist committed to the tradition of Mexican music and culture. While Chente appeals to the rural population and the working class, Alejandro appeals to the urban middle class, the young, and, in particular, women. As one reporter commented:

> Alejandro Fernández is guilty of the fact that the urban middle class and, above all, young people are listening to ranchera music with a naturalness that for many years they only had listening to pop, ballads, rock, and other genres more popular in English music. Not since the time of Pedro Infante and Jorge Negrete has there been a charro costume that has melted as many hearts as Alejandro Fernández's costume.[43]

Alejandro Fernández's popularity as a ranchera singer has surpassed that of his father's, and he is acclaimed as Mexico's hottest male singer. Regardless of his privileged upbringing, Alejandro Fernández, like his father, is committed to the protection of Mexican tradition and music, releasing a disc celebrating one hundred years of Mexican music, including boleros, ranchera, and ballads. Alejandro Fernández refuses to succumb to the pressure of recording in English, as many other Mexican music stars have done, and is openly critical of the lack of recognition Mexican regional music such as ranchera receives at international music award shows.[44] In an interview in 2002, Alejandro Fernández commented that he regrets that in some Latin American countries he is only known as a ballad singer (as a result of one of his two albums of ballads) because his desire is to promote Mexican music, specifically ranchera, in other countries.[45] Incidentally, Alejandro Fernández was selected to represent Mexican music and tradition at the 2000 Expo in Hannover, and more recently he has been cast as the lead in a film on the life of Revolutionary hero Emiliano Zapata. In fact, the Zapata-inspired mustache he grew for the making of the film, which he was sporting during the Lazos Invencibles concert and one of his videos, caused quite a media stir.[46]

Like his father, Alejandro Fernández is not only dedicated to the promotion of Mexican music, but he also promotes images of charros, bullfights, cockfighting, the Revolution, and rural life in his concerts and videos. First and foremost, he almost always performs in the traje de charro, which comes with a strict code of behavior and respect for the charro tradition. He is an accomplished horseman and encourages the use of his nickname, "El Potrillo." In fact, one of his songs that he uses to close his concerts is called "El Potrillo":

> Mi historia ya la saben,
> Soy el hijo de un gran hombre.
> El mejor padre del mundo,
> Él es el Número Uno,
> De esta hermosa y gran nación,
> Soy *El Potrillo* señores!
>
> (You already know my story,
> I am the son of a great man.
> The best father in the world,
> He is the Number One,
> In this beautiful and grand nation,
> Gentlemen, I am the Colt!)

In addition to these similarities, Alejandro Fernández also possesses a similar character to his father due to his expressiveness in concerts, his "explosive temper," and "hot-bloodedness" (he too has also been involved in at least one fight at a palenque).[47]

Alejandro Fernández resembles his father, too, in his reputation as a family man (he married his high school sweetheart and had three children with her) and as a womanizer (now separated from his wife, living with his girlfriend and their two children). The media coverage and gossip regarding his marriage, separation, divorce, and rumors of reconciliation with América (his wife) are plentiful. Considered a fairy tale marriage of true love, it is rumored that the relationship is and will continue to be threatened by Alejandro's (understandable yet tragic) womanizing:

> Their marriage [Alejandro Fernández and América Guinard], began with them in love, has now been through several stages over time

> including the many infidelities of *El Potrillo*. The love between the couple has dissolved . . . but now it appears the divorce has revived the love between the pair . . .[48]

It goes on to report on Alejandro Fernández's dedication to his children and the support he has provided to his ex-wife since their separation.

Unlike his father's concerts, Alejandro Fernández's performances are less gritty but equally as emotive, energetic, and masculine. Largely due to his image as urban and upper class, the connection between the average concert-going fan and Alejandro Fernández is not as viable as it is with Chente. The history of his family is too well known, and any attempt to portray himself as a simple man of a humble background would not only be impossible but ridiculous. Therefore, his show is more elaborate than his father's simple production and includes more stage props (such as large screens), lighting effects, and a regular band to accompany him on his ballads and boleros in addition to a mariachi. While Alejandro Fernández is unable to perform a "del pueblo" or gritty Mexican authenticity, he is able, quite successfully, to perform an overt sexual maleness. The majority of the concertgoers are young women, several of whom will throw their bras, phone numbers, teddy bears, flowers, and, at times, themselves, into the arena where Alejandro Fernández is singing. While Alejandro Fernández is not known to cry during concerts, his performances are gut-wrenching, physically exhaustive, and emotionally tumultuous. By a simple flick of his chin or a turn of his hips, El Potrillo can throw a crowd into frenzy:

> Euphoria is a word too soft to describe this show of three and a half hours. Alejandro Fernández is more than a ranchera singer, he is a dream, a sexual fantasy, an idol sustained by the desperate shouts of thousands of fans.[49]

In the context of their hometown of Guadalajara, the Fernández family is a popular and attractive performance not only of an idealized Mexican masculinity, but also of Guadalajara's claim as cradle to that masculinity. The family's performance of ranchera and their involvement in charrería, cockfights, and soccer games (the Fernández family are avid fans and supporters of the Chivas, one of two Guadalajara soccer teams) are all meaningful acts in an idealized masculine performance in Jalisco. However, underlying this authentic and normative performance of sexuality and Mexican tradition are rumors and criticisms of both artists regarding their authenticity, sincerity, and validity as real charros, real mariachis, and as real Mexican men.

First, Vicente Fernández's dedication to the genre of ranchera and the tradition of the charro is perceived by some as insincere and is particularly undermined by his focus on quantity rather than quality in production of albums and films. Within this critique of commercialism and insincerity he is also accused of merely imitating the authentic man-of-the-people, or "del pueblo," style of ranchera legends from the Golden Age. That is, his performance of a gritty masculinity is a contrived copy of the "real machos" of the Golden Age. Furthermore, his expressiveness during concerts, and in particular the crying, is criticized as contrived to augment his image as a simple man who has gone from rags to riches. For example, during an interview with one local mariachi I asked him what he thought of current ranchera singers, such as Vicente Fernández. In response, the mariachi began to fake cry and then waved his hand as if to dismiss Vicente Fernández, stating that his crying is faked and that by doing so he "fails to show proper respect for the music."

Sincerity and sentimentality, as I mentioned earlier, are important characteristics of an idealized macho mariachi. Yet, paradoxically, another common comment on his crying is that only pathetic men are unable to control their emotions, and his excessive crying is a sign of weakness. In conversation with fans in particular, Vicente Fernández's crying often led to insinuations that he and his son, Alejandro, were gay and perhaps even lovers. As one friend pointed out, "There is something strange going on in that house!" Finally, Vicente Fernández's body, and in particular his manipulation of it, has become part of the circulating discourse regarding his inauthentic, contrived performance of the macho. A newspaper article reporting on Vicente Fernández finally admitting to plastic surgery joked:

> And now that the popular *charro de Huentitlán* has finally acknowledged he uses plastic surgery to look younger, it would not surprise us if he became the official spokesman of the hair dye product, Miss Clairol.[50]

These sometimes subtle and other times overt attacks on Vicente Fernández's manhood by way of jokes regarding his excessive crying and vanity have become, in Judith Butler's (1993) formulation, the failures and gaps that are unavoidable in every performance of gender. In particular, Chente's performance of an idealized masculinity is not only one of excess, but it is also extremely public to an audience (Guadalajarans) whose awareness of alternative performances of masculinities is never far from the surface.

The gaps and failures of Alejandro Fernández's performance of an overt sensuality show themselves in rumors and gossip regarding his sexual preference. Upon discovering that I am a fan of Alejandro Fernández, practically every male friend I have, every mariachi I interviewed, and every music store clerk I did business with in Guadalajara claimed that El Potrillo "es joto" (is a fag/homo). Eager to convince me of the legitimacy of this urban legend I was told many "firsthand accounts" of his attendance at gay bars in Guadalajara and his admittance to a local hospital for injuries sustained during gay sex. My female friends rarely commented or volunteered information regarding Alejandro Fernández's sexuality, either regretfully confirming the rumors with a nod or rolling their eyes in exasperation. Surprised by the consistency of this reaction by my male friends in Guadalajara I decided to ask for explanations of his marriage and his reputation as a womanizer. "It's a cover-up," my friends would reply. "What about his children?" I would ask. "He is bisexual," they responded. Often, my friends would recommend Pepe Aguilar, a ranchera singer from a neighboring state and son of another famous charro cantor, Antonio Aguilar, as a preferable model of the Mexican man. At first I was unsure how to handle these statements within my research until I saw the cover of the tabloid quoted at the beginning of this chapter: "El Potrillo and Chente kiss lovingly on the lips! But they are not GAY CHARROS!"

The Kiss:
A Flash of Mexican Male Sexual Ambiguity in Guadalajara

Finally we can return to the scene that opened this chapter, the kiss between father and son ranchera singers at a concert in Guadalajara and the subsequent shocking tabloid headline. The kiss was not the first, nor the last, between Vicente and Alejandro Fernández in concert, nor is it the first time that a Mexican father and son have demonstrated affection for each other publicly. Regardless, the kiss did create a ripple of discomfort at the concert and caused people to take a second look as they walked by newsstands the following week. A group of fans I met at the stadium, who were offering me both explanations and tequila to aid in my understanding and enjoyment of the concert, were somewhat shocked by the kiss. One man grimaced and shook his head in disgust. Not aware at the time of the implications, I failed to ask anyone at the concert about the kiss. While no one I spoke with the following week actually entertained the possibility of the two singers having an intimate relationship, explaining the kiss as either a European or a rural Mexican custom, the kiss was never normalized. Most took it as an opportunity to share gossip regarding the (homo)sexuality of the singers.

My argument is that the kiss became a flash point of the anxiety regarding male sexual plurality and ambiguity in Mexico and in particular Guadalajara. In his philosophy of history, Walter Benjamin argues that the "true picture of the past flits by. The past can be seized only as an image which flashes up at the instant when it can be recognized and is never seen again. . . . It means to seize hold of a memory as it flashes up at a moment of danger."[51] In light of the battling landscapes of masculinity in Guadalajara, the performance of a hypermasculinity by the Fernández family, and the anxiety and fear of homosexuality in the everyday in Guadalajara, the kiss worked as a flash that illuminated the potential and danger of different possibilities in imagining alternative Mexican male sexualities.

The ambivalent nature of gender and sexuality, the slipping of the macho into the gay and back again, is illuminated by the anxiety produced by the simultaneous performance of masculinity and queerness by the Fernández family. The ability of the Fernández family to perform an idealized and normative masculinity and a queer one simultaneously is a reflection of the complexity and ambiguity of male sexualities in Guadalajara and Mexico in general. This rupture, the seemingly paradoxical performance of the macho gay and the gay charro, is not accidental. Rather, in a performance of sexuality that is as excessive as that of Vicente and Alejandro Fernández in a city whose image of machismo is vital to their place in the national landscape, ruptures, failures, and ambiguity are inevitable.

NOTES

1. In her research on homosexuality in Mexico City, Annick Prieur states that "*Maricón* . . . probably a male-gendered version of *María*, is a pejorative term that they [her participants] would never use to refer to themselves." The term is most often translated as *fag* or *homo*. Annick Prieur, "Domination and Desire: Male Homosexuality and the Construction of Masculinity in Mexico," in *Machos, Mistresses, Madonnas: Contesting Power of Latin American Gender Imagery*, ed. Marit Melhuus and Kristi Anne Stlen (New York: Verso, 1996), 87.
2. Cover of *¡Ooorale!*, April 2002.
3. See references to Guadalajara's comparison to San Francisco in Lionel Cantú, "De Ambiente: Queer Tourism and the Shifting Boundaries of Mexican Male Sexualities," *GLQ* 8, no. 1–2, (2002): 139–66; Joseph M. Carrier, *De Los Otros: Intimacy and Homosexuality among Mexican Men* (New York: Columbia University Press, 1995); and Héctor Carrillo, *The Night Is Young: Sexuality in Mexico in the time of AIDS* (Chicago: University of Chicago Press, 2002).
4. The use of all terminology in regard to Mexican male sexuality is extremely contentious. *Macho, ser hombre, gay, homosexual, bisexual, joto, puto, maricón*, etc., are all terms with contested and multiple meanings. For an excellent overview, see Annick Prieur, *Mema's House, Mexico City: On Transvestites, Queens, and Machos* (Chicago: University of Chicago Press, 1998). Furthermore, those words similar to or drawn from English (such as *homosexual* or *gay*) have very different meanings in Spanish. Therefore, rather than referring to the gay or homosexual community in Guadalajara, I will instead use the Spanish term *el ambiente*, which refers to the community of men who have sex with men, transsexuals, transvestites, and transgender people. Although women who have sex with women are also included in this term, this segment of el ambiente is not as visible as the men. Moreover, this chapter deals exclusively with male sexualities. I intend to examine the sexuality of women in Guadalajara and in production of mariachi and ranchera music in my dissertation.
5. Excerpts from "¡Ay, Jalisco no te rajes!" written by E. Cortázar and M. Esperón. All translation by author unless otherwise noted.
6. In conjunction with the reputation of the macho from Jalisco there is also a saying that the women from Jalisco are the most beautiful women in Mexico, famous for their European features and Christian piety.
7. See Jeffrey M. Pilcher, "The Gay Caballero: Machismo, Homosexuality, and the Nation in Golden Age Film," in this volume.
8. While there was a glorification of the indigenous past, there was a repression of the current indigenous population. Eric Zolov, "Discovering a Land 'Mysterious and Obvious': The Renarrativizing of Post-Revolutionary Mexico," in *Fragments of a Golden Age: The Politics of Culture in Mexico Since 1940*, ed. Gilbert M. Joseph, Anne Rubenstein, and Eric Zolov (Durham, NC: Duke University Press, 2001).
9. Zolov, "Discovering a Land 'Mysterious and Obvious,'" 241.

10. It is important to be clear that *macho*, like all other terms used in Mexico regarding gender and sexuality, is highly contested. As Matthew Gutmann, *The Meanings of Macho: Being a Man in Mexico City* (Berkeley: University of California Press, 1996), and Annick Prieur illustrate in their ethnographies on sexuality in Mexico City, *macho* means many things to many people. It can mean a man of honor, a brute, a coward, or a womanizer, depending on the context and the speaker. For this chapter, the use of *macho* and *machismo* refers to the image idealized in the charro cantor film genre.
11. Efraín de la Cruz González, *El Origen del Mariachi Coculense: una cultura con charros, mariachis y tequila* (Guadalajara: Secretaría de Educación Pública, 1996), 187.
12. Carlos Monsiváis, "Preface: Tequila with Lime and Other Table Talk," in *Tequila: The Spirit of Mexico*, ed. Enrique F. Martínez Limón (New York: Abbeville Press, 2004).
13. Olga Nájera-Ramírez, "Engendering Nationalism: Identity, Discourse, and the Mexican Charro," *Anthropological Quarterly* 67, no. 1 (1994): 1–14; and Anne Rubenstein, "Pedro Infante's Death as Political Spectacle" in *Fragments of a Golden Age: The Politics of Culture in Mexico Since 1940*, ed. Gilbert M. Joseph, Anne Rubenstein, and Eric Zolov (Durham, NC: Duke University Press, 2001), 199–233.
14. Nájera-Ramírez, "Engendering Nationalism," 30.
15. Ibid.
16. Ibid. See also website of La Asociación Nacional de Charros (http://www.asociacionnacionaldecharros.com/blog/).
17. Nájera-Ramírez, "Engendering Nationalism," 27–28.
18. Traditional or indigenous mariachis usually include four musicians dressed in indigenous costumes with two violins, a harp, and a vihuela. For an excellent study of mariachi antiguo, see Arturo Chamarro, *Mariachi antiguo, jarabe y son: símbolo compartidos y tradición musical en las identidades jaliscienses* (Zapopan: El Colegio de Jalisco, 2000).
19. "Mixed" mariachis, or those mariachis that have both male and female musicians, are extremely common in the United States but fairly rare in the mariachis I saw in Jalisco.
20. "Las penas de amor se curan con mariachis," *Público*, September 8, 2002.
21. I heard this statement ("In Guadalajara, men are either mariachis or maricones") several times while in Guadalajara, including from mariachis participating in the Encuentro de Mariachi y Charrería. See also Cantú, "De Ambiente."
22. Vanesa Robles, "Ni San Francisco ni Amsterdam, dicen los *gays* tapatíos," *Público*, July 4, 2001.
23. Carrillo, *The Night Is Young*, 10.
24. Note that most of my discussion regarding el ambiente in Guadalajara is about men, as this chapter is concerned with the reputation of Guadalajara as being home to machos and homosexual men. There has been very little academic

research on the sexual diversity of women in Jalisco or Mexico in general. Many researchers comment on the invisibility of lesbians in this literature. See Cantú, "De Ambiente."

25. Editors' comment: Note the use of language of cultural pluralism—drawing on the European, and particularly the French, model of "sexual diversity." The American use of "pride" is not as widely disseminated in Mexico.
26. Enrique Vázquez, "Nace el movimiento unificado por la diversidad sexual Jalisco," *Público*, July 10, 2002.
27. Vanesa Robles, "Los homosexuales de Guadalajara enfrentan un 'clima difícil,'" *Público*, October 3, 2001.
28. Maricarmen Rello, "Sigue la discriminación a *gays*, dicen organismos," *Público*, December 13, 2002; and "Denuncian ante la ONU," *Mural*, November 1, 2002.
29. Carrillo, *The Night Is Young*, 14.
30. Lionel Cantú notes that Acapulco is also an important destination in gay tourism but that Puerto Vallarta has recently surpassed it in popularity.
31. Cantú, "De Ambiente," 159.
32. *A Man's Guide to Mexico and Central America*, cited in Cantú, "De Ambiente."
33. "Niegan que Jalisco lidere bares gays," *Mural*, January 27, 2003.
34. El Charro de Huentitán (The Cowboy from Huentitán, a small town outside of Guadalajara where Vicente Fernández was born), El Número Uno (Number One), and Chente (Vince, short for Vicente). He is also known as "El Hijo del Pueblo" ("Son of the Countryside/People").
35. This award was somewhat controversial as it was viewed as a long-overdue recognition and inclusion of Mexican regional music at the Latin Grammys.
36. *El Potrillo* means the "The Colt" and was drawn from the name of Vicente Fernández's ranch outside of Guadalajara, which was called "Los Tres Potrillos" ("The Three Colts") and named for his three sons.
37. Anne Rubenstein demonstrates in her article on ranchera legend Pedro Infante how his rural, down-to-earth, hardworking, loyal, and brave persona were an embodiment of Mexico's struggle with gender, tradition, and modernity in its search for a national identity. Originally a carpenter from a poor rural background, Pedro Infante was dedicated to his mother, a womanizer (at the time of his death he was on trial for bigamy and was the father of at least fourteen children), and daring. He bridged both the image of the charro, an image "always receding into the past," and "a risky modernity" portrayed in his love of urban and modern living. See Rubenstein, "Pedro Infante's Death as Political Spectacle," 216, 227.
38. "El hijo de 'Chente,' liberado," *Público*, August 1, 1998.
39. Drawn from my notes and from media coverage of the concert. See Carmen Cruz, "América y 'el Potrillo': Legalmente siguen siendo esposos," *TV y Novelas* 24, no. 17 (2002): 110.
40. "El amo y señor de la música ranchera," Ocio, *Público*, October 17, 1997.
41. "Don Vicente Fernández," *TV Notas*, July 3, 2002.

42. "Hoy platiqué con mi gallo" ("Today I Chatted with My Cock"), written by Vicente Fernández.
43. "Le dicen 'Potrillo,' pero es profeta en su tierra," *Público*, October 16, 1997.
44. "*El Potrillo* desacredita a los Grammy," *Público*, March 2, 1998.
45. "Alejandro Fernández," *Quien* 3, no. 3 (September 2002).
46. After several delays, the film was released in 2005 to a cool reception by critics and the public alike.
47. "Confesiones de un 'Potrillo,'" *Público*, September 22, 1997.
48. Carmen Cruz, "América y 'El Potrillo': Legalmente siguen siendo esposos," *TV y Novelas* 24, no. 17 (2002): 110.
49. "*El Potrillo* causó euforia," *Público*, October 18, 1997.
50. "Vicente Fernández: 'quitar lo que sobra'; El ídolo ranchero admite su cirugía plástica," *Público*, June 12, 1999.
51. Walter Benjamin, *Illuminations* (New York: Harcourt, Brace & World, 1968), 254.

Conclusion

Mexican Masculinities

RAMÓN A. GUTIÉRREZ

THE HISTORY OF MEXICAN MASCULINITIES BETWEEN 1880 AND 1960, as the essays here show, cannot easily be understood as a single, unitary trajectory from a fractured past of enormous regional diversity to a monolithic sense of *lo mexicano* or a singular sense of Mexican masculinity or femininity. Historians have long chronicled the complexity of many Mexicos and have shown how regions evolved with their own particular elites, gender binaries, and discourses of distinctiveness that popularly explained why those born in Oaxaca were unique from those born in Chihuahua, why the *jalisciense* (a resident of the state of Jalisco) was superior to a *chilango* (a resident of Mexico City). What we learn quite precisely here is that for all the speculation about the Porfiriato's creation of a unitary bounded sense of Mexicanness, the reality was the existence of many masculinities and femininities and considerable contestation over lo mexicano.

Scholarship on Mexican culture since the late 1930s had long focused on the presidency of Porfirio Díaz, from 1880 to 1910, as the period when Mexico constructed its distinctive national citizenship, with ideals of proper comportment for women and men. Among those intellectuals who pondered these concerns, Octavio Paz and Samuel Ramos were undoubtedly the most important, writing national character studies that postulated the existence of Mexican hypermasculinity, or *machismo*. The argument about the Porfiriato was that President Díaz and his French-inspired technocrats, his infamous *científicos*, took as their main task the modernization of Mexico into an economically dynamic state. To do this, they forged a national citizenry through space and force, integrating the nation's far-flung regions through a web of roads and railroads that crisscrossed the country and connected local markets to those of national and international import, linking Mexican regional capitalists to those in London, Paris, and New York and offering elites bribes and privileges to make the idea of a unitary nation a reality. Those who resisted were subordinated or eradicated. The disruptions, displacements, and simmering resentments that characterized this contentious process led to the Revolution in 1910. Though the most overt carnage was over by 1917, it took several more decades for a new Mexico to emerge from bloodshed and ashes and even longer for the quintessential Mexican, the national man and woman, to emerge. It took several more decades for Mexican intellectuals to define what compulsions drove this national man and woman.

Octavio Paz, the Mexican poet, essayist, and eventual Nobel laureate, accordingly asked in 1950, "What are we, and how can we fulfill our obligations to ourselves as we are?" In the pages of *The Labyrinth of Solitude: Life and Thought in Mexico*, Paz answered this question in an extended meditation "on the psychology of a nation," carefully examining how the masculine and the feminine had been psychically and historically formed.[1] What characterized the Mexican national character, the personal and collective psyche, opined Paz, was a deep sense of inferiority and solitude, "the feeling and knowledge that one is alone, alienated from the world and oneself."[2] This sense of inferiority and aloneness was born of conquest, nurtured under Spanish and French colonialisms, and deepened as a result of territorial conquest and economic plunder, which historically particularly marked Mexico's relations with the United States.

So far from God, yet so close to the United States, what possible mythic and symbolic stock did Mexico have on which to construct a national identity? This is what Paz pondered. How to fashion Mexican nationalism into a distinct identity, when the Cold War global order of post–World War II projected only two economic systems (capitalism and socialism) and two powerful fathers in the family of nations (the United States and the Soviet Union). And Mexicans? They were *hijos de la chingada*, Paz asserted. To put it crudely, they were fucked, having been born the children of a raped and violated mother. This reality had created an aggressive *macho* male, who relished in ripping "open the *chingada* [the raped mother], the female, who is pure passivity, defenseless against the exterior world."[3]

Paz likened the power and violence of the macho, of the *gran chingón*, to that of the Spanish conquistador, whence devolved the power of caciques, feudal lords, hacienda owners, politicians, generals, and captains of industry. "They are all machos, *chingones*." They were symbols of brutish manliness, closed and controlled.[4] The symbolic national woman, la chingada, was the violated Indian mother, ripped open, pure passivity, her name lost to history. "She is Nothingness," Paz wrote. Thus, when Mexicans yearly inaugurated the celebration of their national independence from Spain by shouting out, "Viva México, hijos de la chingada," they expressed their desire "to live closed off from the outside world and, above all, from the past," continually asserting their manhood, precisely because they were perpetually nagged by a sense of inferiority as sons of nothingness, as hijos de la chingada.[5]

Paz found the metabolic repercussions of Mexico's geopolitical inferiority writ large on the body politic and small, on male and female bodies. Machismo, or hypervirility, was Mexico's defensive response to global inferiority and to its history of colonialism. While a number of other philosophers, psychoanalysts, psychologists, anthropologists, and sociologists spun similarly elaborate webs that characterized Mexican masculinity and femininity, the only major controversy in this literature was about the race and class location of this putative Mexican inferiority. For Paz it was in mestizos, the mixed-blood children of Spanish fathers and Indian mothers, who most compensated for their inferiority through exaggerated machismo. Philosopher Samuel Ramos found the "phallic obsession" among Mexican men of the lowest class, whom he called "*pelados*." Among Mexican men of this class, "the sexual organ becomes symbolic of masculine force. In verbal combat he attributes to his adversary an imaginary femininity, reserving for himself the masculine role." These men constantly asserted that they had *muchos huevos* (much balls), physically locating virility in their testicles. While the French and Germans boasted of their science, art, and technology, Mexicans boasted of their manliness, Ramos complained.[6]

By largely sidestepping these Mexican national character studies and the exaggerated binary gender oppositions scholars like Paz and Ramos advanced, the authors of the essays herein collected demonstrate how from 1880 to 1960 a cacophony of ideas about masculinity and femininity constantly vied for dominance in popular Mexican discourse and action. The cultural construction of Mexican masculinity and femininity was never a linear process. Rather it was always paradoxical and often contradictory, defying easy binaries, as women and men pragmatically negotiated conflicting desires, duties, and notions of decency, respect, and social standing.

The most widely held understanding of gender in Mexico clearly was that it was rooted in reproductive biology, which ostensibly produced male and female bodies, which when properly socialized, naturally resulted in masculine and the feminine selves. But even more important theoretically is the documented discovery that Mexicans often employed gender discourses about the proper relationship between the masculine and the feminine to describe unequal distributions of power among men, among women, and between men and women. Unlike the logic of modern biological science that has long wanted only to acknowledge two sexual bodies (male/female) that embody only two genders (masculine/feminine), Mexican popular understandings of gender reflected variability, recognized wide racial and class differences in gender ideology, and saw gender as fluid, permeable, and negotiated in action. The masculine and feminine were accordingly imagined as anchors of opposite ends of a continuum. The popular injunction that Mexican men should "be very manly" or "*ser muy hombre*" pronounced masculinity's variability; its cultural definition based on a set of behaviors and the recognition that one could, as Robert McKee Irwin has put it, "be very manly, not very manly, or even not manly at all," characteristics which could and often did apply to women.[7]

That men could be feminine, by choice or by force, and that women could be masculine by luck or by demand, is a theme repeatedly noted in these essays. Víctor M. Macías-González shows how the masculinities made popular during the Porfiriato were largely associated with an effeminate France. Masculinity meant civility, refinement, and whiteness, particularly at the bathhouses built in Mexico City in the early 1900s. Bathing in these luxurious edifices became a sign of refinement for the elite, a place for primping and preening, for idleness, and even for indulgence in homosexuality, behaviors that many critics saw as testament of Mexico's increasing feminization. Cleanliness was equated with civilization, and it was to guide the great unwashed, the filthy masses, which patrons of bathhouses saw as their duty, indeed, as their noblesse oblige.

While such behavior led to the generation of caricatures of Mexican elite men as pansies, from afar, from the vantage point of the United States, Mexico was a *bien macho* place for a particular breed of men. Chaffing under the puritanical dictates of domesticity, of prohibition, of Victorian social controls, many middle-class American men looked southward to the vice economies in the Mexican border cities of Tijuana and Mexicali for respite and fortification through liquor and fornication. Mexicali, with its wanton womanizing, it free-flowing tequila, and anything-goes-for-a-price ethos, became the perfect tonic for men feeling emasculated, domesticated, and overly feminized. Mexicali, as Eric Schantz notes, in time became a space of Mexican machismo, a place of male privilege and libidinal license, a site of penetrative influences both for foreign capital and for sex-starved American men.

Jeffrey Pilcher and Mary-Lee Mulholland draw on the work of folklorist Américo Paredes to give us a sense of the historical specificity of the origins of machismo. In his important essay, "The United States, Mexico, and *Machismo*,"[8] Paredes argued that if one studied Mexico's multiple literary and artistic forms from the conquest to the 1940s, there were plenty of examples of bombastic, boastful men who displayed heroism and courage, a supermanliness that could conceivably conceal the inferiority complex Octavio Paz had put at the center of Mexican national character. But nowhere did the word *macho* or any of its derivatives appear in descriptions of such men. "The reader will find no traces of *machismo* in the songs of the colonial period, the war of independence, or even the Reform," wrote Paredes.[9] Images of boastful, brave men proliferated during the Mexican Revolution, but still the word *macho* was never used to describe them. "Not until the 1940s, during World War II, do we begin to run across it." The first instance of the word *macho* that approximated Octavio Paz's use Paredes found in a *corrido* that had been composed sometime between 1940 and 1946, when Manuel Ávila Camacho was Mexico's president.

> Viva el pueblo siempre macho!
> Agustín el general!
> y Viva Ávila Camacho
> y la vida sindical!
>
> (Long live the people, always machos!
> Augustin, the general!
> Long live Ávila Camacho
> and the life of labor unions!)

Paredes suspected that because Mexicans eager to join the Allied cause often boasted that they would beat the Axis powers because their president was "Ca . . . macho!," *macho* entered the popular lexicon rather widely.

Characteristics that previously had simply been described as manly, valorous, and brave were increasingly deemed macho.

> Yo soy puro mexicano
> y me he echado el compromiso con
> la tierra en que nací
> de ser macho entre machos,
> y por eso muy ufano yo le canto a
> mi país.
>
> (I am a true-blue Mexican,
> and I have an obligation to the land
> where I was born,
> to be a macho among machos;
> and that is why I proudly sing to my country.)[10]

According to Paredes, machismo as hypervirility did not appear in Mexico until the late 1930s, after the violent phase of the Mexican Revolution had ended, thus intensifying the memories of that violence. Verbalized in the songs of Pedro Infante and Jorge Negrete, popularly narrativized through Mexican *charro* (cowboy) movies, the violence associated with Mexican manhood grew exponentially, at least cinematically, through the importation and emulation of American cowboy movies of the "Wild West." Ironically, everything about the American cowboy except the revolver was exported from Mexico to the United States in the 1820s and 1830s. In the 1940s Mexicans imported the American movie cowboy. His brutishness became machismo, explains Paredes, due to a growing feeling of nationalism accompanied by sentiments of distrust and inferiority toward outsiders, particularly toward the United States."[11]

Several essays in this collection note that by the beginning of the twentieth century, the strict separation of the social worlds that Mexican men and women had previously inhabited began to break down, precipitating, as Robert Buffington argues, the necessity to create a new male subjectivity in a world dominated by heterosexuality. Since Mexico gained its independence from Spain in 1821, the republic had been a hermaphrodite of sorts, seeking an identity for *la madre patria*, or the mother fatherland. Bequeathed a heritage of powerful feminine icons—the Virgin of Guadalupe (the symbol of Mexican independence and of female modesty) and La Malinche (the emblem of conquest, rape, and *mestizaje*)—Mexico sought a virile identity to cast off its putative colonial impotence and to assert its masculinity. Mexican thinkers of the nineteenth century primarily imagined the nation homosocially constituted, created through brotherly relationships among male citizens. Women were, of course, necessary to the nation's reproduction, but their role in heterosexuality fundamentally threatened civilization, or so a number of intellectuals believed. Heterosexual erotic desire was capable of destroying class boundaries, polluting racial purity, even dismantling the integrity of families through adultery, incest, and fornication. Novelist José T. de Cuéllar articulated such themes in the 1890s, deeming Greek heterosexuality the ideal way Mexican women and men should structure their relationships. The Greeks secluded their women, maintained sexual and pedagogical relationships with young men, and thus avoided prostitution, adultery, and premarital sex. In those nineteenth-century Mexican novels now deemed to have given birth to a distinctive national consciousness through literature, novels such as Fernández de Lizardi's *El Periquillo Sarniento*, José Tomás de Cuéllar's *Astucia*, Manuel Payno's *El fistol del Diablo*, and Ignacio Altamirano's *El Zarco*, membership and belonging in the body politic was created through homosocial, often homoerotic, and even homosexual relations between men. In these works the crude macho was not the idealized man; rather, it was the hombre de bien, the youthful, honest, and true friend given to friendships and love affairs, less to marriage and family, and seldom to fatherhood. Robert Buffington thus chronicles the compulsive, fractious, anxious talk of men on the eve of the Mexican Revolution, negotiating their relationships with women while constantly fearing betrayal by them. The Mexican penny press and records of litigation show how this male anxiety resulted in higher levels of violence toward women, which Buffington calls "the tongue-in-cheek performance of male toughness for the benefit of other men." Modernity, according to Buffington, gave primacy to the heterosexual dyad over a national homosociality that had once reigned supreme.

The spaces where the ideals of such heterosexuality were performed, learned, and reproduced as a distinctively modern Mexican gender system, notes Anne Rubenstein, were the movie theaters of the realm. Theaters were temples of modernity where women and men behaved in new ways largely by observing what was important to their screen idols. The silver screen offered Mexicans ideals of gender comportment, notions of fashion, cosmopolitanism, leisure, and a world full of love and lust rather free of violence and the Mexican Revolution's past. Theaters offered intimate, dark spaces as well, in which men and women could interact erotically, outside the supervision of family and kin and in public. Anne Rubenstein, Jeffrey Pilcher, and Andrew Wood all draw our attention to the important work cinema performed in the construction of Mexican masculinities and femininities. Andrew Wood shows how the onscreen and offscreen life of the singer and film star Agustín Lara rendered him a rather weak, effeminate sort. Lara, who was much older than his beloved María Felix, a gargantuan movie star in her own right, was constantly mocked by her affairs, his crooning songs of love for her, and in the end, their divorce. Agustín Lara was hardly the macho, the demanding and controlling jealous lover. Rather, he was the effeminate, controlled instead by a domineering wench, or that is how the press and the cinema had him performing his manhood. Jeffrey Pilcher's analysis of the Mexican film history discovers various forms of masculinity. In Pedro Infante films, one sees elegant fops (*catrínes*); boisterous, dissipated, often alcoholic flirts; and touchy, often pretentious but usually impecunious ranchers. In Mario Moreno, who played the role of Cantiflas in hundreds of films, one sees the Mexican country bumpkin, the pelado, who mocks elite ways, subverts society's hierarchical order, and, at least in his films, usually wins the woman from more macho competitors.

The profound cultural changes that this volume chronicles in the representation of masculinity and femininity answers the questions, What changed and what remained the same? Kathryn A. Sloan shows that a high regard for female virginity before marriage and fidelity within matrimony remained hallmarks of female and familial honor across society as a whole, particularly in the more rural Mexican states that were far from Mexico City. In places like Oaxaca, the documentary evidence shows that distinct class-based forms of honor existed. The honor of working-class women was just as complex as its elite analogue but undoubtedly more dynamically negotiated. Women of this class often did not have male protectors who would readily come to the defense of their reputations. If young women wanted to be deemed honorable, they had to fend for themselves, openly defying gender prescriptions and asserting their autonomy. The example of a fourteen-year-old laundress named María, who was being wooed and pursued by a young man named Francisco in Oaxaca, is particularly illuminating. "[S]he spurned him and pelted him with rocks to make him go away, in effect, staking her claim to honor." Working-class women in Oaxaca, at least in 1899, were playing masculine roles in their relationships with men, refusing orders, articulating sets of matrimonial demands, and in essence, wearing the pants, as Mexicans might have said.

The research herein presented by Kathryn A. Sloan also clearly shows that marriage by the beginning of the twentieth century ceased to be an exclusive affair of parents who arranged economically advantageous matches for their daughters and sons. This transformation had been occurring in Mexico since the 1770s. By 1900 the discourse of romantic love became the raison d'être for compassionate marriage based on personal desire and individual choice. Even among the lower classes the idiom of romantic love suffused relationships between young women and men. From the chronicle of the elopement of Josefa Calvo and Manuel Vivas in Oaxaca, we learn of their burning love for each other through their handwritten missives, which describe their desire to live as husband and wife, whatever parents might think about the match. As we glean from this story, Josefa was not the passive female pawn one might have imagined a century earlier. She orchestrated the time, place, and terms of her elopement, with her lover Manuel doing exactly as she demanded.

While in the nineteenth century honor was the collective ideology of social personhood that defined a person's place in a hierarchically organized society, prescribing ideal gender norms for what was deemed masculine and feminine, by the beginning of the twentieth century, James A. Garza and Robert Buffington show that honor had been complicated by a sense that what was most important in life was that one should be *gente decente*, or decent people. This is an intriguing passing reference in both essays that requires more attention and considerable future study.

In sum, what the authors of these essays repeatedly show is that regional, class, and ethnic stereotypes about masculinities and femininities in Mexico have long existed. Mexican women have most often been depicted as virgins or as whores, as the asexual Virgin of Guadalupe or as the treacherous doña Marina, La Malinche of indigenous betrayal; men were constrained and defined by their hypermasculinity, or their machismo. What these essays instead clearly demonstrate are many masculinities, masculinities that were class inflected, that varied substantially by race, and that were animated differentially according to time, space, and place. Masculinity was always constructed oppositionally in relationship to femininity, either by degrees, by inversions, or by subversions of the gender order that produced new and distinct forms of person.

NOTES

1. Octavio Paz, *El laberinto de la soledad* (Mexico: Cuadernos Americanos, 1950). All citations herein are to this English-language edition, *The Labyrinth of Solitude: Life and Thought in Mexico* (New York: Grove Press, 1961), 9.
2. Ibid., 195.
3. Ibid., 77.
4. Ibid., 82.
5. Ibid., 86.
6. Samuel Ramos, *Profile of Man and Culture in Mexico* (Austin: University of Texas Press, 1962), 59–60. This title was first published in Spanish in 1933.
7. Robert McKee Irwin, *Mexican Masculinities* (Minneapolis: University of Minnesota Press, 2003), xx.
8. Américo Paredes, *Folklore and Culture on the Texas-Mexican Border* (Austin: University of Texas Press, 1993), 215–34.
9. Ibid., 217.
10. Ibid., 220.
11. Ibid., 233.

Contributors

Robert Buffington, associate professor of women and gender studies, University of Colorado at Boulder, has done extensive work on the histories of crime and sexuality in Mexico and Latin America. His books include *Criminal and Citizen in Modern Mexico* (University of Nebraska Press, 2000); *Reconstructing Criminality in Modern Latin America* (Rowman & Littlefield, 2001), which was coedited with Carlos Aguirre; and *True Stories of Crime in Modern Mexico* (University of New Mexico Press, 2009), coedited with Pablo Piccato. He is currently working on *A Sentimental Education for the Working Man: Mexico City 1900–1910*, which will analyze the impact of modernity on working-class masculinities.

James A. Garza is associate professor of history and ethnic studies at University of Nebraska–Lincoln, where he heads the program in nineteenth-century studies. He is the author of *The Imagined Underworld: Sex, Crime and Vice in Porfirian Mexico City* (University of Nebraska Press, 2008). Dr. Garza's current studies focus on Mexico City's environmental history as well as Mexican American and borderlands history.

Ramón A. Gutiérrez is the Preston & Sterling Morton Distinguished Service Professor in United States History at the College at the University of Chicago, where he directs the Center for the Study of Race, Politics and Culture. He is the author of *When Jesus Came, the Corn Mothers Went Away: Marriage, Sexuality and Power in New Mexico, 1500–1846* (Stanford University Press, 1991) and numerous other publications, including *Contested Eden: California Before the Gold Rush* (University of California Press, 1999), coedited with Richard J. Orsi, and *Mexicans in California: Emergent Challenges and Transformations* (University of Illinois Press, 2009), coedited with Patricia Zavella. His research specialties include Chicano history, race and ethnicity in American life, Indian-white relations in the Americas, colonial Latin America, and Mexican immigration. Dr. Gutiérrez has received numerous academic awards, including a MacArthur Foundation Prize Fellowship (1983), the John Hope Franklin Prize from the American Studies Association (1992), and the Frederick Jackson Turner Prize from the Organization of American Historians (1992).

Víctor M. Macías-González is associate professor of history and women's, gender, and sexuality studies at the University of Wisconsin, La Crosse, where he directs the Institute for Latina/o and Latin American Studies and the Eagle Mentoring Program. He has published on art, consumption, diplomacy, education, etiquette, gender, society, and transnationalism in nineteenth-century Mexico and has an interest in the history of Mexicans abroad. Macías-González is presently completing a cultural history of the Mexican aristocracy, tentatively titled *Gentes de grandes nombres.*

Mary-Lee Mulholland is an instructor in the Latin American Studies Program at the University of Calgary. Her research focuses on themes of popular culture in Latin America, and her doctoral thesis, *Mariachi in Excess: Performing Race, Gender, Sexuality, and Regionalism in Jalisco, Mexico* (2007), examined mariachi as a site of the production and contestation of identities in Jalisco, Mexico.

Jeffrey M. Pilcher, professor of history at the University of Minnesota, is the author of *¡Que vivan los tamales! Food and the Making of Mexican Identity* (University of New Mexico Press, 1998), *Cantinflas and the Chaos of Mexican Modernity* (Scholarly Resources, 2001), *The Sausage Rebellion: Public Health, Private Enterprise, and Meat in Mexico City, 1890–1917* (University of New Mexico Press, 2006), and *Food in World History* (Routledge, 2006). He is currently writing a book about the globalization of Mexican cuisine entitled *Planet Taco.*

Anne Rubenstein is associate professor of history at York University in Toronto. She is the author of *Bad Language, Naked Ladies, and Other Threats to the Nation: A Political History of Comic Books in Mexico* (Duke University Press, 1998) and coedited *Fragments of a Golden Age: The Politics of Culture in Mexico since 1940* (Duke University Press, 2001) with Gil Joseph and Eric Zolov. Her recent articles and current research focus on gender, sexuality, fans and audiences, and moviegoing in Mexico since 1917, which will eventually result in a book tentatively titled *Going to the Movies in Mexico.*

Eric Schantz has taught Latin American history at California State University, Los Angeles. He has been a participating scholar at the Seminario Externo Permanente of the Instituto de Investigaciones Históricas of the Universidad Autónoma de Baja California since 2008, where he also serves in the editorial board of the historical journal *Meyibó.*

Kathryn A. Sloan is associate professor of history at the University of Arkansas and the author of *Runaway Daughters: Seduction, Elopement, and Honor in Nineteenth-Century Mexico* (University of New Mexico Press, 2008). She is currently writing *Women's Roles in Latin America and the Caribbean,* a book-length synthesis of Latin American and Caribbean women's history.

Andrew G. Wood is associate professor of history at the University of Tulsa and a social and cultural historian of modern Mexico and the U.S.-Mexican borderlands. He is interested in the history of music, tourism, civic celebrations, urban social movements, public health, and pirates. He was born in Montreal, Canada.

Index

Other titles in the Diálogos series available from the University of New Mexico Press:

Independence in Spanish America: Civil Wars, Revolutions, and Underdevelopment (revised edition)
—Jay Kinsbruner

Heroes on Horseback: A Life and Times of the Last Gaucho Caudillos
—John Charles Chasteen

The Life and Death of Carolina Maria de Jesus
—Robert M. Levine and José Carlos Sebe Bom Meihy

¡Que vivan los tamales! Food and the Making of Mexican Identity
—Jeffrey M. Pilcher

The Faces of Honor: Sex, Shame, and Violence in Colonial Latin America
—Edited by Lyman L. Johnson and Sonya Lipsett-Rivera

The Century of U.S. Capitalism in Latin America—Thomas F. O'Brien

Tangled Destinies: Latin America and the United States
—Don Coerver and Linda Hall

Everyday Life and Politics in Nineteenth Century Mexico: Men, Women, and War
—Mark Wasserman

Lives of the Bigamists: Marriage, Family, and Community in Colonial Mexico
—Richard Boyer

Andean Worlds: Indigenous History, Culture, and Consciousness Under Spanish Rule, 1532–1825
—Kenneth J. Andrien

The Mexican Revolution, 1910–1940—Michael J. Gonzales

Quito 1599: City and Colony in Transition—Kris Lane

A Pest in the Land: New World Epidemics in a Global Perspective
—Suzanne Austin Alchon

The Silver King: The Remarkable Life of the Count of Regla in Colonial Mexico
—Edith Boorstein Couturier

National Rhythms, African Roots: The Deep History of Latin American Popular Dance
—John Charles Chasteen

The Great Festivals of Colonial Mexico City: Performing Power and Identity
—Linda A. Curcio-Nagy

The Souls of Purgatory: The Spiritual Diary of a Seventeenth-Century Afro-Peruvian Mystic, Ursula de Jesús
—Nancy E. van Deusen

Dutra's World: Wealth and Family in Nineteenth-Century Rio de Janeiro
—Zephyr L. Frank

Death, Dismemberment, and Memory: Body Politics in Latin America
—Edited by Lyman L. Johnson

Plaza of Sacrifices: Gender, Power, and Terror in 1968 Mexico
—Elaine Carey

— continued on next page —

Women in the Crucible of Conquest:
The Gendered Genesis of Spanish American Society, 1500–1600
—Karen Vieira Powers

Beyond Black and Red: African-Native Relations in Colonial Latin America
—Edited by Matthew Restall

Mexico OtherWise: Modern Mexico in the Eyes of Foreign Observers
—Edited and translated by Jürgen Buchenau

Local Religion in Colonial Mexico
—Edited by Martin Austin Nesvig

Malintzin's Choices: An Indian Woman in the Conquest of Mexico
—Camilla Townsend

From Slavery to Freedom in Brazil: Bahia, 1835–1900
—Dale Torston Graden

Slaves, Subjects, and Subversives: Blacks in Colonial Latin America
—Edited by Jane G. Landers and Barry M. Robinson

Private Passions and Public Sins: Men and Women in Seventeenth-Century Lima
—María Emma Mannarelli

Making the Americas: The United States and Latin America
from the Age of Revolutions to the Era of Globalization
—Thomas F. O'Brien

Remembering a Massacre in El Salvador: The Insurrection of 1932,
Roque Dalton, and the Politics of Historical Memory
—Héctor Lindo-Fuentes, Erik Ching, and Rafael A. Lara-Martínez

Raising an Empire: Children in Early Modern Iberia and Colonial Latin America
—Ondina E. González and Bianca Premo

Christians, Blasphemers, and Witches:
Afro-Mexican Rituals in the Seventeenth Century
—Joan Cameron Bristol

Art and Architecture of Viceregal Latin America, 1521–1821
—Kelly Donahue-Wallace

Rethinking Jewish-Latin Americans
—Edited by Jeffrey Lesser and Raanan Rein

True Stories of Crime in Modern Mexico
—Edited by Robert Buffington and Pablo Piccato

Aftershocks: Earthquakes and Popular Politics in Latin America
—Edited by Jürgen Buchenau and Lyman L. Johnson

Black Mexico: Race and Society from Colonial to Modern Times
—Edited by Ben Vinson III and Matthew Restall

The War for Mexico's West: Indians and Spaniards in New Galicia, 1524–1550
—Ida Altman

— continued on next page —

Damned Notions of Liberty: Slavery, Culture, and Power in Colonial Mexico, 1640–1769
—Frank Proctor

Irresistible Forces: Latin American Migration to the United States and its Effects on the South
—Gregory B. Weeks and John R. Weeks

Cuauhtémoc's Bones: Forging National Identity in Modern Mexico
—Paul Gillingham

Slavery, Freedom, and Abolition in Latin America and the Atlantic World
—Christopher Schmidt-Nowara

A History of Mining in Latin America: From the Colonial Era to the Present
—Kendall W. Brown

Modernizing Minds in El Salvador: Education Reform and the Cold War, 1960–1980
—Héctor Lindo-Fuentes and Erik Ching

SERIES ADVISORY EDITOR:
Lyman L. Johnson,
University of North Carolina at Charlotte